CHRISTIAN LOVE

PAUL E. JOHNSON

Christian Love

ABINGDON-COKESBURY PRESS
NEW YORK • NASHVILLE

CHRISTIAN LOVE

COPYRIGHT MCMLI 1951
BY PIERCE AND SMITH

SET UP, PRINTED, AND BOUND BY THE
PARTHENON PRESS, AT NASHVILLE,
TENNESSEE, UNITED STATES OF AMERICA

Preface

Christian love may be approached from many vistas. A theological approach will interpret the nature of God and the revelation of his love in creating and redeeming man by divine initiative. A biblical exegesis will begin with the text and discover the meaning of love to the biblical writers and the sources from which they drew inspiration. Historical investigation will trace the developing Christian ideas of love in broadening movements. Sociological studies will explore the social patterns and institutions that have arisen expressly in the activities of such love. Ethical studies will consider the human values at stake in living together to weigh the potential good and evil in the coming and going of this love.

Another approach, and the one to be pursued in this book, is a psychological study of Christian love. Psychology deals with human experience in contrast to the supernatural questions of theology. Yet belief in God is a central fact in the human experience of Christian love. To give an accurate description of Christian behavior we may not ignore the data of theological, biblical, historical, sociological, and ethical studies. For as Christian love consists of religious and social experiences, no psychology that excludes social and religious behavior is prepared to cope with the subject at hand.

A psychology of Christian love consequently stands in a vulnerable position, exposed on all sides without being able to satisfy anyone. It will be too psychological for those who have a predominantly religious interest, for they will miss a theological consideration of supernatural issues. It will not be psychological enough for those who have a predominately scientific interest, for they will expect a specialized treatment of laboratory or statistical procedures. Under this cross fire one cannot but feel the force of both charges; I welcome the criticism and recognize the difficulties.

My position is that the subject of Christian love can best be investigated by a psychology that is social and religious. If others find it fruitful to study the nature of love from a scientific method more narrowly conceived or a religious method more broadly conceived, I shall do everything in my power to encourage their work. For only by many hypotheses and methods can the truth of any subject be adequately explored. May I also invite the exchange of research designs, methods, and conclusions among all who are drawn to study Christian love from whatever approach. For without faithful co-operation little of consequence has ever been discovered. The most that we know about love is tragically meager; the least that we can do in so urgent a quest is to share what we can find with one another.

This study will be pursued from the viewpoint of interpersonal psychology, which to me is a social and religious psychology, therefore qualified to find meaning in Christian love. As a preliminary statement let me define interpersonal psychology as the scientific study of persons interacting with other persons. The methods of the social sciences are numerous; as I view them, they are essentially empirical in description, dynamic in cause-effect relations, systematic in interpretation. The actual results may not justify these expectations, but they constitute the aims for this sudy of love in interpersonal relationships.

Interpersonal psychology has certain emphases to be noted as the study unfolds. (1) Persons are the central focus of this psychology. (2) Persons confront each other in I-Thou relationships. (3) Personal motives are responses to significant persons in one's social orbit. (4) The desires and efforts of persons are aimed toward goals valued by other persons. (5) Persons work for values in order to share them with, or keep them from, other persons. (6) From defensive tactics come fear, rivalry, and poverty; from sharing come mutual confidence, co-operation, and growth. (7) The health of persons and societies depends upon the kind of relations persons develop toward each other; when interpersonal relations are insecure, hostile, and predatory, the society declines and its members suffer nervous disorders; when interpersonal relations provide security, love, and mutual aid, the society prospers and its members mature in creative wholeness.

Interpersonal relations are woven into the texture of this book, for many minds have exchanged ideas on the subject for centuries, while in our time research in related fields has contributed to our view of Christian love. Colleagues and students have participated in the consideration of these topics: Seward Hiltner suggested the need of such a study; Albert F. Bramble conducted preliminary research in a doctoral dissertation; Edgar S. Brightman, Peter A. Bertocci, and Walter G. Muelder gave helpful criticisms; Florence N. Lund and Lois K. Larue assisted in preparing the manuscript. These valued services are gratefully acknowledged. Evelyn Grant Johnson, my wife, has shared as always in the preparation of the manuscript and even more in the discovery of the meaning of love.

PAUL E. JOHNSON

Contents

I

Words of Love

1. HUNGER FOR LOVE

The human need for love is at last self-evident. The race in its long march from the past, as well as each person in his adventures of growing up, has experimented with loveless ways of living. But these ways have all failed to win the good life, until at length by the overwhelming evidence of experience we turn to love. We may be stubborn and deny that we shall ever yield our rebellion against love, or braggart enough to boast we are too strong to ask for love, or foolish enough to deceive ourselves that love after all is not for our style of life who are clever enough to live by our wits.

But who refusing love can escape the bitter harvest of consequences? To suffer the lonely void, the raging hostility of this bitterness, is to know the distress of life without love. And the social consequences are as devastating as the personal distresses. Kagawa set these forth poetically in his *Love, the Law of Life*, describing the famine of love among the people of the world:

Ah, this famine of love! How it saddens my soul!
In city and country, in hospital and factory, in shop and on street, everywhere this dreadful drought of love! Not a drop of love anywhere: the loveless land is more dreary than Sahara and more terrible than Gobi. When the last drop of love has dried away all men will go mad and begin to massacre all who have ever thought of love or appreciated it. Behold them armed with guns, swords, spears, and even ancient maces, hating and suspecting one another! [1]

[1] Tr. J. F. Gressitt (Philadelphia: John C. Winston Co., 1931), p. 41.

How quickly the prophecy was fulfilled! Almost instantly came the invasion of Manchuria, then of Ethiopia, Czechoslovakia, Poland, and France, and the whole world was drawn into a raging conflict. New weapons added cunning to fury until the devastation surpassed anything the human race had known or ever imagined. The massacre was not limited to the combatants as in former wars. Whole populations were obliterated without consideration of guilt or innocence; "all who ever thought of love" were caught in the flames of total destruction.

Then followed the cold war, a cessation of bombing but not of hostilities. Never have more people demanded peace or longed more ardently for a world community of justice and security. With grim determination the peoples of the world have been forming a United Nations, to seek peaceful solutions to national rivalries; but every step of progress is hounded by fearful reluctance, "hating and suspecting one another." Until love comes to replace hate and trust rises above suspicion, the outlook is dark and foreboding for this planet called Earth. The world population of two billion, taken as a whole or one by one, has a need more desperate than any other thing. Without food the body may perish; without love soul and body perish together. With food the body may languish in bitterness and despair; with love souls feed bodies and share joys and sufferings in the elation of comradeship. If love is so urgently needed, why is it so delayed and denied?

This is the question that engages our study in this book. It consists of other questions that will be pursued chapter by chapter in detail. What is love psychologically, religiously, and ethically? What is the Christian meaning of love? From what energies does love gain its motive power? Is it possible to educate children in love more persuasively than we do? How can the Christian family be a more adequate home for love? How may Christian experience bless sex and marriage? What are the human explosives that defeat love? Is it possible to have a beloved community that will meet in larger ways the hunger for love?

For a beginning we may define love as *growing interest in, appreciation of, and responsibility for, other persons*. From this first step in definition [2] we shall seek by other steps to understand love more adequately. But love is a mystery, even as life is a mystery, larger than our knowledge. If we start out to explore one dimension of love, before we reach that ultimate goal, we see that love has other dimensions also to explore, no one of which is complete without the others. Perhaps no other human experience is more varied in multiple meanings than love. To declare what love means to me in one situation is not to say exactly what love means to you in this or other conditions. We speak of love as if everyone had the same idea, but all the time we find different meanings in love and consequently do not speak the same language when we talk of love. This tendency to hold different meanings in our private worlds keeps us apart and leads to misunderstandings and widespread confusion about love.

2. Confusion of Loves

We are told that love is blind. There is evidence to the contrary, for love often sees better than hate or indifference. But failure to love is a blindness that closes eyes to the best life has to offer. This paltry love is blinded by our own confusions in loving. What word has a larger variety of meanings? These four letters of Anglo-Saxon origin *l-o-v-e* spell different meanings to different people in different circumstances. Consequently, when it is love we refer to, who knows exactly what we mean? When a girl confesses that she "just loves" olives and "adores" pickles, would you believe she could be in love with a vegetable? When a man meets a girl walking the street of a strange city and offers to pay for a one-night bed, is that love? If so, it is quite different from his love for his mother or his sister. Love of a brother is not the same as love of one's wife. This love again is different from love of country, and neither is love of country identical

[2] "A feeling of strong personal attachment induced by that which delights or commands admiration, by sympathetic understanding, or by ties of kinship," is the first of several definitions of love given in *Webster's New International Dictionary of the English Language* (Springfield, Mass.: G. & C. Merriam Co., 1935), p. 1462.

with love of friends and neighbors. Love of nature, as mountains, lakes, and trees, has another meaning; as also has the love of music, art, or literature. And the love of one's job, lifelong devotion to a chosen vocation, is something else—not to forget love of strangers and enemies. Beyond all of these is love of God.

Love is used in current speech to cover a multitude of dissimilar attitudes, as: (1) taste, (2) lust, (3) filial devotion, (4) family loyalty, (5) conjugal union, (6) patriotism, (7) friendship, (8) neighborliness, (9) admiration of nature, (10) artistic appreciation, (11) vocational interest, (12) philanthropy, (13) forgiveness, and (14) religious reverence. There are common elements to be sure: personal feelings of attraction, admiration, gratitude, and obligation. But every one of these fourteen attitudes has unique nuances of meaning not identical with the others. The distinctions are subtle but obvious to anyone who has experienced each of these situations. And they do not stand apart in opposition, for they overreach and intermingle in blends of meaning.

Is it any wonder that love is a complex of intricate designs in human experience? To love we need to know what love is. Yet love means so many things, how can we know which love is what and what love means? Consequently our love is confused, and the art of loving is lost in bewildering dilemmas.

It would be less ambiguous if love had but one meaning. And if our language were clear-cut enough to chisel out a separate word for each situation, then we might know what we were talking about. To invent a series of such words is not beyond human ingenuity. The linguist could then as in a cemetery walk along geometrical paths between rows of stone markers, each one labeled to indicate a separate identity. The only disadvantage about a cemetery is that the people who live there are dead. A language of abstractions is also a city of the dead. Nothing yields more neatly to orderly arrangement than abstract symbols (words, figures, designs), but life defies perfect classification. It is too complex, too dynamic, too versatile. It overflows every line of demarcation and refuses to stay supinely in any mold. Life is one surprise after another—from the unpredictability of bacteria to the astonishing behavior of men. In so far as love is alive, it breaks over the boundaries of language in the wealth of its moods and meanings.

Intriguing as the language of love may be, it does not alone go deep enough to sound the living experience we seek to understand. To comprehend the inner meaning of such living experience calls for a social psychology of love. One must of course admit that psychological studies may be abstract and lifeless. Academic psychology has dealt exhaustively with trivia and vacillated energetically between the obvious and the obscure. But in the recent developments of psychology there are dynamic concepts and tools to fathom better the zestful activities of living persons. Not that any tools are adequate or any concepts sufficient to do justice to the vital experiences of love. Yet love is inherently a product of dynamic needs arising through interpersonal relations. And consequently no psychology that is not dynamic and interpersonal will offer appropriate tools by which to explore the living experience of love. Not the brass instruments and artificial experiments of the departmental laboratory, but investigation of human situations will better enable us to see how and why persons act as they do toward other persons.

It is true that the human scene is more confusing than the scientific laboratory or library where every item is labeled, classified, and quantified. The facts of life are not so orderly or sterile as the ivory towers of pure research. But they may be more significant, at least more urgent. The time has come to take our scientific tools to people where they are in the slums of the city, the grime of the factory, the squalor of rural poverty, the passions of lust, anger, and greed, the fury of war, the sullen resentments of race and class. This is what the social sciences are seeking to do. Here the destinies of men, women, and children are being decided for good or ill. Yet face to face with persons in dynamic interaction our scientific tools fail us. They are too rough and rigid to measure the delicate counterbalances of human motives. Finding our best tools inept, we shall need to

15

invent better ones as we confront these people in their daily activities.

To observe and describe is not to understand. The scientist of human love will employ action research by participation in group dynamics. He will need empathy to know how persons feel about love, and cultural appreciation to see what it means in their social expectations. He may employ psychoanalysis to reach unconscious motivation, or psychodrama to practice the roles of social interaction, or diagnostic testing and projective techniques to assess the structure and forces of personality, or counseling and psychotherapy to release emotional tensions and affirm growing insights. He may survey attitudes and opinions, examine populations and cultures, conduct statistical measurements and correlations, examine personal documents, consider social constellations and cultural patterns. Or he may invite artistic expression, occupational therapy, recreation and group therapy to develop spontaneity and social interests.

Human relations are confusing. They are complicated by the inner motives and outgoing activities of persons who constantly interact with each other. In the welter of these human relations love rises and falls. Baffled by this confusion some flee and others repress such disturbing situations, but to understand love there is nothing to gain in escape or deception. The student of love will need to come into the midst of this confusion to see it, to feel it, and to participate in it himself to know the meaning of love.

3. Love as Weakness

Love fails by popular confusion as to its meaning. It is also rejected as a form of weakness. Love yields; it may even appear as a surrender. Love melts the resistance of one person against another; it softens the hardhearted, indulges the offender with forgiveness, tempers stern justice with mercy.

Virtue stands for strength. We honor the person who is strong to do his duty and insist that a person uphold virtue at any cost. Love often seems to betray virtue. A virgin may fall in love and surrender virginity before marriage; a married woman may be overpowered by love for a man who is not her husband. A married man may go into bankruptcy and lose his business to please the expensive tastes of his beloved wife; an indulgent father may so love his child that he neglects to discipline him to the detriment of the son's character. In these and other ways virtue may be betrayed by love. Not all love is like this, but overindulgent love is weakening.

Again love may weaken independence. A child becomes so dependent upon a loving mother that he cannot be happy when she is away; a pair of twins may become so dependent on each other that life is unbearable when they are separated; a grandmother may be so hungry for affection that she becomes an invalid dependent on the family who wait upon her. Charity may pauperize families who grow dependent on social agencies for the necessities of daily life, unable to support themselves. Love is not always like this, but dependent love is weakening.

Love is offensive to pride, and pride often denies love. A schoolboy who has been ridiculed for his eyeglasses and large ears may be too proud to play with his schoolmates and so bury himself in books. The young swain who is jilted may suffer a wounded pride that prevents his asking any girl thereafter. The friends who quarrel may be too proud to admit they could have been wrong; the haughty aristocrat feels too superior to love his neighbor; the self-righteous man has little sympathy for the poor sinner. The soldier will defend himself at all costs and fear to give comfort to the enemy; the proud race or nation wastes little love on the alien. Where pride rules, love is unwelcome as a weakness to be feared and resisted.

This is another confusion of love. It is *false* love that betrays virtue, overindulges dependence, or defends itself with fearful pride. The weakness of love arises from misunderstanding and contradiction of its true nature, from too little rather than too much love. A drop of love in a bucket of pride is not a strong solution of love. When love is outweighed by other motives, it is weak, for the mingling of conflicting interests cancels the power of any motive and leads to impotence. The fate of love in human life is often to be overpowered

17

by its enemies. The power of love is to change the recalcitrant and warring impulses of life to its own likeness.

4. LOVE AS STRENGTH

Why is man ascendant over other animals? Many answers have been offered. He is more cunning and invents better tools to serve his needs. He binds space and time together, remembers the past and plans his future. He records his knowledge and teaches each new generation the accumulated wisdom of former ones. He is sensitive to spiritual values and aspires to attain higher levels of emerging development. He also organizes social groups for mutual aid and co-operation.

These are good answers, and there is truth in each of them. But there is another answer that may outweigh all the rest—*because he learns to love.* The mammals who suckle their young show tender feelings of interest in and concern for the welfare of others. They nourish the helpless little offspring at their own breasts; they nestle and cuddle them and come to feel pity and affection for them. It is in such animals that the law of sacrifice appears where parents lay down their lives for their young. The unselfish desire to sacrifice for others has become the greatest strength of the mammals. With this motive they have outlived other species with greater agility, strength, or defensive and offensive armor.

In *R.U.R.*,[3] an allegorical play by Karel Capek, the robots manufactured to serve as soldiers arise and overthrow the human race by reason of human divisions and betrayals. In the final assault the secret formula for making the mechanical men is lost, and as robots do not reproduce, their future is doomed. One surviving human scientist devotes his life to improving the race of robots until in the last scene two of them fall in love. This is of course a fantasy to show that a machine culture may threaten spiritual values. The fatal limitation of machines and mechanical products is their inability to love. The dramatic fiction of the play is to show how empty and suicidal is a civilization that cannot love. If robots learn to love, they are not

[3] *Rossum's Universal Robots* (New York: Doubleday, Page & Co., 1923).

mechanical inventions but creative human spirits. Without love the human race will perish. If men are to survive, love must be stronger than all other motives.

Love to be strong must be unified. It must be of one mind, heart, and strength; for conflict and confusion weaken love, as we have seen. If our survival hangs upon the purity of our love, it is evidently a slender thread; for love is seldom without doubts, temptations, and struggles. Every human relationship is subject to changing gusts of emotional impulses, interests, needs, and aims in endless variety. Love is always unfinished business, with a future yet to be decided again and again. The rise of love is not an individual decision alone, but the constant interplay of responses among persons. Nor can two people keep their love apart from the social influences of other persons who participate with them in their community life. For love is no Cellophane-wrapped package untouched by human hands. It is rather a constantly changing and interchanging stream of life shared by all who have any part in it.

The strength of love is not in its simple purity so much as in its complex wholeness. The unity which love requires is more like a democracy than a monarchy demanding instant obedience to decisions handed down from above with no questions asked. It is the unity of a majority vote in which the constituency of love holds a plurality over its rivals. Where love struggles against hatred, anger, and resentment, it must hold a decisive, though not a safe, margin of power. Where love proves constant, its faithfulness rises to ascendance over fickle moods and vagrant lusts; where love is unselfish, it gains a balance of purpose that holds a slight edge over selfish desires. The larger the majority the stronger the party, we are apt to assume; but that does not comprehend the dynamics of human energy. The most alert, agile, and persistent strength is a strenuous effort in issues hotly contested with vigorous opponents. Only when challenged by opposition does a man or a group exert its full strength.

Karen Horney describes three tendencies in human motivations: to move against others, to move away from others, and to move toward others.[4] These tendencies evidently struggle for ascendancy in each of us. If unimpeded the first flies to aggression, the second withdraws in escapism, while the third leans upon another dependently. But the healthy person is saved from these neurotic extremes by counterbalancing these tendencies in dynamic equilibrium. So every strength in personality is a meeting of resistances in counterbalances of energy. The unity of love gains strength in such a balance of opposites, with a margin of control in the direction of values shared affectionately with other persons.

5. CHRISTIAN LOVE

Christian love is not a clear record of simple purity. For this too is a constant struggle against doubts and temptations. Christians have had their doubts and difficulties in living up to a holy love for all people. Such love has been despised as a weak "slave morality" for subdued victims who were not strong enough to conquer and dominate others.[5] And the Christian virtues of humility have appeared humiliating to the man who wants to be a superman, or the "go-getter" who is out to win ahead of everyone else. Love, he contends, is a handicap for the strong who can take what they want. Not a few Christians become wise in these ways of the world and forget to love the enemy or competitor beyond their doors.

Love is consequently deceived by hypocrisy. We speak eloquently of love, read beautiful passages of Scripture, esteem lofty ideals, worship the man on a cross, and depart our separate ways. A coin may be left as a token, after which there is little else to do; we do not apply these teachings to the markets or battlefields of everyday living, where theory meets the test of practice. A chasm is apt to separate words from deeds, while the ideals of religion sicken and grow feeble from lack of exercise. So our love becomes a sham show of false appearances, as futile as it is pious. There is a strange blindness that prevents men from seeing their own hypocrisies. Our enemies, even our best friends, see the inconsistencies between practice

[4] *Our Inner Conflicts* (New York: W. W. Norton & Co., 1945).
[5] Friedrich Nietzsche, *The Genealogy of Morals.*

20

and profession; they may tell us in kindness or scorn, but we only resent the criticism and regret they do not understand us.

If at length we do see our failure to love as Christians should, we calculate what is required of us and often decide that the cost is too high. It is unreasonable to ask so much. After all the needs of myself and family are met, we must save against a rainy day in the future. Too bad there is nothing to spare; we would like to be generous, we say, if it were not so costly. Love is a lovely ideal, but is it really worth the sacrifice? Because we fear the wolves in sheep's clothing, we act like sheep in sheep's clothing, timidly saving our own skins and scarcely daring to raise a hand on behalf of fellow sufferers. Christian love in these ways fails by neglect, a kind of inopportunism that seldom comes to the right opportunity to express love in affirmative action.

Yet there are glorious chapters in the history of Christian love. Mary visited by the Most High cherishes in her heart a divinely unselfish love for her son Jesus. As Jesus grows in wisdom, stature, and in favor with God and men, he goes about his Father's business of love. The twelve disciples who answer his call forsake all to follow him and learn together how to live in this love. Other disciples after the Pentecost form a beloved community, sharing all things in common, rejoicing, and serving God. In the face of persecution many Christians are faithful unto death, like torches in a dark world bearing witness to a new light of love. Convinced believers in this way of love lay aside property and position to become little brothers of the poor, going forth to minister to any in need. Missionaries give up home and security to live in foreign lands as messengers of the gospel of love. Reforming spirits called Protestants are determined to correct the evil abuses of their day and create new communities where love and democracy unite in freedom to worship God. Churches and schools rise on the frontiers, social settlements in the slums, to bring life to new birth in spiritual love. Fellowships of suffering and service raise funds and bring vital goods to starving and homeless enemies in the reconciling forgiveness of love.

But Christian love is needed more than ever today. It has not yet prevailed over hate, cruelty, or the lust for power. We need to love in larger ways, going farther and deeper into the experience and expression of love. Otherwise love will be too little and too late to meet the crises of our time.

We shall need to see what this love is that people so hunger for. We need to understand its motives and dynamics in persons and groups. We must detect its failures and inconsistencies, diagnose its weakness and strength. We must experiment with love in our time in the crowded places where we live among our fellow creatures. From wise and generous experiments we will need to assess values and test methods to bring love to fruition in deeds and in relationships of lovingkindness. We must offer love anew to heal our world sickness in practice as well as principle. Yet not as a rival against other ways of life, for love is a divine overflow of light into darkness, a growth of health over disease to save and sanitize, to create and share a more wholesome life with all.

II

The Christian Meaning of Love

We have seen the confusion of many diverse meanings in the language of love and sought to find a preliminary definition of what in general we are to mean by love. Now we come to love in the distinctly Christian sense. How does Christian love differ from other kinds of love? To answer this question calls for historical investigation, beginning with the New Testament as containing the earliest sources of Christian teaching and tradition.

Christianity is generally known as the religion of love. "See how these Christians love one another," was said of the early Christian communities in the Mediterranean world. The disciples of Jesus were moved by a new spirit of devotion to follow him and learn of him that love is the law above all other laws. More than a law, it is the joyous experience of mutual affection that changes life from a dreary treadmill to adventures in discovery. For love discovers surprising values of understanding, appreciation, and service otherwise unknown. The disciples found in Christian living a new love, not easy to describe yet quite unique in meaning, clearly distinguishable from other loves. This love is new in two senses, depth and range. In depth Christian love is called divine—as coming from God, who takes the initiative in loving man and sharing that heavenly love with him. In range it is universal, excluding no one but reaching out to love all people in whatever conditions they may be.

1. LOVE IN THE NEW TESTAMENT

There is no theme in the New Testament more persistent than love. It flows like a stream of refreshing water throughout the

Gospels and epistles. To count the many references to love does not represent their significance. For love, as we have seen, is more than a word; its meanings exceed linguistic dimensions. Love is the motif of the New Testament, and it will be fruitful to explore it as the dominant theme of the Christian symphony. There are three movements in this symphony of Christian love: (*a*) God's love for man, (*b*) man's love for God, and (*c*) man's love for man.

a) *God's love for man.* The entire life and teaching of Jesus rests upon the hypothesis that God is a loving Father. The parables of the prodigal son (Luke 15:11), the lost sheep (Matt. 18:12), the good Samaritan (Luke 10:30), and the laborers in the vineyard (Matt. 20:1) stress this love of God. We are invited to be merciful as God is merciful (Luke 6:36), perfect as he is in loving enemies (Matt. 5:48), forgiving as he forgives (Matt. 6:12), generous as he is in giving good gifts to his children (Matt. 7:11). Paul finds the supreme revelation of God's love in the fact that while we were yet sinners, he sent his son Jesus Christ to die upon the cross to save us (Rom. 5:8). Nothing can separate us from the love of God (Rom. 8:39). John declares that God is love (I John 4:8), who first loved us (I John 4:19) and gave his Son that we should not perish but have eternal life (John 3:16). The love of God for his chosen people as revealed in the history and covenant of the Old Testament becomes a new covenant in the mission of Jesus to redeem all people by his unfailing divine love.

b) *Man's love for God.* Jesus places love for God above all other obligations. In this he carries on the emphasis of his Hebrew heritage, the *Shema* (Deut. 6:4-5), by which every Jewish service of worship is opened: "Thou shalt love the Lord thy God with all thy heart, and with all thy soul, and with all thy mind" (Matt. 22:37). To love God means to serve him with faithful devotion in life and death. From his first recorded words, "I must be about my Father's business" (Luke 2:49), to his final breath, "Father, into thy hands I commend my spirit" (Luke 23:46) the life of Jesus spelled devotion to God. For love is manifest in deed more than in word. "Not every one that saith unto me, Lord, Lord, shall enter . . . ; but he that doeth the will of my Father which is in heaven." (Matt. 7:21). The epistles bear similar testimony. Those who love God are called in terms of his purpose (Rom. 8:28). Love to God means keeping his commandments (I John 5:3). To love God is to dwell in his love and show that love to others (I John 4:7-8). Faith in God means trust in his love and faithfulness in doing his loving will (I John 4:12-16).

c) Man's love for man. "Love thy neighbour as thyself" (Matt. 22:39) is the second great commandment which Jesus joins with the first duty of loving God. In the parable of the good Samaritan he answers the question "Who is my neighbour?" by pointing to the wounded stranger overlooked by priest and Levite (Luke 10:30). In the Sermon on the Mount he enjoins this same love to enemies. If you love them which love you, what do you more than others (Matt. 5:43-47)? Paul writes to the Thessalonians that instruction upon brotherly love is not needed, for they are taught by God to love one another (I Thess. 4:9). His hymn of love gives the best definition of Christian brotherly love (I Cor. 13). Whatever we may have or do accomplishes nothing without love. Love never fails. Follow God and walk in love, as Christ has also loved us (Eph. 5:1-2). John offers a new commandment to love one another as Christ loved us (John 13:34-35). Love of God is demonstrated in love of brothers; otherwise God is not truly loved (I John 4:7-8, 21).

2. CHRISTIAN EXPERIENCE OF LOVE

The distinctive character of Christian love is in loving as an experience. To Jesus and his followers love was a way of life to be discovered in practice more than in theory. The New Testament is not a textbook of theology but a record of vital experiences as told by persons who lived through them. It is exactly such experiences that we seek to comprehend. Others may approach love from abstract principles or theological presuppositions to argue a thesis in favor of this or that. But we shall want to bring doctrinal controversies to the test of actual experience as the source and guide to understanding. Experience is the crux of all knowledge, and study of Christian love will seek to understand the experience of love in what it means to Christians.

Christian love is growing interest in, appreciation of, and responsibility for every person as a member of one family of God.[1]

God's love for man is *parental love.* To the Christian, God is the heavenly Father of all. He is revered as the creator who gives birth to new life, who develops potential into actual life, who awakens interests and invites enlarging responses. He is gratefully acknowledged as the nourisher and sustainer of life, who protects, yet encourages experiment and educative adventures. He is loved for the greatness of his love, impartially bestowed on all his children, faithful even to the unfaithful, blessing the just and the unjust, striving to turn evil intentions to good and make the useless fruitful in value. He is praised for his redemptive purpose in seeking to make the unworthy more worthy.

To experience God as heavenly Father is to find our highest human knowledge of fatherly love enlarged to universal dimensions. The earliest experiences of most children are of parents who give them loving care, supplying warmth, nourishment, and affection. Parents may sometimes punish, deprive, or go away; but children come to accept these as necessary events in a larger purpose that means to do the best possible for their growing welfare. The very errors and evils of human parents give rise to longing for a more perfect heavenly parent. Faith rooted in such experience flowers in the aspiration of a more-than-human Father. "If ye then, being evil, know how to give good gifts unto your children, how much more shall your Father which is in heaven give good things to them that ask him?" (Matt. 7:11.) In the joys and sorrows of human family love there comes a sense of greater responsibilities, a perfect Father who never fails or forgets his children. "When my father and my mother forsake me, then the Lord will take me up." (Ps. 27:10.)

Psychologist E. M. Ligon considers fatherly love the most constant

[1] A Christian family is a society of interrelated persons responding to each other by sentiments and services of active Christlike love. For discussion see Chap. V.

and dependable of all human motives.[2] It is one of the basic drives in human nature, and it provides a dynamic for unselfish devotion to weaker members of society. Parental love is the most sustained motive in human life. The most difficult problem in the psychology of motivation is how to sustain effort. It is easy to arouse momentary excitement leading to action, but very difficult to maintain enthusiasm day in and day out. Of all loves the most faithful is parental love, and around this dynamic the energies of Christian personality are best integrated. Fatherly love is so meaningful to the little child and so capable of expanding discovery that it becomes the great theme of Christian experience—God is our loving Father.

Mother love is also noted for unselfish devotion. It is natural that appreciation for motherhood holds a high place in the history of religions, deified as goddess in some, enshrined as angel, saint, or holy mother in others. Hindus pray, "Thou art the father and mother of all that thou hast made." Buddhists offer devotion to a goddess of mercy, ancient Mediterranean religions to the Great Mother (Magna Mater). Roman Catholics give a large place in worship to Mary, the blessed mother of Jesus. The Christian God, however, is not represented as either male or female. He rises above sex distinctions to the more complete nature that includes the spiritual virtues of both father and mother. The masculine pronoun is used in the generic sense that refers to a loving personality in utmost completeness. God as Father signifies the faithful strength of father love and the gentle mercy of mother love. It is our language, not our intention, that limits the overflowing vastness of divine love.

The Greek New Testament word for this overflowing divine love is *agape*. As Anders Nygren expounds it, *agape* is God's own love spontaneously flowing to all creatures, not by reason of their worth or merit, not moved by any gain for himself, not caused by any external force or value, but coming freely from his boundless gen-

[2] *The Psychology of Christian Personality* (New York: The Macmillan Co., 1935), pp. 63-91.

erosity.[3] Such love is creative, bringing new value to every object of God's love. It reaches across all chasms and barriers to us and opens a way between God and man. Jesus came not to call the righteous but sinners (Mark 2:17), not because they are deserving, but because it is God's nature to love. To Paul it was a continual amazement that he who persecuted Jesus should be saved by Jesus. Not by any merit of his own, but rather by God's love there opened a way to him. "By the grace of God I am what I am." (I Cor. 15:10.) All have sinned and fallen short of the glory of God (Rom. 3:23), yet, "God was in Christ, reconciling the world unto himself" (II Cor. 5:19). *Agape* is fatherly love on a universal scale.

Man's love for God is *filial love*. Jesus often speaks of God as Father. "Our Father which art in heaven, hallowed be thy name." (Matt. 6:9.) His every attitude toward God is filial as with complete trust, obedience, communion, and devotion he seeks to do his Father's will and work. "I can of mine own self do nothing. . . . I seek not mine own will, but the will of the Father which hath sent me." (John 5:30.) In every deed he is conscious of representing his Father. As a son resembles his father in manner and viewpoint, so Jesus is related to his Father. "He that hath seen me hath seen the Father." (John 14:9.) In these attitudes of unswerving devotion we can see the deep reservoir of his filial love. Apart from the Father life has no meaning, no vocation, no resources. All that he is or ever hopes to be, all that he asks or seeks in life, all that he does and says arises from the filial experience. "I am in the Father, and the Father in me." (John 14:11.) "I am not alone, because the Father is with me." (John 16:32.)

It is this filial relationship to God that Jesus invited others to experience. First of all privileges is to love God as a heavenly Father; when one seeks foremost this relationship all other values of life will be added (Matt. 6:33). To live with God is the pearl of great price, the hidden treasure which one will eagerly sell all else to obtain. There is no higher blessedness than to become children of God in

[3] *Agape and Eros*, Vol. I tr. A. G. Hebert; Vol. II tr. P. S. Watson (London: Society for Promoting Christian Knowledge; New York: The Macmillan Company, 1932-1939).

the full spiritual meaning of that filial love. The Beatitudes lead up to this climax in "Blessed are the peacemakers: for they shall be called the children of God" (Matt. 5:9). They suggest laws of cause and effect in the spiritual life; by sowing humility, sympathy, meekness or mutual respect, righteous hunger, mercy, purity or wholeheartedness, peace, and reconciliation we may reap a harvest of happiness as children of God. To be a child of the Father in heaven one must love fellow men, even enemies and evildoers, as God does, and by so living and loving take an active place in the family of God (Matt. 5:43-48).

Nygren overlooks this filial love in his monumental treatise on Christian love. In Nygren's emphasis on *agape* God is ever the one who initiates love; man is only the receiver from God, not the giver to God. There is no way from man's side by which he can attain God.

> Between God and man there is an impassable barrier, which man from his side can never cross. Every effort of man to exalt himself to the Divine is regarded as an act of presumption like that of the Titans; so far from bringing man into a right relation to God, it is the extreme of godlessness. The gulf between God and man can only be bridged by God himself.[4]

We are not in a position to speak with such finality about God. But we can point to the teaching of Jesus as he urged men, "Seek ye first the kingdom of God, and his righteousness" (Matt. 6:33); "Ask, and it shall be given you; seek, and ye shall find; knock, and it shall be opened unto you" (Matt. 7:7). There is no indication in the life or teaching of Jesus that man is helpless to seek, or separated by an impassable gulf from God, or obliged to wait in sorrow and sin with no effort to remedy his situation. There is New Testament evidence that God initiates love for men, but no evidence that men are unable to return love for love. It is taken for granted that we can and should love God because he first loved us (I John 4:19).

We are not invited to become God, as some mystics in Greece and India have sought to do. The presumptuous sin of the Titans in Greek legend was their attempt to overthrow and replace Zeus. This may be the aim of pantheists who seek the loss of personal identity in

---

[4] *Ibid.,* I, 163.

ecstatic union with God. Both of these efforts to become God, whether by revolt or absorption, deny the kind of filial love taught in the New Testament. A filial son does not revolt against his father to replace him, as in the Oedipus motive expounded by Greek tragedy and Freud. Such rivalry and revolt is unfilial. Neither does a filial son lose his identity, but rather will he honor and serve the father in his own way by fulfilling sonship in the largest sense.

Nygren insists that nothing a man can do will open the way to God. He points to the failure of self-abasement and amendment, as well as righteousness and merit, to secure God's favor. A man's efforts in any direction may be false or futile, but it would be a hasty generalization to conclude that all efforts are useless. There are devious ways of seeking God, many of which the New Testament rejects. Jesus casts the money-changers out of the temple, agreeing with the prophets that mercy and prayer are better than sacrifices of slain animals (Matt. 21:12-13). He rejects legalistic ceremonies such as tithing herbs (Luke 11:42), washing of hands (Matt. 15:20), and nonactivity on the Sabbath (Matt. 12:12), in favor of weightier matters such as the love of God, feeding the hungry, and healing the sick. But nowhere does he recommend doing nothing. There are weightier things to do, more urgently needed and more appropriate toward God.

The New Testament does not teach that what men do makes no difference to God. To the contrary what man does is presented as of the utmost importance to God. "Not everyone that saith unto me, Lord, Lord . . . ; but he that doeth the will of my Father." (Matt. 7:21.) Verbs characteristically appear in the active voice: do, go, come, follow. The disciple is known by what he does, for actions speak louder than words. God's love is active; so must ours be. "My Father worketh hitherto, and I work." (John 5:17.) The love of God is portrayed as impartial; to him the sinner is as dear as the righteous man. Yet sinners are to repent, the sick are to get well, the unjust are to restore and be just, the woman in adultery is to go and sin no more. And whoever would have a place in God's family must do their best to be worthy and useful, not unprofitable servants and sluggards, but

30

earnest followers ready to give up private plans and fortunes to follow the way of the Cross to serve and save others.

The truth is that filial relationships have responsibilities as well as privileges. To love God is to keep his commandments, to continue in love, to abide faithfully, to bear much fruit, to be pruned sacrificially, and even to lay down life for love (John 15:1-13). Three times Peter is asked, "Lovest thou me?" Each time the answer is to do something about it, prove his love in deeds, be an effective workman in the cause of love (John 21:15-17). The prodigal son took the steps to return home, and to maintain his place in the family he would need on the next day to join in the responsibilities of a son at home. There is nothing so inexorable or so inescapable as the requirements of love.

True love is mutually responsive. If the father loves the son, how does that excuse the son from loving the father? If family love reaches cosmic perspective, is there any reason to doubt that the Father's love to us does not invite our filial love to him? Spinoza held the highest good to be the intellectual love of God. But love that is only intellectual is abstract and theoretical. Nygren may also be pursuing the fallacy of abstraction when he takes love as one-sided, coming down only from God to man. The experience of Jesus and New Testament writers, as well as the witness of most of the voices in Christian history, points to love as a mutual meeting of God and man, each loving the other with all his heart, mind, and strength.

Man's love for man is *fraternal love*. In the religious perspective of Christian faith this likewise enlarges family love to universal dimensions. Brotherly love (*philadelphia*) is the keynote of Christian ethics and social action. Beginning with himself as each person inevitably does, he learns in the family to share with brothers and sisters. The only child is at a disadvantage in such learning, for the daily routine of family living puts him at the center of receiving with less demand upon him to share. When a younger baby arrives, he is apt to receive quite a shock in seeing the family attention move to the newcomer. He is apt to resist the imposter and even play the part of a helpless or screaming baby to regain the favored position. Such rivalries are a heavy strain on the family ties; they make family love grow more

31

generous or break down in the members' struggles for ascendancy over one another. These rivalries and conflicts infect society at large, until our entire civilization is threatened by explosive strife.

Christian love pulls affection outward from self to others. Self-love moves out to love of brothers and sisters. Sibling rivalry yields to sibling love. Brothers are not rivals but comrades; sisters are not objects of envy but of tender affection. Children are shown parental love in faithful protecting care and merciful kindness. Older members of the family are shown filial love, respect, and consideration. "Honour thy father and thy mother." (Exod. 20:12.) "Children, obey your parents in the Lord. . . . And, ye fathers, provoke not your children to wrath: but bring them up in the nurture and admonition of the Lord." (Eph. 6:1, 4.) But the traditional family is not to build a wall around Christian love. Jesus asked: "Who is my mother, or my brethren? And he looked round about on them which sat about him, and said, Behold my mother and my brethren! For whosoever shall do the will of God, the same is my brother, and my sister, and my mother" (Mark 3:33-35).

This evidently was not intended to reject his blood relatives but to enlarge family love to include others. For blood relationship is only one of the ties that relate us to each other. Many social and spiritual interests may bind us even more closely together. Those who do the will of God, Jesus indicates, are children of one cosmic Father, united by that larger family tie, sharing a common fatherly love from above, a filial love in response to him, and a brotherly love for each other. "Love goes outward," said the Chinese sage Chu Hsi. To prevent this outward expansion of love is to cripple its freedom and deny its true nature. Christian love goes outward to all people as members of one family under one Father. "God that made the world and all things therein . . . hath made of one blood all nations of men for to dwell on all the face of the earth." (Acts 17:24, 26.)

Jesus started a moral revolution when he advocated, "Love your enemies." Even to this day it comes as a shock to the smug complacency of our narrow-walled living. It has always been customary to love the few who are near by ties of family and community, but to reject all claims from others. Strangers are alien; they do not belong. Therefore ignore them, scorn them, and distrust them. The typical tendency has been to class strangers with enemies, for they are unknown, different, and dangerous. The Hebrew instruction is a long step forward when it teaches that one is to open his hand to the stranger that is within his gates, but it is an inferior charity to give him meat that is not fit for the household to eat (Deut. 14:21). Jesus sets aside all shrewd moral calculations and cautious restrictions.

Ye have heard that it hath been said, Thou shalt love thy neighbour, and hate thine enemy. But I say unto you, love your enemies, bless them that curse you, do good to them that hate you, and pray for them which despitefully use you and persecute you; that ye may be the children of your Father which is in heaven: for he maketh his sun to rise on the evil and on the good, and sendeth rain on the just and on the unjust. (Matt. 5:43-45.)

This is dangerous doctrine. In our time men have been abused, imprisoned, and murdered for trying to practice it, as Gandhi and other pacifists have. For it is contrary to the accepted mores of nations and people, who feel threatened by such an ethical revolution. But the saying of Jesus is remarkable as well for the reason on which he rests his case. This is the way God loves, for he is the Father of all, the evil and the good; he cares for the just and the unjust. The argument follows that as God loves, so we ought to love in order to be worthy children of such a Father. To acknowledge God as the Father of the human family on this planet is to accept all as our brothers and sisters to share in universal family love. What a difference on earth when this heavenly love is extended to all! Then we may pray: Thy family come on earth as it is loved in heaven. Suspicion, strife, hatred, and indifference—the four terrible horsemen that ravish our planet today— will then yield to their long-awaited successors—trust, sympathy, sharing, and love.

> I heard a child crying with hunger outside my door,
> And I went out into the night,
> And I said, "Why, this is my child!"
> And I took him in and gave him food.

I saw a young Polish girl crying her
Heart out in a camp in Germany—expecting
A baby, without a stitch of clothing for it, with
No one in the whole wide world to turn to
In her hour of need . . .
And I said, "Why, this is my sister!"
And I gave her clothing, and I gave
Her care and comfort in my home.

I stood beside a boy in a Displaced Persons
Camp, and I saw his shoulders shake with sobs
When they told him he had failed the
Semester's work in the temporary university
Inside the camp. And I said, "Why, this is my brother!"
And I took him to a youth hostel and gave
Him food and rest and friendship.

I knelt beside an old Chinese woman
Where she lay swollen with disease
Beside the road near Kwantung,
Abandoned by the living who feared
To catch the plague—and I said,
"Why, this is my mother!" And I took
Her to a Chinese mission and
They placed her on a clean bed
And washed her tired and filthy body
And gave her tender, loving care.

I sat before a haggard, haunted man
Who'd come to ask for seed and
Farming tools to make up the
Shortages of seed-grain, eaten
To keep alive during the nightmare winter months,
And the loss of breeding stock, slaughtered
In desperation. And I said, "Why,
This is my father!" And I gave him
Implements and food and went to
Visit in his home with gifts of
Clothing for his wife and children.

I heard the music of many voices singing hymns of worship
In a city of Europe where the war had been.
And I thought, "I will go to church," and
I went, and there were only the ruins of a church,
And pale and shabby people were the singers
And the worshipers. I sat with them
On the crude benches in the cleared place
Before the altar. And I said, "Why, this is my church!
And I arose and said aloud, "We must rebuild it.
Let me help to lift the stones." [5]

In the fourth century B.C. a Chinese seer, Mo Ti, caught this vision.[6] His country was ravaged then, as now, with civil strife, army warring against army, the strong exploiting the weak, the rich forgetting the desperate plight of the poor. He journeyed up and down the roads from village to village proclaiming that the will of heaven is universal love. Heaven loves all people, and wills that we also love all people. Loving our father we are to love all fathers as our own. Loving our mother we are to love all mothers as our own. Loving our brother we are to love all brothers as our own. Then large states will no longer devour small states or strong households exploit weak ones. When we treat all people as members of our own family, love will become universal and cure the social ills of suffering humanity.

Toward this larger family loyalty the wise seers and altruistic doers of all ages have been moving. As pioneer explorers grope their way through tangled jungles and rock-strewn canyons up the sides of a lofty mountain, so come the prophets of love. They approach from different lands by the pathways of different religions. Some rest or settle a short way up the mountain; others press on higher. At the summit of the mountain all paths converge above the strife and sordid rivalries of the half-gods and half-slaves below. Now it is unmistakably clear from the mountaintop that there is one heaven and one earth.

[5] Printed anonymously in *Lest We Forget*, the June, 1948, newsletter from the Congregational Christian Committee for War Victims and Reconstruction. Used by permission of the Missions Council of the Congregational Christian Churches.

[6] *The Ethical and Political Works of Motse*, tr. Y. P. Mei (London: Arthur Probsthain, 1929).

One God nourishes all people as heaven touches the whole earth. One Father loves every man, woman, and child—two billion members of one human family.

3. WHAT OF SELF-LOVE?

What becomes of the self in Christian love? Voices are lifted against the self as an obstacle to Christian altruism. Jesus is quoted as saying, "If any man will come after me, let him deny himself" (Matt. 16:24). Self-love is an attachment that often hinders freedom to grow. Psychologists call self-love "narcism," a term derived from the Greek story of Narcissus, who fell in love with his own reflection in a pool of water. Self-love is a natural stage in the early period of childhood when one is showered with attention and feels himself to be the center of his world. As he discovers other persons who are not his puppets but have wishes and ways of their own, his own omnipotence will usually shrink to the size of one person among many. As he learns to return love to others, he outgrows the danger of fixation at the stage of self-love and becomes a ready member of an interacting society. But selfishness yields reluctantly and contrives to threaten the larger dimensions of social love.

For this reason Christian teaching accents the need of overcoming selfish impulses by vigorous methods. To be a disciple means to discipline oneself, and the followers of Jesus had few illusions of self-indulgence. Their self-denials were decisive and immediate in terms of giving up competing interests to follow the Master. Those who wanted to postpone the discipline or turn back were not encouraged to be disciples. Even the disciples who saw the present denials as a prelude to future gains of power and prestige in the kingdom, as sitting at the right or left in seats of honor, were corrected promptly by Jesus (Matt. 20:20-23). They were instead to take up a cross and follow in the way of sacrifice (Matt. 16:24) as a privilege to be accepted gladly without reward as the world may give for services rendered.

Does this mean that self-love is completely rejected? There are earnest Christians who answer Yes. Away with all love of self. Nygren takes this stand that Christian love (*agape*) has no place for self-love.

Christianity does not recognize self-love as Christian. It recognizes love to God and love to one's neighbour; but self-love is the great enemy which must be overcome. Self-love separates man from God; it blocks the channels of self-spending and self-offering, both toward God and toward man.[7]

Self-love is to him the very essence of *eros*, which he finds in constant opposition to *agape*. *Eros* is the Greek word from which *erotic* comes, and though often sublimated above sex desire it remains for Nygren a self-seeking love. Every desire has self-reference to satisfy the cravings of the self. He notes the ways in which *eros* has infiltrated into the pure *agape* stream of self-giving love and counts it the enemy with which Christianity cannot afford to compromise. The self-desires are the root of very sin; they must yield to God until the egocentric becomes theocentric and God's love (*agape*) can then save us from self-love (*eros*).

Augustine (354-430) sees it differently. To him all love is acquisitive, a craving that rises from our lack of some good. The quest for good (*bonum*) is the most fundamental urge of human life. For we are created as finite beings insufficient in ourselves; we must desire in order to love, and love to complete our incompleteness. Every good desired satisfies the self, and consequently all love is by that much self-love. Love of neighbor and love of God are not free of self-love because the self rightly enjoys such a privilege. To Augustine even God in the Trinity is a community of self-love. Therefore self is not denied but fulfilled in Christian love. For instead of the lust (*cupiditas*) of selfish desire we are led to higher unselfish love (*caritas*) in the Christian way of loving.

For the most part Christian tradition has followed Augustine in fulfilling rather than rejecting the self in love. There are rigid ascetics who prefer the negative path of Buddhism in cutting off desire as the source of all evil. But desire is also the source of good, and to deny all desire is to ask for unconscious Nirvana. To deny the self

---

[7] *Op. cit.*, I, 170. For contrary views see A. C. Knudson, *The Principles of Christian Ethics* (New York and Nashville: Abingdon-Cokesbury Press, 1943), pp. 118-34; and J. L. Liebman, *Peace of Mind* (New York: Simon & Schuster, 1946), pp. 38-58.

completely is to prefer death to life, a strange falling in love with annihilation. This is not the Christian way as we understand it. The self in Christianity is not rejected but purified of selfishness, lust, and pride. The Lord's Prayer does not ask God to deliver us from self but to "deliver us from evil." It is the evil of false selfishness that cries out for deliverance, and from such temptation the prayer leads to the social values of God's family—"for thine is the kingdom, and the power, and the glory, for ever."

Such prayer strengthens rather than abnegates the self by leading the self to active participation in a larger cause of social love. In the family of universal love every self is strengthened by mutual respect and approval, human and divine. There is nothing a person hungers for so much as approval, to be accepted by others as a worthy member, not to be rejected or condemned, but affectionately treated with understanding and appreciation. In the human family parental love strengthens the growing selves to be good citizens taking their active part for the welfare of all. Parental rejection makes neurotics and criminals who are unable to work or play constructively with others by reason of their self-rejection and emotional insecurity. What a difference family love makes in the ascendancy of good over evil in each self!

Christianity exalts the self in interpersonal relations. To accept oneself as a child of a heavenly Father who loves, cares, and values him is a significant experience. To feel oneself related to the larger family of God's children, a member of an intimately sympathetic fellowship, enhances one's own worth together with the worth of every other self in this beloved community. To be needed by the Father and useful in service to others is another exaltation. "He that is greatest among you shall be your servant." (Matt. 23:11.) This is not exalting oneself; it is rather humbling oneself in a service that is exalting. This is not a striving to rise above others in ruthless competition or selfish lust for power. It is rather the desire to decrease that others may increase, to rise only in company with others who share fairly in the progress of the whole community. If righteousness exalts a nation, it is because its citizens are exalted in service for the good of all. And beyond the nation are other members of the one family to whom our service is due that they may be exalted with us.

To "love thy neighbour as thyself" is the ethic Jesus offers for the family of one Father (Mark 12:31). To Nygren this means a rejection of the self in a larger love that transcends it.

When love gains its new direction, when it is turned away from the self and directed to one's neighbour, then the natural perversion of the will (self-love) is overcome. Thus, so far from love to one's neighbour presupposing and including self-love, it excludes it and overcomes it.[8]

But this interpretation distorts the obvious meaning of Jesus. The text does not read, Love thy neighbor *instead* of thyself, but, *As* you love yourself, love *also* your neighbor. Self-love is actually the standard by which to love others. It not only assumes a self-love but even takes it as the measure of neighbor love. If I think meanly of myself, there is no reason to think better of my neighbor. This is psychologically true; self-love is the foundation of love for others. A person who despises himself will be very likely to respect and value other persons to the same extent.

Furthermore, Christian love enhances the value of the self by virtue of the Father's love for every self. How can I despise or reject a self, whether my own or another, whom the Father values enough to love? Is it not an affront to God, contrary to his will, blaspheming his wisdom and purpose to reject what he loves? To reject myself is to negate the potential goodness that is in me and reduce it to evil. For self-rejection is morbid, repressive, and crippling to my confidence and efficiency. It makes me less useful to the Father and less valuable in service to the neighbors I want to love. Self-love is the seed from which is produced the fruit of brotherly love.

But it needs to grow. If my love is fixated on myself, it fails to grow and so defeats the larger usefulness it might otherwise have. Self-love needs to outgrow self-centered fixation, to become free to turn outward to brothers and upward to God. When our love grows up and

[8] *Op. cit.,* I, 72.

out, it becomes mature enough to be filial and brotherly love. The self is not thereby rejected but rather matured in growing to the larger interests of social love. As the seed becomes the fruit, so the self grows into the nourishing delight of Christian love.

Those who condemn self-love seem to confuse it with selfishness. To respect and care for oneself (self-love) is not identical with egotism and arrogance (selfishness). It is vanity to think more highly of oneself than the truth allows, but it is also folly to have an inferiority complex in anxious misery and scornful rejection of self. Humility is to see oneself in true perspective, not to cudgel oneself into degradation to the point of nothingness. This was the error of Calvin that has bequeathed a bitter heritage, the "total depravity" of man.

For I do not call it humility if you suppose that we have anything left. . . . We cannot think of ourselves as we ought to think without utterly despising everything that may be supposed as excellence in us. This humility is unfeigned submission of a mind overwhelmed with a weighty sense of its own misery and poverty.[9]

Selfishness is disregard of others. It has traditionally been set in opposition to unselfishness as the disregard of oneself. A deeper psychological understanding will show that, instead of opposing each other, selfishness and unselfishness are both likely to arise from hostility rather than love. To reject any self, whether my own or another, is an act of hostility. It would be naïve to assume that by hating myself I thereby love others, or by hating others I love myself. Attitudes are not so easily deceived, and neither are persons by a quick change from one object to another. No amount of despising adds up to love simply by turning from me to you. The mother who showers attention upon her child in overprotective ways is trying to conceal and compensate for her hostile impulses to reject the child. Children see through the disguise, and instead of returning the mask of love they return the hostility more deeply sensed. Calvin, who so despised

---

[9] John Calvin, *Institutes of the Christian Religion*, tr. John Allen (Philadelphia: Presbyterian Board of Christian Education, 1928), III, 681.

himself, also despised his fellow man (Servetus) to the point of wishing him to burn at the stake.

Erich Fromm shows that selfishness is in reality the opposite of self-love.

The selfish person does not love himself too much but too little; in fact he hates himself. This lack of fondness and care for himself, which is only one expression of his lack of productiveness, leaves him empty and frustrated. He is necessarily unhappy and anxiously concerned to snatch from life the satisfactions which he blocks himself from attaining. He seems to care too much for himself, but actually he only makes an unsuccessful attempt to cover up and compensate for his failure to care for his real self.[10]

Self-love is the psychological complement of loving other persons. These are not alternatives between which we choose. Instead of being contradictory they are conjunctive loves. All who are capable of loving others will be capable of loving themselves also. Love is an indivisible relationship between selves that does not reject one for the other, but that holds both in mutual esteem. To love another enhances the worth of the lover as well as the beloved. For genuine love, as Fromm shows, is an expression of productiveness, a cherishing and sharing of values by which each self is enriched. In so loving, all persons come to a worth they would not otherwise have. As Kierkegaard shows in his *Works of Love* (1874):

If anyone, therefore, will not learn from Christianity to love *himself* in the right way, then neither can he love his neighbor. . . . To love one's self in the right way and to love one's neighbor are absolutely analogous concepts, are at bottom one and the same. . . . Hence the law is: "You shall love yourself as you love your neighbor when you love him as yourself." [11]

Paul writes to the Corinthians of this more excellent love. In fact nothing else counts but love, without which one is futile and empty

---

[10] *Man for Himself: An Inquiry into the Psychology of Ethics* (New York: Rinehart & Co., 1947), p. 131.

[11] *A Kierkegaard Anthology*, ed. Robert Bretall (Princeton: Princeton University Press, 1946), p. 289.

as a noisy gong or a clanging cymbal. No sacrifice or deed is useful without love.

If I give away all I have [ascetic denial], and if I deliver my body to be burned [martyr complex], but have not love, I gain nothing.
Love is patient and kind; love is not jealous or boastful; it is not arrogant or rude. Love does not insist on its own way; it is not irritable or resentful; it does not rejoice at wrong, but rejoices in the right. Love bears all things, believes all things, hopes all things, endures all things. Love never ends. (I Cor. 13:3-8, *R.S.V.*)

4. THE DYNAMIC OF CHRISTIAN LOVE

What keeps Christian love alive? What causes a Christian to love? How does love activate Christian fellowship? What motives exert dynamic influences in a loving Christian community?

Nygren insists that Christian love (*agape*) is uncaused and unmotivated. Spontaneous and overflowing, God's love comes to the Christian and through him as a channel to others. By this he means that divine love is a spontaneous expression of God's nature, not called forth by anything outside itself. It appears to him that God is indifferent to human merit; he loves the sinner as much as the righteous, not by reason of either's condition but by his own loving nature. In the same way a Christian is to love others unconditionally, regardless of their unworthiness, if the *agape* love of God is to flow through them.

We can agree that the highest love is spontaneous and impartial. A mother by her own parental devotion will love the crippled child as much as the strong and beautiful one. But we do not agree that spontaneous love is uncaused. Even when it may be hidden from us, there is a cause for every event. Otherwise this is not an orderly, dependable universe but a chaos of unpredictable and accidental happenings. There is a theology that holds miracle more significant than law, contending that caprice is more divine than faithful order. But to us this seems to fly in the face of all experience of a trustworthy Providence. If the supernatural is really above the natural, it will express a larger order of cause and effect, by which higher good is to become more effective. To say, as Nygren does, that *agape* love flows from God's own nature is to indicate a causal relationship. In our language it would be clearer to say that God's love is evidently caused or motivated by his desire to create and sustain better life.

If love is pure giving (*agape*), there must be a motive that causes one to give. It is hardly adequate to say that love is piped in and through one by divine plumbing. To love is not so mechanical as this; it is more dynamic and expressive of the spiritual resources of personality. In psychological terms love is a deepening interest of one person in another to express affection in appropriate actions. Such giving is more than a generous impulse; it is a consistent purpose of love to share significant values with another person.

Augustine gives a psychological account of Christian love. As noted above, he traces all love to the basic motive of desire. And desire is traced back to our lack as finite creatures forever incomplete and seeking goods to meet our insufficiencies. Temporal goods are only partially satisfying; human love is never quite complete; so we are moved to seek higher and eternal values. "Our hearts are restless until they find rest in Thee." Not by human love alone do mortals reach God. This, as Augustine sees it, is possible only by the grace of God's love to us. He thereby achieves a synthesis between *eros* (the aspiring love of man) and *agape* (the overflowing love from God).

The love of good desire (*caritas*) offers a basis for analysis of Christian love. To love God with all the heart is an expression of desire. But this view is open to criticism. In the first place it rests upon the hedonistic premise that craving for pleasure is the chief motive of life. This, in the second place, provides no valid distinction between lust and love except the object chosen. And in the third place it makes all love acquisitive seeking to enrich oneself. It is not adequate to reduce Christian love to desire; yet it is not evident how love can be dynamic without desire. Is there perhaps another form of desire not directed to self-satisfaction in this acquisitive way?

We find such another desire in *creative relationship*. To be confronted by a Personality who loves is a relationship that cannot but be creative of new life. To desire to give oneself to such a Person is not acquisitive desire. It is rather a desire to enter a mutual relation

that makes life altogether different through interpersonal co-operation. To a Christian like Paul this meeting was the most real and
significant event of his life and, as he saw it, of all history.

> For we preach not ourselves, but Jesus Christ the Lord; and ourselves
> your servants for Jesus' sake. For God, who commanded the light to shine
> out of darkness, hath shined in our hearts, to give the light of the knowl-
> edge of the glory of God in the face of Jesus Christ. But we have this
> treasure in earthen vessels, that the excellency of the power may be of
> God, and not of us. (II Cor. 4:5-7.)

Does Paul refer to his conversion on the Damascus road? To that
and more. The meeting with Jesus there was to him a continuous
event that occurs wherever a man is confronted by a Person in creative
relationship. The significance of that event was not only a vivid experience of the moment. It might have been a hallucination if it happened once and not again. Paul was convinced and changed by a
continuing creation which confronted him anew each day, a transforming relationship which added a new dimension to life and which
he could only believe to be communion with a divine Person.

The divine-human encounter reveals a God of love (*agape*) who
meets man at the turn of every road.[12] And those who respond to
the divine visitation find that truth is active to search and change the
whole meaning of life. For the truth is the communication of one who
offers unconditional love to every creature, an act of God to be met
by an act of man in mutual giving. Here we move beyond psychology
to theology. The experience of this encounter is psychological; the
interpretation of meeting the God of love is theological. A psychologist, however, can observe the results of such experience in the behavior of Paul and others who show the evidence of new life. And
the resources of this love go further to create a community of persons
who share a larger life.

Human love aims to achieve mutual affectionate response. Is this
also characteristic of Christian love? We believe it cannot be other-

[12] Emil Brunner, *The Divine-Human Encounter*, tr. A. W. Loos (Philadelphia:
The Westminster Press, 1943).

wise. For love that is unilateral is crippled and one-sided, it lacks the give and take essential to growth. In human life unilateral love usually withers and declines for lack of encouraging response and mutuality. There is of course magnanimity in love that is faithful even though unrequited. But if no response ever comes, even faithfulness is tragically unfulfilled. Faithful love is never wasted, even though it may appear to be a total loss; for we do not see the invisible consequences of such love or know at what time or in what unexpected ways persons remember and are blessed by manifestations of unfailing love. The mother who faithfully loves, serves, and prays for an alcoholic son even while he fails her by wayward irresponsibility, nonsupport, and ridicule does not love in vain. Such love has a redemptive influence, if not obviously for the son, whose disease has such a firm grip on him; yet in spite of himself he is blessed by forgiving mother love, and others looking on are likewise encouraged by such faithfulness.

Yet as we understand Christian love, it is more than pure giving. It is giving to invite a response. Does God love only and forever in lonely grandeur with no concern for the response to love? If so, it is contrary to empirical evidence and all we know about love. Such love is psychologically and ethically untrue. Jesus suggests otherwise in the parable of a shepherd rejoicing to find the lost sheep: "I say unto you, that likewise joy shall be in heaven over one sinner that repenteth" (Luke 15:7). Again the love of God is portrayed in the father of the prodigal son running to welcome him home (Luke 15:20). In Christian love there is no intention that *agape* means sending best wishes with no return address. The remote grandeur that makes an offering of love to the unworthy and goes away with no answer desired is far from the spirit of Jesus. "Therefore if thou bring thy gift to the altar, and there rememberest that thy brother hath ought against thee; leave there thy gift before the altar, and go thy way; first be reconciled to thy brother, and then come and offer thy gift." (Matt. 5:23-24.) More important than prayer or sacrifice is it to reconcile a brother. *Agape* is redemptive love that invites a response of love. Thereby is love increased and shared in growing fellowship.

The motive of creative relationship is different from acquisitive love of self-seeking and self-satisfaction. It seeks to satisfy and develop another through mutual devotion. It is not a one-way activity, however, that insists upon giving with no receiving. If it is more blessed to give than to receive, then that blessing is to be shared that others may also have the joy of giving. Only haughty pride refuses to receive in exchange for giving. A Christian community cannot long endure if founded on one-way giving. There is need for mutual giving and receiving, without either of which the community fails.

Creative relationship is the essential motive of Christian love. It represents God's love to man inviting his response in deeds worthy of repentance. It presents man's love to God in prayer that seeks a response of divine giving, or faith that anticipates continuous fatherly love. It reaches out to the enemy to reconcile him, to the stranger to make him a friend, and to the neighbor to unite in creating a beloved community. Not every mutual response is love, but at the level of Christian aspiration love has divine qualities of giving and receiving the values of eternally abundant life.

The great discovery of life is what Martin Buber calls the *I-Thou* relationship. To every thing my relationship is merely to *It*. But to another person *I* come to a *Thou* and find a relationship mutually giving and creative.

The *Thou* meets me. But I step into direct relation with it. Hence the relation means being chosen and choosing, suffering and action in one. . . . The primary word *I-Thou* can be spoken only with the whole being. . . . All real living is meeting.

Love is responsibility of an *I* for a *Thou*. . . . Relation is mutual. My *Thou* affects me, as *I* affect it.

He who takes his stand in relation shares in a reality, that is, in a being that neither merely belongs to him nor merely lies outside him. All reality is an activity in which I share without being able to appropriate for myself. Where there is no sharing there is no reality.

Every particular *Thou* is a glimpse through to the eternal *Thou*. . . . If you hallow this life you meet the living God.

You know always in your heart that you need God more than everything; but do you not know too that God needs you? . . . You need God, in order to be—and God needs you, for the very meaning of your life.

46

Creation happens to us, burns itself into us, recasts us in burning—we tremble and are faint, we submit. We take part in creation, meet the Creator, reach out to Him, helpers and companions.[13]

There are two impediments to the perfect fulfillment of mutual love.[14] First, there is no certainty of equality in giving and taking love, or that love will always be returned. Second, there is a barrier which no human person is quite able to cross. "We share but in part, and are left lonely." By such failures many lovers have despaired of mutually perfect love. And here is where divine love surpasses human frailty and fickleness. To find God a loving Father perfect in love meets human needs otherwise unmet. Those who come into this filial relationship report that God responds faithfully as the eternal Companion. This Jesus confesses in the hour of trial. "Behold, the hour cometh, yea, is now come, that ye shall be scattered, every man to his own, and shall leave me alone: and yet I am not alone, because the Father is with me." (John 16:32.) On the cross there was a cry wrung from his lips in the words of the psalmist: "My God, my God, why hast thou forsaken me?" (Matt. 27:46). But then in another breath he cried, "Father, into thy hands I commend my spirit" (Luke 23:46).

If Christian love is truly represented in the life of Jesus, it is a divine-human creative relationship. The Father and the Son meet constantly in prayer, teaching, healing, and dying upon the cross to point the way by which others may co-operate with God in a family of love. There is no need to say more or construct specious arguments in its defense. For Christian love is an experience. It is an open secret

[13] I and Thou, tr. R. G. Smith (Edinburgh: T. & T. Clark, 1937), pp. 11, 14-15, 63, 75, 79, 82.

[14] M. C. D'Arcy, The Mind and Heart of Love (New York: Henry Holt & Co., 1947), p. 322. Some Christian mystics have reported periods of dryness in prayer, dark nights of the soul when God seems to have withdrawn his presence. Psychologically this would seem to be a projection of subjective difficulties as feelings of guilt, despair, or indifference resulting from moods and temperamental disturbances. "Only one Thou never ceases by its nature to be Thou for us. He who knows God knows also very well remoteness from God, and the anguish of barrenness in the tormented heart; but he does not know the absence of God: it is we only who are not always there." (Buber, op. cit., p. 99.)

47

to those who are ready to enter as Jesus and others have into such transforming relationships.

How is Christian love different from other loves? Historically Christian love rises from Jesus, who loved God as Father and every person as inseparably related in one family of God. It is as unique as and no more than the spirit of Jesus shown in attitudes of appreciation and deeds of service to other persons everywhere. Religiously this spirit of love has much in common with the highest aspirations and deepest devotions of other religions: the law and prophecy of continuing Judaism, the Bakhti and Yogi devotion of Hinduism, the brotherhood and mercy of Buddhism, the reciprocal relationships of Confucianism, the Taoist kindness in return for injury, the universal love of Mohism, the sacrificial love and faithfulness of the Moslem, Parsee, Sikh, Jain, and Shintoist. Ethically Christian love is distinct from all secular loves by its inclusive outreach to the Kingdom of God to bring the whole world into God's realm of creative-redemptive love. Psychologically Christian love is interpersonal in searching the larger possibilities of human-divine relationships, a trifocal motivation of *I* and *Thou* and *We*.

III

Motive Power of Love

Love is more than a word. It may be enshrined as chief in a list of abstract virtues, but in life love is no abstraction. Love is an energy. Energetic love is one of the most powerful motives in human actions. For love of woman or child, or country or God, men have devoted their utmost powers. What then is the power of love? What forces are at work when we love? How is love possible? Can we understand its causes and conditions? In Chapter II we found this energy responsive to Christian ideals that created communities of mutual affection and service. By other names and standards people have also learned to love and unite in community life. We shall need to examine the motives that give rise to love.

1. Is Love an Instinct?

Love has often been described as instinctive. William James in his pioneer work, *The Principles of Psychology*, refers to love as an instinct.[1] Parental love and sexual love are prominent in his list of instincts. Sex impulses are apparently instinctive as acting blindly and automatically without one's foresight or previous education. But James goes on to show that sexual instincts are modified by experiences according to individual stimuli, inward condition, habits acquired, and the clash of contrary impulses. Instinct was a popular concept in that time, accepted naïvely by most writers as the readiest cause to explain animal and human behavior. It is notable that while James

[1] New York: Henry Holt & Co., 1890, II, 437. See also A. Sutherland, *The Origin and Growth of the Moral Instinct* (New York: Longmans, Green & Co., 1898), who traces the rise of altruism from the maternal instinct.

did employ the concept of instinct, he was alert enough to see the absurdity of unlearned tendencies. He calls the earlier writings on instinct "ineffectual wastes of words" that "smothered everything in vague wonder." An instinct of maternity "represents the animal as obeying abstractions." [2] In the critical analysis of James instincts look much as they do to modern psychologists—too complex, modifiable, and abstract to serve as the simple explanatory principle of behavior.

The instinct theory was further developed by William McDougall. He considers the maternal instinct the most powerful of all, able to override any other, even fear.[3] Of great importance also is the sexual instinct or instinct of reproduction. These together with a gregariousness or herd instinct are motives which seem to support love. McDougall defines instinct as "an inherited or innate psycho-physical disposition which determines its possessor to perceive, . . . to experience an emotional excitement . . . and to act." [4] After thirty years of critical study and discussion he rejects the mechanistic view of behavior determined by an innate push from behind, and replaces the term "instinct" with "propensity." McDougall's later emphasis is on goal seeking as the basic motivation, with adaptive learning and adjustment to reach desired goals. A propensity is such a "disposition . . . of the mind's total organization . . . which, when it is excited, generates an active tendency, a striving, an impulse or a drive towards some goal." [5] This goal seeking need not always be conscious. But when working toward a foreseen goal it is a *desire;* when accepted and approved it is a *purpose.* Love becomes more intelligible in this later

[2] *Ibid.,* pp. 383-85. He notes instincts as an "a priori synthesis" and says, "To the broody hen the notion would probably seem monstrous that there should be a creature in the world to whom a nestful of eggs was not the utterly fascinating and precious and never-to-be-too-much-sat-upon object which it is to her" (p. 387).

[3] *An Introduction to Social Psychology* (Boston: J. W. Luce & Co., 1908, 1918), p. 70. In his *Outline of Psychology* (New York: Charles Scribner's Sons, 1923), p. 130, he refers to the parental instinct as "nature's brightest and most beautiful invention."

[4] *Ibid.,* p. 30.

[5] *The Energies of Men* (New York: Charles Scribner's Sons, 1932), p. 40. Instinct he calls a "vague explanatory principle" (p. 31). By this time he calls his psychology hormic, from the Greek *horme,* meaning purpose.

view as seeking, desiring, and purposing the goals of interpersonal relationships.

Freud sees love arising from the biological urge of the sex instinct as the basic drive of life. Yet in human development love is far more than a biological urge of inherited prepotency. The tendency to love is called "libido," by which Freud means a psychological interest in persons and objects that bring satisfying experiences. Many attacks upon Freud come from a misunderstanding of his basic concepts, such as sex; it is claimed, for instance, that he reduces the higher interests of life to animal lusts. A closer study will show that Freud is moving in the opposite direction; he elevates sex to the larger and higher meaning of love in social dimensions. In his extension of the term "sexual" Freud refers not only to genital function but to any life functions having pleasure as their goal, and not only to body pleasure but to all affectionate impulses. Though Freud does not surrender the instinctive basis of love, he does not confine it to the blind impulse of unlearned tendencies. Rather he shows again and again how love is modified by outgoing interest in other persons (object love) or in-turning interest as self-love (narcism); how love may be arrested by unhappy social experiences (fixation) or returned to earlier stages of development by rivalry for attention (regression) or dammed up by social and self-disapproval (repression) or directed into other more socially acceptable channels (sublimation).

The libido of Freud is therefore a broad and flexible stream of human energy consisting of biological urges and psychological interests that seek many goals and are modifiable by social influences and self-chosen adjustments. There has been confusion in this larger view of sex motivation, due in part to Freud and in part to the difficulties of translation from another language. But surely Freud is contending that love is more than an instinct; he is emphasizing the psychosomatic character of love and showing how significant love is to persons, as other persons are to the development of love. In his later writings the life instinct seeks to overcome the death instinct. He gives the impetus to trace the motivation of human life as a biosocial process in which love is formed and reformed by the constantly growing influence of interpersonal relations upon native impulses.[6]

2. LOVE A DYNAMIC NEED

Let us not overlook the dynamic nature of these psychologies of James, McDougall, and Freud. They are all motor psychologies of action in revolt against the static, artificial patterns of the earlier structuralists. From mechanistic causes that push and drive they move to goals which organisms seek. This active reference to goals is a larger perspective in which instincts are superseded by desires and purposes.

From this we see that love is dynamic. It is psychic energy that responds to attractive objects; that selects, prefers, and chooses what to love. Dynamisms of goal seeking explain love better than mechanisms of inherited drives. And when love objects are desired and selected, the response is more than organic. Desires and choices are conscious; they direct as well as express unconscious urges. Love is drawn by attraction more than it is propelled by blind impulse. The goal of a loving relationship is the controlling cause. Love is a going concern of inner tension and outgoing intention.

Love is therefore natural. Living creatures have an innate capacity to respond. Heredity plays its part in preparing mammals for love. What we inherit, however, is not a mechanism predetermined to love but an organism predisposed to respond to affection, not an instinctive drive that automatically discharges sex impulses blindly regardless of the object but rather a capacity to respond favorably to attractive organisms that show affectionate interest. Does this mean that love is inevitable because we inherit capacities to love? No, that would oversimplify the interpersonal situation in which interest is highly selective of persons to love and societies that invite responses of love. We inherit capacities to respond in kind to attitudes shown us. It is natural to show affection to one who shows affection to us. It is also natural to hate and resent those who resent and hate us. But human nature is ready for love and is frustrated when denied its expression. To reject

[6] See *The Basic Writings of Sigmund Freud.*

an unwanted child is to repress and cripple the child's capacity to love by social conditioning to hostility. To provide affectionate attitudes toward a child is to develop and enlarge the native capacity to love.

Love is consequently a basic need in human development. Every person needs to love and to be loved. With mammals the infant is invited to love first by the mother in suckling and caressing. The infant needs affection in order to develop its inherited capacities to motor response (as in play), attentive response (as watching the mother), and emotional response (in returning affection). The need for affection is recognized by psychiatrists and child psychologists as one of the most essential needs of normal personality, indicating that the denial of affection is the major cause of neurotic and antisocial behavior.[7] To our view need is a better concept than instinct because it is a conscious seeking. In needs we find the primary source of religious experience.[8] Out of the depths of human need men pray to a Creator of values. Unconscious needs exert their influence in organic tensions; conscious needs by open goal seeking, planning, and organizing energies.

In this conscious seeking love grows by experience. James, McDougall, and Freud recognize that innate tendencies are modified by learning experience; other social scientists increasingly emphasize the ways in which experience enters into goal seeking purposes. Love is not present at birth, but it is learned by the interchange of friendly interest and affectionate responses with other persons. Erogenous zones and glands are prepared to respond to love; but unless the subject becomes aware of a loving person, the physiology does not become the psychology of love. It is by experiences of affectionate responsiveness—such as fondling and play in infancy, mutual interest in

[7] Horney, *The Neurotic Personality of Our Time* (New York: W. W. Norton & Co., Inc., 1937), p. 44, says, "In examining the childhood histories of a great number of neurotic persons I have found . . . the basic evil is invariably a lack of genuine warmth and affection. A child can stand a great deal of what is often regarded as traumatic—such as sudden weaning, occasional beating, sex experience—as long as inwardly he feels wanted and loved."

[8] P. E. Johnson, *Psychology of Religion* (New York and Nashville: Abingdon-Cokesbury Press, 1945), pp. 38-45. A need is a psychomotor tension to attain an essential value-goal.

adolescence, courting a mate or developing friendly interests in maturity—that love develops.

3. EMOTIONS AND RESPONSES

The nature of emotions is one of the vaguest and most vital subjects of psychology. For two centuries it has been customary to classify psychological faculties as intellectual, emotional, and volitional. This appears artificial today as we find these processes mingling and interacting together constantly. For logical convenience they may be separated, but in living activity they are inseparable. P. T. Young defines emotion as "an acute disturbance of the individual, psychological in origin, involving behavior, conscious experience, and visceral functioning." [9] This indicates the range and unification of processes involved in emotion. The whole personality is affected, body as well as mind, behavior as well as experience. To Young emotion is always disturbing, upsetting, and disintegrating.

I agree with Young in the unitary view of emotion as affecting the whole personality, but I do not agree that emotion is always upsetting. Violent emotions do disturb our poise and may upset efficient performance or prevent progress toward a goal. But emotional undertones constantly support effective behavior. Emotional overtones give brilliance, interest, desire, valuation, and motive power to the attainment of goals. I have previously defined emotion as "the qualitative experience of tension toward goals." [10] The tension is psychosomatic, appearing in organic functions and psychic energies of attraction or aversion. Emotional energy is qualitative, not quantitative, and defies exact measurement, for it is embedded in and diffused throughout the whole of life. It is motivating as dynamic and telic tendencies toward goals, a by-product of values sought or evils avoided. The intensity of emotion is thus dependent upon the value-significance of the goal, the eagerness to attain it, and the facilitation or frustration of purposive goal seeking. When goal seeking is overexcited eagerness or distressing anxiety as to reaching the goal, it will be disturbing and

[9] *Emotion in Man and Animal* (New York: John Wiley & Sons, Inc., 1943), p. 51.
[10] *Op. cit.,* p. 50.

upsetting. When the goal seeking proceeds efficiently, the emotional responses are supporting and satisfying. Love is then satisfying and supporting in reference to the person loved.

What becomes of "will power" in recent psychology? The will is no longer viewed as an independent agent that works on its own circuit. Dynamic psychology takes the whole self into action ceaselessly in motor tendencies to choose and seek goals. Goal seeking includes intellect, will, and emotion in one dynamic process. To recognize and approve a goal is cognitive; to need-want-choose it is volitional; to feel qualitative satisfaction in approaching it is emotional. This is a positive goal-response; a negative response would disapprove, reject, and feel distress in approaching a goal. Love is a positive motor response of approving, desiring, and sustaining other persons. To say that love is the whole self acting with good will is to mean a positive response to the other person as a value-goal.

This dynamic unitary motivation is best called a "response." To respond is to answer back or react to a specific goal-oriented stimulus. A readiness to respond is an "attitude," a favorable or unfavorable set toward a specific object. "Appreciation" is a constellation of favorable attitudes, primarily cognitive, toward an object. "Sentiment" is a constellation of positive or negative attitudes, primarily emotional, toward an object. "Intention" is a constellation of purposive attitudes, primarily volitional, toward an object. This division is one of emphasis only, for attitudes are never wholly of one kind or another, but each is somewhat cognitive-volitional-emotional.

Love is a whole response of one person to another in which interest grows into obligation by a feeling of belonging to each other for good. I am his as he is mine, whether he is my friend, lover, relative, or fellow countryman. This sense of responsible association does not arrive instantaneously; it is the product of interweaving common interests in which the significance of belonging together is strengthened by many experiences of sharing a common life in a relationship of enduring values. A Christian love will leap over man-made barriers of in-groups when the sense of belonging to all men arises from deep and vivid experiences of one human family of God, in which the love of a heavenly Father for all requires that his earthly children love and forgive one another as he loves and forgives them. Love is motivated by attitudes of appreciation and desire to respond to a beloved person or group of persons. Every constellation of attitudes is governed by its object as well as its subject, and therefore it is a dynamic responsiveness between a subject and an object. Consequently love is always a unique experience of an I and a Thou. Strictly speaking one does not love a thing, for it does not respond with emotions and attitudes that are mutual. Indirectly, however, cherished objects gain in value of appreciation, but always and only because a person appreciates them with a value that derives from association with persons.

One who responds is responsive; when he responds faithfully, he is responsible. At this point psychology merges with ethics, where description meets value. Interpersonal psychology works with values as well as facts, for persons are interested in and motivated by efforts to gain value-goals in association with other persons. We have seen that love grows from interest and appreciation to responsibility for other persons. Let us define "responsibility" as the undertaking to do one's best for another person so far as possible at all times. The accent is on persistent, voluntary, best possible, interpersonal action. Such behavior is psychologically describable; it is also ethically valuable. Love without responsibility is little more than a romantic thrill. Therefore love is essentially an ethical experience between two or more persons in social relationships. To give an accurate description of Christian love we shall have to recognize its religious and ethical values.

4. Love as Affection

Affection is here used to specify the emotional responses of love. Love is no simple feeling but a constellation of many psychosomatic responses to valued persons. It arises from attitudes and sentiments in response to the tension of inner needs and the stimuli of attractive relationships with other persons. Such emotional responses focus upon love objects as dynamic systems strengthened by increasing bonds of meaning and value, arising in goal seeking purposes and satisfying social experiences. Affections are therefore the dynamic harmony of desired responsiveness.

In a psychological analysis of the dynamics of love the chief danger is oversimplification. Love is one of the most complex dynamic systems, consisting of the most varied and intricate compositions to be found in human behavior. Most attempts to dissect and explain the psychology of love suffer from easy abstractions that conceal rather than expose its true nature. Without presuming to reveal the whole meaning of love we may recognize the deceptions of simplicity and search for deeper sources and larger interpenetrations of these baffling affections. Affections are not exhausted in quantitative measurements or external observations of behavior. They are not to be fully understood by factual description of social processes without reference to values and personal meanings. Depth psychologies are having success in exploring the elemental motivations of love, and yet there is more to love than libido and id. This Freud has recognized in his analysis of the ego and superego as controlling, modifying, and sublimating the native impulses. Other psychoanalytic investigations also recognize and expound the complexities and counteractivities of human affections.

Another investigator to recognize the complexity of affections is Emanuel Swedenborg (1688-1772). In his *De Anima* [11] he brushes aside the faculty psychology of his time and views the mind as consisting of three dynamic interacting systems: (1) animus or "inferior mind," (2) mens or "rational mind," and (3) anima or "superior mind." The affections originate in the animus and the anima, while the mens, having no intrinsic affections of its own, is a battleground "between inferior and superior loves which combat against each other and endeavor to possess" it. One may note the similarity of this outline to Freud's portrayal of the id, ego, and superego, as well as to Jung's conception of personal unconscious, persona, and collective

[11] First written in 1742, unpublished until 1849 in Latin, translated into English as *The Soul; or, Rational Psychology* by Frank Sewall, and published in New York by the New Church Board of Publications in 1887.

unconscious.[12] The affections according to Swedenborg are not fixed in number or pre-existent or independent of each other as were the generalized capacities of faculty psychology. He lists numerous affections in each region, as a wide range of emotions in the lower mind and a constellation of loves in the higher mind. Freudians begin with the lower region of primitive impulses striving for expression and gratification, the sex drives of libido and the selfish demands of the id. Whatever conduct and character develop are modifications of this basic unconscious striving of the lustful pleasure principle. The conscious ego and the conscientious superego seek to mediate between the amoral demands of the id and the moral requirements of society. But the psychology of Swedenborg reverses the tendency. The dynamic forces of life originate in the higher region of the anima and are modified by the desires of the animus, mediated by the activity of the mens. Both recognize conflicting tendencies mediated, but for Swedenborg the spiritual loves are more fundamental than the sensual lusts.

From comparing loves together, the spiritual and the corporeal, for instance, it becomes evident enough that spiritual loves are the fountain of all corporeal loves; consequently that no corporeal love can exist unless a spiritual love pre-exists.[13]

The success of any individual life requires the harmony or integration of the emotions guided by the higher loves of the soul. Like the depth psychologists he recognizes that the rational mind is not the whole story. Emotional desires and affections are deeper than reason in human motivation. Or more exactly, reason mingles with desires and affections in every experience of life. "In our rational mind loves perpetually reign, nor would there be any mind without loves." [14] The dynamic of the rational mind as of all activity is the motive pow-

[12] H. D. Spoerl, "Dynamic Aspects of Swedenborg's Psychology," *The New Philosophy*, XLVI (Jan., 1943), 259.

[13] *The Soul; or, Rational Psychology*, sec. 457, pp. 284-85.

[14] *Ibid.*, sec. 315, pp. 196-97. The superconscious in Hindu psychology is equivalent to the anima of Swedenborg and is regarded as able to control conscious and unconscious impulses by its dynamic religious experiences. See Swami Akhilananda, *Hindu Psychology* (New York: Harper & Bros., 1946), pp. 150-98.

er of love. The objects of attention, knowledge, and activity are its loves. Without love there would be no desire, for "we desire what we love." Love is the basic energy of human life.

5. Religious Motivation

Freud and Swedenborg have stated—unintentionally it may be— the human predicament that religion seeks to cope with. Both men, though representing different centuries, national and religious cultures, were honest scientists who gave careful and systematic analyses of the human mind. Each of them found personality to be a dynamic complex of conflicting energies, in which the rational mind is not the whole mind but a surface manifestation of deeper, more urgent psychic forces. The power of this impulsive life is at once the hope and despair of man. Out of the depths of human impulses spring every desire for good and every temptation to evil. The psychologists' exposé of this inner conflict of irrational forces in man has shocked our modern pride in reason. But this unbridled surge of the impulse to evil is nothing new to religion. Most religions from earliest records have profoundly felt and described these invasive forces.

Not only have these religions acutely described the impulsive tendencies to good and evil; they have placed this struggle at the center of life as the most significant of all decisive issues in life and death. Not merely for the moment but for all eternity the destiny of the soul hangs upon its own inner struggles between impulses to good and evil. The basic problem of every ethical religion is how to cope with these overpowering impulses so they may not deceive or destroy but reveal and develop the best possibilities of which life is capable.

And religious beliefs differ at the same crucial point where Freud and Swedenborg differ—whether to view the higher or lower loves as predominant. Buddha, for example, agreed with Freud that the lower impulses are basic in life, that they constantly threaten the soul's higher potentiality and are to be restrained only with the greatest difficulty. To this prince, who renounced every comfort and pleasure to cope with seductive temptations, all suffering was rooted in desire. Therefore all desire appeared to him evil and must be cut

59

off by complete renunciation. Theologians in other religions have insisted that man is essentially a creature of evil desire, so totally depraved that his impulses are not to be trusted.

Jesus, on the contrary, believed as Swedenborg that the higher impulses are most natural to life; that even though they may be threatened by lower impulses to evil, they may keep the upper hand by resources available from above. For to Jesus man was a child not of the devil but of God, the heavenly Father who created man in the image of his own goodness and loves him with unfailing redemptive love. Not that Jesus was naïve about human nature; he was as fully aware of evil desires as Buddha and saw the soul as an endless battleground of conflicting tendencies. In a day when good and evil were judged by outward performance he saw that such issues are decided in the motives of the heart. "Thou shalt not kill" is an external prohibition, but murder arises from anger, and he that is angry with his brother has murder in his heart. "Thou shalt not commit adultery" is another external code, but adultery arises from lust, and he that looks on a woman lustfully has already committed adultery in his heart. The inner law of motivation is central, while the outer law is dependent upon the inner as effect comes from cause. To discover one's duty to others one must consult the inner desires as to what one would have them do. In this Jesus was speaking as a Jew to sift out the best of Judaism, and of other religions as well in which motives are often tangled in a confusion of external prescriptions and inner desires.

It is in the dynamic study of these deeper motives that religion and psychology meet. The recent depth psychologies of Freud, Jung, and Künkel are closer to religious experience than the rationalistic philosophies of many theologians. Paul and Augustine portray the conflict of desires in the soul of man in the vital insights if not the vocabulary of dynamic psychology today. The motive power of every human life is found in the loves that passionately stir within the soul. That there are lower amoral desires in conflict with higher spiritual desires is as well known to religious leaders as to the depth psychologists.

MOTIVE POWER OF LOVE

How then does religious love arise? Evidently in a victorious struggle over the lusts of the flesh which war against the higher desires for spiritual values. To Buddha as to Freud the religious love wins to the extent that it censors and represses the pleasure-seeking lusts. But Freud is more discriminating than Buddha in seeing the id as neither good nor evil but a lusty set of impulses that may be sublimated and transformed into the pattern approved by the social conscience. Instead of cutting off all desire to gain peace, Freud knows the morbid undermining resistance of impulses so ruthlessly repressed. He seeks a workable compromise in which the higher love may channel and express in acceptable ways the elemental passion.

To Jesus the major thrust of life is not from below but from above. The higher impulses to love as children of God are more natural than the perversions of anger, enmity, and lust. His effort is therefore to release by faith and encouragement, by forgiving and accepting love, the higher impulses that have been restrained by the lower. He has a cathartic method of releasing the tensions of fear and hostility—casting out demons is the colloquial equivalent—by reducing them to impotence in the presence of a stronger expulsive affection. The direction of his healing therapy is affirmation of the best tendencies by appreciating the potential possibilities of immediate growth into their fulfillment. He casts out evil impulses by confronting them with an overpowering stream of creative goodness (*agape* love) from the heavenly Father flowing in and through the awakening personality. While negative, fearful religions and psychologies concentrate on defeating evil impulses by restraint and suppression, positive faith-filled religions release good impulses by creative trust and transforming love.

Such religious motives to love are spontaneous, not coerced or restrained but overflowing in trust and good will. Spontaneity is the capacity to respond to stimuli, not automatically by reflex action but with interest by impulsive desire. Jesus was so spontaneous in his overflowing love that he did not limit his good will to those who loved him as the custom was, but he also loved his enemies and forgave those who crucified him. Such love is unconventional, not to be different but to be unlimited by narrow calculations, not to destroy but to fulfill the law in a larger sense. Spontaneous love rises from deeper sources than calculating love, and these larger resources give impetus to more generous devotion to others. Where do these resources come from? Jesus finds the creative initiative in God, renewed by frequent communion. "As the Father hath loved me, so have I loved you." (John 15:9.)

The sense of need is active in religious motivation. All life is in need at all times, for it is incomplete and dependent on larger resources. These insufficiencies are psychic as well as somatic; hunger for love is as urgent as hunger for food. With no language but a cry, infants cry for someone to come and meet their needs. As they grow stronger and strive to be independent, they are apt to feel ashamed of their insufficiencies and seek to appear more self-sufficient than they really are. The religious emphasis is to confess one's needs and be more honest about one's inadequacies, thus to penetrate self-deceptions and lead one to ask openly for what he lacks. Jesus teaches men to be as little children in this way, to pray for their daily bread, not in fearful anxiety or helplessness but in trust that the heavenly Father knows what his children need and is ready to give to them that ask aright if they do their part to work with him for the larger good of all.

A vital sense of need prompts one to search for ways of meeting it. Complacency arises from dullness that is not alert to actual needs confronting life every hour. The person aware of these vital needs will be active in a persistent seeking for solutions to fulfill them. "Seek, and ye shall find" (Matt. 7:7) is a characteristic saying of Jesus, recalling the promise, "Ye shall seek me, and find me, when ye shall search for me with all your heart" (Jer. 29:13). This activism is the exploratory mood of growing life and ceases only to decay. Love is a growing experience of seeking and finding a response, of trusting and expecting trustworthy fidelity. Without constant rediscovery love fades; the seeking is as necessary as the finding, the trusting as essential as being trusted. Jesus, aware of his need for God, sought communion with him by day and night. Augustine after many hesitations confessed, "Thou has touched me, and I am on fire for thy peace."

Interpersonal attraction is essential to love. How are persons attracted to each other? Not by mechanical forces like the mass attraction of sun and planets or the electrical charging of electrons around neutrons. In human motivation the whole personality is invested in every act by attention and intention. Persons are attracted by desirable values that awaken interest enough to select them as preferred goals to orient responses in their direction. A person who is primarily interested in himself has introvert tendencies, as Jung explained, giving attention to his inner occupations.[15] Religious exercises may cultivate the inner life as a preparation for turning outward to extrovert activities in company with others. When social interests are weak or insecure or unpleasant, a person is likely to withdraw into himself and become self-centered. Religious conversion is often noted as a decisive turning away from selfish egocentricity to a genuine unselfish interest in other persons. One of the chief hazards in growing from childhood to maturity is a social insecurity that prevents a confident turning outward to effective interpersonal relations with others. Religious trust in a heavenly Father gives needed security; prayer practices interpersonal communication; unselfish service activates interest in others; and religious fellowship draws the individual into satisfying membership in the group life. Jesus learned to love in the intimate association of a genuinely religious family, growing "in favour with God and man" (Luke 2:52). When a Christian views every person as a child of God in one family, interest turns outward, appreciation heightens, and love develops in the sense of belonging together in a value-creating fellowship. We respond to significant persons, and the Christian experience of love enhances the significance of every person.

Love is learned in situations where love is expressed. Human motives are constantly modified by learning through experiences of living with others. Early Christians confessed, "We love him, because

[15] *Psychological Types*, tr. H. G. Baynes (New York: Harcourt, Brace & Co., 1923), pp. 412-517.

he first loved us" (I John 4:19). As a child finds parents loving him, it is natural for him to respond in loving ways. So religious persons who feel that they are sustained by the love of a heavenly Father learn to respond in loving attitudes toward him. And as they learn of his faithful love and care for every person, they also seek to love and serve others in his spirit. The central fact in Christianity is the life of Jesus, who demonstrates the dynamic possibilities of love. It is the conviction of a Christlike God who loves every creature in this redemptive way that shows the meaning of Christian love. Learning develops insight to understand and skills to practice the new discoveries. Christians understand God as a loving Father who calls them to love to the uttermost every person and to practice that love in the saving fellowship of one family. "Love one another." (John 15:17.)

In these ways love develops responsibility. At birth life has the capacity to respond. The first responses are random kicks and cries with little co-ordination. By trial and error, fumble and success, the range of human responses is unbelievably extended, to play endless variations of hostility as well as love. How do these responses turn from hostility to love? We have noted the motivating tendencies of spontaneity, need, search, interpersonal attraction, learning, growth of insights and skills. The most difficult and distinctive of all motives in Christian love is responsibility. How does this develop? Responsibility develops from responsiveness, not inevitably but only when appropriate conditions produce it by effective learning. The sense of ought is defined and directed by social causes and effects as other persons act in consistent ways faithfully to express love and reduce hostility, by attitudes of approval when love is present and disapproval when love is absent.

A person who finds security and satisfaction in being faithfully loved learns how to love in willing responsibility. It was so with Jesus, who felt himself loved of family and God. His intention was thus to seek valuable goals with and for, instead of against, other persons. He desired to make the best of all opportunities to enjoy values with others and to care for the valued persons more than valued things. He therefore felt inclined to work for the satisfaction of interpersonal needs and to increase spiritual values in the sharing of love. He came to value giving as more desirable than receiving: "It is more blessed to give than to receive" (Acts 20:35). As a boy he found the joy of partnership with his heavenly Father: "I must be about my Father's business" (Luke 2:49). He called others to join him in this work for heavenly treasure, and he lived with them faithfully and developmentally in a family of God. Rejecting popular demands for political leadership in an earthly kingdom, he chose the part of a suffering servant who is ready to give his life for the saving of others. When despised and crucified he did not revile his enemies or curse God but compassionately prayed God to forgive them, "Father, forgive them; for they know not what they do" (Luke 23:34).

In our time the spirit of this responsible love is well demonstrated by Gandhi and Schweitzer. Gandhi so identified himself with the poor and oppressed of South Africa and India that he took their burdens upon his slender shoulders with unflinching courage, until by prayer and social organization he released soul force enough by non-violent methods of fasting and death to set his people free at first spiritually and at last politically.

Schweitzer, at the height of popular acclaim as organist and theologian, felt upon himself the burden of the sufferings of the poor and sick until, no longer able to endure the comforts that were his privilege in Europe, he turned to heal and teach the neglected children of God in Africa and to demonstrate that reverence for life which is the spirit of one family and the hope of one world, blood-drenched with conflict and exploitation, yet throbbing with growing life and spiritual aspirations toward God as Father and men as brothers.

Such love is contagious. Its power is multiplied by the stirring emotional appeal of heroic examples, with rising tides of enthusiasm to sacrifice personal gains for the larger good in social resonance that magnifies through expanding public movements the slightest vibrations of generous altruistic love. When popular enthusiasm, instead of turning to violence and resentment, can be channeled into spiritual devotion to a heavenly Father that overflows into forgiving, reconciling love for enemies, there will be energies released in the world that will be stronger than atomic bombs or hatred and vengeance. To maintain the strength of this or any spiritual movement, however, the emotional tides must be renewed by interpersonal reinforcement through constant sharing of enthusiasm, by a redefining of common goals, and a rededication of personal commitment. In fact the contest between hate and love is ever tilting in the balance and will have to be decided by each person again and again. No gains or losses are therefore final, whatever they may be; the cause of love is always hard pressed, forever in need of stalwart support by every person in every hour.

IV

Education for Love

The hunger for love is as natural and necessary in human life as the hunger for food. This we find in the newborn infant as well as in the lonely aged person. Yet there is one important difference: the newborn is empty with no knowledge of what he is lacking, while the lonely elder is full of memories of persons and relationships that add up to love. The infant has not yet learned how to love; the aged person has learned through countless real and vital experiences in relation to other persons what it means to love and be loved, to give up and do without the visitations of love. Hunger is the absence of that which we need; it prompts us to search and hope to find, but it is not yet the reality we desire. For love is more than hunger; it is the truest fulfillment of our deepest human need.

If love is the highest good and deepest need in human life, then why should love fail? Because love is a product of learning. As the hungry infant will starve until he learns to eat the food that others prepare for him, so will he suffer loneliness until he learns to participate in the social joys that come to him through the invitations of loving parents and friendly playmates. Everyone has capacities to love, but they develop only in response to love from others. For love is interpersonal learning. If love fails, who is to blame? The child is usually blamed as unresponsive, naughty, negativistic, or incorrigible. He is often punished to "make him good" and teach him to love. But the actual fact is that the responsibility is a social one. The whole family has failed, and the whole of society needs to learn the lessons of love, to show the individual how to love even as he is loved.

1. How Does Love Fail?

To see how love fails we need to recognize the dynamic interplay of desires in the intricate network of social relations. Like a vast system of radio communications society beams messages to individual persons on standard wave lengths. Each person may turn his radio on or off and choose the station he will listen to; he may if he desires telephone or write the station to request or object to programs. But the radio messages always come in on publicly defined broadcasting beams, and if anyone wishes to hear, he will turn the dial to select the given wave length. So in every society the members are held together by communications in which standard beams are used as regulated by the authority of that society. We hear what society has to say over and over until we have learned the codes of our cultures. The standards of the society thus regulate the individual, and the individual person learns to select the cultural beam that society expects him to hear.

The school is not the only educational device in any community; it is but one of many agencies engaged in the process of learning. All forms of communication are educators, whether by printed words in newspapers, or pictures shown on screens and billboards, or sounds issued over radio and telephone systems. All forms of observable behavior are educators, as one person watches another express himself in various ways. All approvals and disapprovals are educators, whether from parents or playmates, private or public opinions, current slang or traditional wisdom. These social influences add up to what is known as culture. Every society has a culture that represents its common body of interests, beliefs, and demands. It is no inert deposit of lore gathered into one place for safekeeping but a pervading spirit that characterizes one group as distinct from another. When a culture represents the accepted and established interests of a society, it has the regulating force of social expectations. Conscientious persons feel impelled to live up to what the group expects of them.

When a society demonstrates hostility, its children try to live up to those social expectations. This is clearly seen in the culture of the

Dobu islanders, southeast of New Guinea.[1] Their social organization is based upon traditions of hostility in every relationship. These traditions put a premium upon treachery and ill will as the standard virtues to be attained if one is to be counted a success in this society. The largest social organization is a group of four to twenty villages in a named locality which represents a war unit on a permanent basis of hostility to every other locality. Within each village there is a daily struggle of everyone against his neighbor in destructive competition for the goods and ills of life. The only religion, if any, gropes for supernatural powers in the form of secret magic, by which each person seeks to gain private advantages for himself and work disaster on others. The chief source of food is yams, which are supposed to grow only by magic. Each person guards his secret incantations by which he causes yams to leave other gardens and come into his own. So each one tries to ruin the harvests of others by rival magic that adds to his own harvest.

Diseases and other misfortunes are not due to natural causes, they believe, but to evil incantations. Each person is busy, therefore, in magical practices to cast evil charms upon others and ward off the diseases that others are casting by incantations upon him. They live in constant fear and mutual suspicion, maliciously exerting every effort to destroy others and protect themselves by these paranoid activities, in a desperate round of ceaseless enmities.

Marriage is likewise founded upon hostility. Every woman is the prey of every man's aggression, and it is never safe for a woman to go out alone even to work in her own garden. Neither is the man safe, for if he is discovered in a woman's hut, he is trapped by her mother at the doorway, and this enforces marriage. But as marriage is prohibited between members of the same village, it brings together representatives of two hostile groups. Each party to marriage owes first allegiance to the family of his own mother, an ancestry known as the "susu." To settle the conflict of "susus" each family lives for one year alternately in each village. When the couple live in the

[1] See Ruth Benedict, *Patterns of Culture* (Boston: Houghton Mifflin Co., 1935), ch. v.

wife's village, her "susu" rules, and the husband is treated as an outsider to be humiliated and scorned. The following year they live in his village under the rule of his family, where the wife is scorned and abused until at length the union is broken.

In this society there is a fatal lack of procedures to foster love. There is no organized religion, morality, political government, or economic production of goods to promote good will and co-operation. Every tradition and code of the Dobuan culture prescribes hostility, rivalry, and aggression. Where every man's hand is raised against his neighbor, there is little communal life and nothing for people to share with each other. Consequently they dwell in poverty, lonely fear, desperate competition, distrust, and displeasure.

Dobuan life reveals how significant culture is in the formation of character. Its cultural pattern involves suspicion, distrust, fierce competitiveness, brutal possessiveness, exclusiveness, fear, hatred, dishonesty, trickery, and destructiveness. Dobuan life idealizes these hostile virtues, and character forms accordingly. This indicates how cultural patterns serve to develop hate or in other conditions love. It is obvious that the Dobuan cannot love in the sense of significant and abiding mutual affection which results in appreciation and respect, kindness and sympathy, mutual aid or unselfish service.

Without love no love can grow. For a loving society is the nourishing soil of a loving person. It is true that every society is composed of persons interacting one with another. Persons can change societies even as societies can change persons. But love must begin somewhere and go forth somewhere. Love begins where persons appreciate each other and express their affection in social interaction that communicates love. Where love is absent in the family or a larger society, the individual is deprived of essential security and satisfaction. In place of love suspicion and hostility will then flourish, as demonstrated on the island of Dobu. Persons and societies with loving attitudes are prerequisite to the growth of love in the newborn. Love is not a magical explosion that springs out of nothing. Love comes from love.

Feelings dwell in man; but man dwells in his love. That is no metaphor, but the actual truth. Love does not cling to the *I* in such a way as to have the *Thou* only for its "content," its object; but love is *between I* and *Thou*. The man who does not know this, with his very being know this, does not know love.[2]

Love is not in the person as a complete unit in himself. Even self-love is a reaction to other persons who teach him to love and reveal the value of a person by their attitudes toward him. It is more adequate to see the person in love as one who is responsive to another person, and, as Buber says, the love is actually between them. The loving person is created by love, and he in his way creates a loving society where mutual responses of love establish relationships of interest, appreciation, and responsibility.

But when a person falters in love, he is usually given the full weight of censure as if he were the only one at fault. It is assumed that he knows better, and whatever errors he commits in loving are charged strictly to his bad intentions or the willful neglect of his good intentions. The little boy who openly declares he will grow up and marry his mother may be excused as too young to understand, but he will be promptly hushed, if not by attitudes of horror, then by embarrassed giggles or polite explanations that it is never done that way. The adolescent boy who revolts against parental discipline and wishes his father were dead will either hide such secret wishes or state them at the imminent peril of violence from the indignant parent. The young woman who falls in love with a man of another social class or religious or racial group is asking for trouble from offended defenders of both groups. The woman taken in adultery would have been killed except for the intervention of Jesus.

It appears that love in our society must walk a straight and narrow line of circumspect prudence defined by social expectations, or run a gauntlet of abuse and punishment from the guardians of these

[2] Buber, *op. cit.*, p. 14. Note also the We Psychology of Künkel. "The real Self therefore is not 'I'; it is 'We.' "—*In Search of Maturity* (New York: Scribner's Sons, 1943), p. 76.

expectations. Each person may properly love only certain other persons in ways approved for each relationship. Love for a mother is not to be confused with love for a wife, nor is love for a neighbor with love for one's own husband. Society defines rigid limits within which we may love, in ways specified for each occasion. In the network of our diverse social relationships it is a complicated business to love each person as society prescribes in the exact amount and flavor approved for that and no other situation.

Hostility is also defined and channeled into rigid patterns by the expectations of one's social group. Not only in a Dobuan culture is this true, but also in a culture like our own where love and hostility are intermingled in intricate contradictions. In time of war one is expected to hate the enemy, kill him if possible, dispossess him of property, blacken his reputation with propaganda, hold him and his culture in bitter disrespect, abuse and exploit his family, starve or bomb his children, force him to unconditional surrender, then impose upon him harsh terms in restraint of trade, dismantling of productive industries, exacting of tribute or reparations, changing boundaries to deprive him of land, or uprooting populations and forcing displaced persons to march elsewhere as homeless refugees. Yet none of these hostilities are to be shown to one's own family, friends, or countrymen. In peacetime such hostilities are severely punished, and in wartime they are defined as unlawful and criminal toward members of the in-group. What wonder that persons are confused by such inconsistencies and torn apart by conflicting impulses to love and hate destructively when the same set of rules compel such contradictory behavior! To kill is a crime when defined as murder; to refuse to kill is a crime when defined as conscientious objection to military service.

The individual person is therefore not the only one to be held responsible for his errors in love and hostility. The society that teaches him to love and to hate is equally accountable. There is undoubtedly confusion in knowing how to love, but fully as disastrous are the conflicts in feeling how to love. For motives, as we have seen, arise from emotive energies that shape and weigh every

72

attempt to reason. When I feel deep resentment, it is not easy to reason it away, until emotional re-education is employed to reconstruct the whole personality to participate in reasonable behavior. If a Christian is to love his enemy as Jesus taught in the Sermon on the Mount, he will need to untangle the conflicting emotions of self-against-enemy or my-country-right-or-wrong until he can feel with predominant conviction that the enemy is his brother in the family of God.

Love fails when it is outvoted by other interests and goals that are considered more important. Among the interests that outvote love in our culture is a craving for *superiority*—the desire to get ahead and rise above our fellows. This is one of the most persistent viruses that infect us with a fever of discontent and ruthless competition. In the race to get ahead even our best friends are our subtle rivals and potential enemies. We try to keep this rivalry on the sporting level, but deeper within us is a serious and hostile determination to prove our superiority at any cost.

Another interest is the hunger for *power*—the aggressive drive for conquest and control of other people. It may be well concealed and exert its momentum in subtle ways, like the pampered child who holds its mother by helpless weakness or the orator who speaks so eloquently for God or political party that audiences yield to his spell and do his bidding. But the power drive is not love for others; it is lust for control to dominate others.

Another ambition is *wealth*—the acquisitive craving to gather possessions, evident in the child's collecting toys as well as in the capitalist who spends his life collecting stocks, bonds, and real estate. It may be a need for security that makes us so insatiable in our demand for material goods, or it may be an urgent rivalry to keep ahead of the Joneses. When wealth means this much, then love of persons yields to lust for things, the number of which in our society is the label of respectability.

Cleverness—the need to be smart enough to outsmart others—is another rival of love. It rises from the fear that someone may take advantage of you, hurt you, or deprive you of your rights and gains. To the clever love is vulnerable; it makes you an easy mark for the clever, who turn every kindness to their own profit. It would be folly to forgive or to be generous or unselfish, for the unscrupulous will only use it to their gain and to your loss. To be clever is to be a superior rival who gets ahead, holds power, and accumulates wealth.

There is also a popular fantasy of *success*—the hunger for personal gain and conspicuous achievement in our society. It feeds the ego on superiority and power over the less successful; it marks the wealthy and the clever by the outstanding results that make them the envy of their neighbors. The great legend of American culture is the success story from the bootblack to the millionaire, from a log cabin to the White House. It is natural to want success, but the lure of it may outweigh love and every other motive.

American culture glorifies *independence*—the myth of splendid isolation that one can be so strong, superior, or clever that he needs no one but can stand alone in lofty grandeur. This is the myth that troubles nations who refuse to yield sovereignty when world government is desperately needed, or churches and denominations who dwindle in tragic decline when unification is offered. It gives a false sense of security and self-sufficiency to men who know not how to love but only to defend.

Then there is the lure of *glamour*—the longing to exhibit one's beauty or skill which is the imprint of Hollywood reflected under the spotlight of stage and sports, beauty contest and radio quiz. We know the deceptions of the make-up and the show-off; but we hold to our illusions, whatever the cost, as more comforting than dull reality. That glamour will eventually fade and let us down we do not stop to think, in the popular social whirl that prefers the thrill of the moment to the real love of a lifetime.

There are other interests more popular than love, and the reader may prefer to make up his own list. Whatever they are, these motivating interests must be strong to outvote love. For love is probably the deepest need of human life when seen in true perspective. But not always do we have this perspective; more

74

often we are urged by the impulses of the moment to follow the will-o'-the-wisp of popular fancy. Fancied because popular no doubt, and popular because it is easier to follow the crowd blindly, even to destruction or the less dramatic but just as crucial denial of the best interest of all.

Love fails by education that favors these unloving interests. Can we not sum them all up in the one word "pride"? Why do we crave superiority, power, wealth, cleverness, success, independence, and glamour? In each case is it not because it appeals to our vanity? We can see this in others; we know that vanity is as deceitful as it is in vain. But the blind spot in our own eye prevents our seeing the pride we conceal so well in ourselves from ourselves. Why the vanity and pride? The psychological cause is an oversensitive ego, wounded in the scuffles of competition, starved for genuine affection, fascinated by the fear of blame and rejection. The anxious ego is the product of an anxious, competitive society which makes false pride a nervous virtue.

Pride is the mortal enemy of love. It polishes the mirror of selfishness and clouds the window of seeing out to others. It unlocks the inner door to self-indulgence but locks the outer door by which we move in love to another. It sweetens the cup of foolish vanity and poisons the well of overflowing regard for others. Pride goes before a fall. And the downfall of love is the betrayal of the self to bitter loneliness and impotence. It is the breakdown of the common life that would share with others the values of the community.

2. LOVE IS LEARNED

The New York State Training School for Girls at Hudson, New York, was a closed community of 505 girls living in sixteen cottages when Dr. Jacob L. Moreno began his sociometric experimentation in 1932. The girls were sent to Hudson by courts from all parts of the state for delinquency or inadequate home situations. They remained for several years at the training school to attend classes, work in industries, and live with a housemother and other girls in cottages where they assisted in the preparation of meals and upkeep of the cottage. They were often unhappy and unco-operative, for they were forced to remain in cottage groups, work, or classes without consulting their choices and desires. At the suggestion of Moreno the social groups were reconstructed according to their own choices. Each student was asked to write the names of five girls in order of preference with whom she would like to live, and the names in rank order of five girls with whom she would not want to live in the same cottage. The same procedure was followed in reconstructing work groups. Each girl was then interviewed to learn the reasons why she chose or rejected these other students.

From this sociometric testing came a number of significant results.[3] The limits of emotional interest were shown in failure to use all the possible choices; that is, 240 choices or $9\frac{1}{2}$ per cent were unused. There was a gradual decline of emotional expansiveness from 500 girls participating in the first choice to 300 girls having sufficient interest to make the fifth choice. The number of choices was not equally divided among the girls; some received as many as forty choices (the stars) while others received none (the isolates). By listing the location of choices it was possible to diagram the network of attractions and repulsions among the students of the same and other cottages, to see where each one stood in the eyes of her associates, and to study the emotional character of the girls in each cottage, workshop, and the community as a whole. By repeating these tests at regular intervals the progress or decline of group interest and the social relations of each student could be measured and charted in sociograms. It was shown that each girl was living in a "social atom" composed of relations to other persons with whom she had emotional attractions and repulsions, mutual or one-sided. Her behavior varied directly with the emotional character of her social atom.

The aim of regrouping was to provide the best possible psychological home for each personality. A girl who was isolated, fearful,

[3] J. L. Moreno, *Who Shall Survive?* (Washington, D. C.: Nervous and Mental Disease Publishing Co., 1934), pp. 70 ff.

or hateful in one group would develop wholesome emotional attitudes when changed to another group. When new students came to Hudson, they were given a "parent test" by visiting with each housemother in whose cottage there was a vacancy, after which the girls and the housemothers would each record their choices for living together. A "family test" was also given by holding conversations with a representative student from each cottage and registering preferences for living together. In this way each new student came to a cottage where a housemother and one girl were in favor of living with her and would be emotionally disposed to help her make a good adjustment in the group. When a girl was not thriving in one group, she was given new sociometric tests and assigned to another cottage where she could make a new start with better prospects of emotional success.

Every individual gravitates towards a situation which offers him as a personality the highest degree of spontaneous expression and fulfillment and he continuously seeks for companions who are willing to share with him. The psychological home is his goal.[4]

We learn to love in such a psychological home, where we are free to express affections spontaneously without fear of rebuff, in relation to companions who share positive emotional responses mutually. To free individuals from rigidity and insecurity Moreno has developed methods of spontaneity training. Two or more persons are brought together on a stage or elsewhere and invited to act out their emotions toward each other. Role training is provided by inviting a person to take the role he will have in real life in applying for a job, and practice with someone who takes the part of the employer how he will act in that situation. When quarrels or misunderstandings arise, each party is asked to reverse his role and play the part of the other one until he feels what it means to have that point of view. This method of learning by acting out roles and spontaneous emotional responses

[4] *Ibid.*, p. 203. See also his *Psychodrama*, 3 vols. (New York: Beacon House, 1945), and *The Theatre of Spontaneity*, tr. from the German (New York: Beacon House, 1947).

is known as psychodrama, and it is proving widely useful in catharsis and learning situations.

In the Hudson experiment spontaneity training was found to improve the social relations among the girls, as they were stimulated to uncover hidden aspects of their personalities and utilize hitherto neglected resources for social adjustment. Because the stay at Hudson was temporary, it was also important to prepare them to take well their place in communities to which they would go by practicing in situations as close to reality as possible. The girls chose the situations and roles in which they wanted to act as well as the partners to act opposite them. Conduct in a life situation is irrevocable, but here it can be tried, criticized, and corrected without serious consequences from mistakes. Social life confines us to one role, which others expect us to play invariably, thus causing anxiety and frustration. Here the girls can try a variety of roles, gaining spontaneity, release, and flexibility for the unexpected nature of future events. In actual life it is difficult to learn from one's mistakes because they are serious enough to produce anxiety by which they are repeated helplessly. Or if successful the efforts become stereotyped and are performed without further learning or sidetracked to a single way of doing it. Spontaneity training is a play situation not too serious for anxiety-free experiment, yet with enough emotional expression and variety for one to learn new roles and find undiscovered personal resources. By these choices and roles each person learns how to take new interest in and responsibility for himself and the others with whom he associates.

Another significant experiment in learning to love has been conducted since 1934 by the Jewish Board of Guardians of New York, directed by S. R. Slavson.[5] Activity group therapy has been provided for 750 children between the ages of nine and eighteen in fifty-five groups. The children were delinquent or neurotic boys and girls who did not prosper well in their homes, schools, street gangs, or playgrounds. They were referred after psychiatric and social case study as needing group therapy to develop their social attitudes. Each

[5] *An Introduction to Group Therapy* (New York: The Commonwealth Fund, 1943).

club was composed of five to eight members of about the same age and sex carefully chosen to counterbalance instigators with isolates and neutralizers. Letters were sent first to invite a child to join a group, then before each meeting for five weeks, and also after each absence reminding him of the next meeting and inviting him to attend.

When the children arrive at the clubroom, they find the adult leader already there at work on some project of his own. Handicraft tools and materials are spread out on a large table with various games also laid out for use. The leader greets each member warmly but makes no effort to guide the conversation or direct activities. When asked what they shall do the leader informs the boys or girls they may use any of the tools and games in any way they desire. As they try out their freedom, at first they may waste or throw around materials recklessly, curse and use vulgar language, or quarrel and strike one another. Some children take no part in group activities at first but work or play alone in fear of the group. When the leader serves refreshments the first time, there may be a wild scramble to get there first or retaliative throwing of milk and crackers. At the end of the period the children may rush out in a storm with no thought of the mess they leave behind them. But as they come together again, they adjust to each other by actions and reactions until they create their own order and organize their own proceedings. They lay out and put away supplies, plan activities and field trips, accept each other as comrades, and learn to work and play together responsibly.

The club eventually becomes a "family" by the spontaneous development of the children's appreciation for each other through shared experiences and social activities. The leader takes the role of the parent who never scolds, never shows anger, ridicule, or rejection but always accepts each child no matter what he does. If riotous play and fighting become group hysteria, he may adjourn the meeting, but without complaint or criticism. He does not take a passive role, for he offers genuine friendliness to each member, responds to questions, praises handwork, and keeps an alert interest in what goes on with good-humored tolerance. When action is called for, he acts, but not to dominate, for he is a nondirective leader whose function is to encourage the development of democratic freedom and responsibility by group dynamics.

There is a reason for this permissive attitude toward maladjusted children. They have been subject to dominating social pressures from parents, teachers, social workers, and officers of the law. To them every adult is a prohibitor who is always saying No, or a rejecter who turns away in dislike and criticism. Against these social pressures and the prohibitors and rejecters who coerce them they rebel in hostility or withdraw in fear and isolation. Even the playmates of their own age bully them, ridicule them, or invite their aggressions. What they need is a permissive society like an ideal family where the parent faithfully accepts without scolding or punishing, and the members appreciate and share activities with growing interest and comradeship. The accepting, praising attitudes of the leader are taken up by the children in appreciating one another.

The results are very gratifying. With few exceptions the children thrive on the diet of *unconditional love,* as Slavson names the basic principle of this group therapy. Attendance is regular, interest is keen, children release pent-up and negative emotions and learn to play and share together. They learn to love by membership in a social atom where love is the characteristic attitude first on the part of the leader, then in mutual response among the members. And learning to love in one group, they are more at home in other groups as they grow in confidence, spontaneity, and regard for others.

Love is what love does. There is no better way to learn than by doing, unless it is doing with other persons who encourage learning by social interest and responsiveness. Learning to love is a larger adventure than learning a multiplication table or the books of the Bible. It is emotional learning in a social context. A person's interpersonal relations, as well as his entire personality, are involved in his learning to love. Love is not learned by coercion, command, or external pressure. It must arise spontaneously from within when social pressures are removed and the person is free to choose his own responses to whom he desires. Coercion produces frustration, resentment, hatred, and revolt, which deny love in the stresses and strains of conflict.

This does not mean, as many falsely assume, that freeing people to do as they please will solve all problems in a laissez-faire paradise. To let people alone is a negative gain in removing coercive pressures, but it is not an adequate incentive or education in good social living. The myth that everybody's self-interest will add up to the social welfare of all is a glaring fallacy disproved by the failures of selfish individualism in ruthless competition and the anarchy of sovereign irresponsible nations without international government. The democratic way of life is interaction where individuals and groups plan and participate together in social action for the community of interests they share.

The school, as we have seen, is a replica of the society it represents. Most schools look backward to the old world from which they have come. In this way errors and tangled conflicts of the past are passed on from generation to generation. What we need to have is schools that point forward to a new and better world, or we do not move in that direction. Our schools have been truncated and broken images of the traditional society. We need schools that have a life of their own, where social impulses can be expressed spontaneously and social interests may develop through democratic interaction. Each school will then be a living society, a social atom within the larger world, where the future citizens can practice freedom and responsibility in growing appreciation and mutual affection. Schools can teach love, but not in the same way that they teach Latin. If love is to be learned, it must be practiced in constructive interaction in which each person takes his part and responds spontaneously to others in social attitudes of co-operation.

3. Opportunities for Christian Education

There is no denying that education for love is urgently needed in our time. Whose business is it to teach love?

The home is a natural setting for love. Established by two lovers who pledge their faith in each other and take vows to hold love forever sacred, whose love procreates children welcomed into the household of love, whose daily tasks are services of love one to another—here if anywhere love can be learned. But the home today is shrinking. Spacious dwellings and large families with grandparents, uncles, aunts, and many children have now become three-room apartments and small families with one, two, or no children far removed from grandparents and relatives. Instead of serving one another in love each member of the family is hurrying off to pursue his own interest. The mother is apt to be working in the city, coming home late and tired. The father is tied up in business, golf, lodge, and civic organizations with scarcely an evening at home. The children spend the day at school, come home to an empty house, and dash away to meet the gang at the hangout. When the family comes together, it must be an accident or some unusual occasion, and there is little time to practice the lessons of love.

The community is an interdependent social organism of persons and institutions held together by the bonds of common interest. For protection, economic trade, utilization of natural resources, social support, recreation, education, and government people are united by many bonds of mutual advantage. By trial and error they learn to live together as neighbors and increase the capital values of their common enterprises. In the community lovers meet and marry; children play and learn together; workers unite in barn raisings, factories, and public works; citizens hold political assemblies and vote upon issues of common concern. Here is a real-life situation to serve as a training ground for love. And love grows in the good community. But it has to compete in a fierce struggle with other motives such as greed, envy, jealousy, hypocrisy, rivalry, acquisitiveness, exploitation, conquest, lust, aggression, fear, resentment, and revenge. Feuds arise, rivals strive to get ahead, competition becomes destructive, passions break forth in anger or smolder in sullen hatred, graft and corruption infest business and public office until the good of the community is choked by an undergrowth of social evils. The community teaches a confusion of conflicting lessons, and love is often overgrown and hemmed in by selfish cunning or lusty pride. People who live in cities are mostly anonymous to each other, fragmented and segregated, caught in a civil war of opposition, indifference, and dispersion. Whether the balance of these conflicting influences in the community teaches love more than other motives is a doubtful question.

The school has the growing child during the best hours of his formative years from six to sixteen. He is at school to learn; his teachers are trained to meet state requirements, using textbooks written by experts. Many things are learned in our schools, and they are not altogether barren of love. But we have seen how ineffective is the school learning of love by formal and factual methods of studying isolated abstractions. It is no secret that many children grow weary of the dull repetition of the traditional school routine and come to resent the hours of involuntary confinement. There are teachers whom they admire and classmates whom they enjoy; it is not their fault that education tastes like castor oil, when the system is bound by oppressive, authoritarian rules of an unloving society whose flavor is distilled with anxious fears, guilts, and rigid restraints. The possibilities of teaching love by participation in loving activities are boundless, but the schools are just beginning to explore them.

The church is the guardian of the Christian heritage of love. It cherishes the literary sources and historical records of the Judaeo-Christian adventures in love. Through worship, instruction, fellowship, and service the church has kept alive the eternal flame of love. But cherishing a heritage is often a handicap in moving forward. The weight of tradition is heavy with formal requirements of ritual and dogmas that seem to many the matters of greatest significance. Creative as they may be when expressing vital experience, yet ritual and dogma may be a substitute for adventurous religious interests and stifle the growth of love. For no treasure of the past has currency unless it is put into the circulation of the present. Otherwise its value is merely sentimental, holding a memory to the denial of actual participation in the living issues of today. Love is not learned until it is practiced. And the practice of love will take the lonely individual into social activities with other persons for the joy of comradeship. To love God is a social act which moves one to love the children of God and devote one's life with them in social experiences of sharing and serving.

Can the church, school, and home work together for the growth of love in the community? If so, their united efforts could bring forth fruits worthy of the Christian heritage. But the present scene reveals a tug of war between church and state with demands for tax funds to aid church-sponsored education, legal disputes over the use of school time and buildings for religious education, threats of sectarian rivalry and control, mutual suspicions and hostilities among secular interests engaged in political struggles. The schools have promoted parent-teacher associations to gain co-operation, but parents are busy elsewhere or so caught in inertia that attendance is poor and activities are frequently at a minimum. The churches offer family pews, but many of them are empty most of the time. They plan family nights to have recreation for the whole family together, but it is not convenient for families to come. Modern life is centrifugal; it sends us flying off in all directions. How can we set in motion centripetal forces to draw us together around common centers of attractive activities? There is no use in drifting along, for we only drift farther apart. To create genuine community (the unity of life shared in common) we shall need to put our oars in these drifting currents and pull together to a well-chosen and agreed-upon destination. Democracy does not work itself, nor is self-government automatic perpetual motion. The persons must take an active hand to govern themselves. So to learn love is no random collection of impressions blown up by a fickle wind like a heap of leaves. The learning of Christian love is a joint enterprise of faithful planning and participation together in growing experiences that express love.

It is tragic to see how many parents believe that sending a child to Sunday school for one hour a week will adequately develop his character and furnish his religion. We have taken far too lightly our responsibility in the character education of our children. And the price of this neglect is a dubious harvest that threatens the decline of such civilization as our fathers labored for generations to build. Not until the home, school, and church actually undertake a thoroughgoing scientific analysis and a never-give-up brand of teamwork can the job of character building be accomplished. If we want love in our society, you and I and our neighbors will have to join hands and work for it.

Such teamwork is actually going on in churches and schools where the need for it has been realized. For example, in the churches that co-operate in the Union College Character Research Project, directed by Ernest M. Ligon, is a program worthy of consideration.[6] An extensive study by survey and questionnaire methods was made of the attitudes of character most to be desired as aims of character education. A list was made of over three hundred attitudes of wholesome personality most lacking and in need of development in children. At what age levels can these attitudes best be taught? By factor analysis the list was combined into some twenty-seven trait-factors and then organized by two-year age steps under eight general traits. These eight general traits represent the Christian hypothesis as taught by Jesus and summed up in the Beatitudes. Jesus evidently aimed to develop character in two major qualities, faith and love. The eight traits are listed as follows:

I. Traits of Christian Faith

1. A dominating *purpose* in the service of mankind ("Happy are the pure in heart"). Its forty-five specific attitudes fall into four major groups:
   a) Purposiveness of action
   b) Persistence and dependability
   c) Self-confidence
   d) Vocational choice
2. *Vision*, a genuine belief that one can so live his life as to make the world a better place to live in ("Happy are the poor in spirit"). Its forty-two specific attitudes are grouped under four factors:
   a) A wholesome curiosity
   b) Creative imagination
   c) Growth in inspiration
   d) Vocational vision

[6] Ligon is professor of psychology at Union College, Schenectady, New York. He describes the project in *A Greater Generation* (New York: The Macmillan Co., 1948) and in *Their Future Is Now* (New York: The Macmillan Co., 1939).

3. *Love of right and truth* ("Happy are they who hunger and thirst after righteousness"). Its thirty-five attitudes are divided into two factors:
   a) A genuine desire to know the truth
   b) A positive, challenging concept of right and wrong
4. *Faith in a Father-God, the friendliness of the universe* ("Happy are the meek"). Its twenty-four specific attitudes are divided into two factors:
   a) Adjustment to the fear which results from a sense of personal helplessness
   b) Faith in a Father-God

II. Traits of Christian Love

5. *Sensitiveness* to the needs of others ("Happy are they that mourn"). Its twenty-six attitudes are listed in three groups:
   a) Social confidence
   b) Social skills
   c) Sympathy
6. *Determination to see that every man gets his chance* at happiness and and success ("Happy are the merciful"). Its thirty attitudes are listed under four factors:
   a) Democracy of contacts
   b) Sportsmanship
   c) Unselfish helpfulness
   d) Social vision
7. *Determination to resolve the conflicts within and between and among men* ("Happy are the peacemakers"). Its forty-four attitudes fall into four groups:
   a) Becoming a part of the family team
   b) Becoming a master of one's temper
   c) Conforming to the stresses of being educated
   d) Adjusting to the restrictions imposed by society on its members
8. *Christian courage*, with the determination to serve men whether they want to be served or not ("Happy are they who are persecuted for righteousness' sake"). Its sixty-three attitudes constitute four factors:
   a) Courage
   b) Reaction to injustice
   c) Vicarious sacrifice
   d) Courageous leadership[7]

[7] Ligon: *A Greater Generation*, copyright 1948 by Ernest M. Ligon and used with the permission of the Macmillan Co.

Character traits are less apt to develop when unintentional, so a precise aim is set forth in every lesson planned. In order to learn one must obey the laws of learning. To learn a generalized concept like a character trait a student must know what to look for, be challenged to want to learn, and then apply it in as many different situations as possible. The lesson must be adapted to each individual at the age when he is most open to learn it, with application to his life situations seven days a week. The successes and failures of the learning process must be evaluated at regular intervals to detect futilities and revise methods and materials continually. Human nature is not simple, and character education must be as complex as the laws of character development.

To fulfill these conditions the church-school year is divided into three curricular units of three months each. This provides six teaching units in each two-year cycle, beginning with the nursery of two- and three-year-olds up to the senior high-school level. In each unit specific attitudes are taught which have been calibrated for that age level and which lead to increasingly mature traits. At the beginning of each unit teachers interview the parents of the children to fill in an attitude scale, indicating in what ways each child needs to learn each of the attitudes to be taught. Parents are asked to describe the typical reactions of the child in behavior areas of attitudes studied and to make a rating of the degree to which these attitudes are present or lacking. A similar interview is held at the end of each unit to rate the child again on these attitudes and to evaluate progress. At the beginning of each year the parent-teacher interview also surveys the child's interests and abilities, as well as his social adjustments at home, at school, and elsewhere. A testing battery is given to make up a personality profile for each child.

When a child is enrolled, the parents are asked to promise four things: (1) to encourage regular attendance of the child at church school as faithfully as at public school, (2) to carry out the home assignments with each lesson as indicated in the Guide for Parents, (3) to make a regular report to the church-school office of practical daily ways they use in teaching the specific attitudes to the children at home, and (4) to participate fully in the parent classes, meeting each week usually before or after the church-school period to discuss with departmental supervisors the learning progress of their children. Parents were shown that without their co-operation no character gains could be accomplished, and beyond all expectations they have shown keen interest and volunteered even more time and co-operation than has been asked of them.

From the data gathered in the interviews and conferences with parents the teachers then prepare lessons and projects, not wholesale but on the basis of individual needs. On the lesson form the attitude to be emphasized appears at the head. Below is a space for each student for his name, address, age, grade, aptitudes and interests, adjustments or need for them in specific situations as learned from the parents. Opposite this is a space to list the initial attitude scale description, such as "Will tell the truth only if questioned," or "Will lie if he thinks he can get out of punishment." Then a space in which to write the lesson adaptations such as "What would you do?" in a situation typical of his home interests and activities. Beyond that is a space to be filled in after the class session, indicating evidences of success.

On the other side of the form is space for planning the lesson in which the individual needs of each student are brought together in a general plan for the class as a whole. Here the teacher writes down in appropriate spaces the common interests of the class, the present behavior in the class relating to the attitude, additional instructional material, and additional project materials to change the attitude. Then follows space to outline the lesson plans for the class session and the evaluation of the success of the lesson. In the class the teacher invites discussion, reading of Bible passages, participation in drama, and the like, following the plans to adapt instruction to the individual needs of each child. Records of the discussion are made during the class period by the assistant teacher. Often a husband and wife whose children are in the church school teach a class together.

These records together with all other records come to the psychology laboratory for evaluation, where methods and materials that are ineffective are revised or replaced. Trained psychologists, religious educators, and curriculum writers participate in the project. The homes are fully as significant as the church and the school in this program, for the children and their parents carry on projects throughout the week to learn the attitudes desired as goals of character development. Worship services are planned to express the attitudes learned during the instruction periods, led by the students themselves voicing the feelings of the entire group, leading to a climax of dedication when each one pledges himself to carry out his share of doing God's will in this Christian social action. The leaders of this research project believe that prayer is one of the major sources of dynamic energy in the development of character. For character education will find its central dynamic in religion, and the task requires the faithful co-operation of church laymen and ministers if it is to succeed. This program has been criticized at some points, such as its trait theory, the accuracy of its rating, and the adequacy of its teaching materials. But a closer study convinces many that character does develop from clear aims, specific life situations, democratic participation, careful evaluation of results, and co-ordination of major social and religious influences. When science, education, and religion work together in the church, the school, and the home, the results are promising.

4. GROWING INTO LOVE

From birth to love is not a single step. The phrase "falling in love" is misleading. It suggests a sudden tumble with no effort but letting go, a slipping back involuntarily from a higher to a lower state. But love is a growth, and like any growing experience it is a gradual development by nourishment and exercise. Organic growth in plants and animals proceeds by unconscious maturation. But psychological growth is different. It requires conscious interest in other persons, growing appreciation of their worth, responsible attitudes of upholding them as belonging to each other in one family. Growing into love is no escalator that takes you for a free ride after the first step. We climb into love by a succession of steps taken at considerable effort, with stresses and strains, crowding and jostling or waiting in turn for others, slipping back and starting again. Some climb only a few steps and stop; others keep on and reach the higher altitudes of love. Birth is not the stamped and certified one-way passage to love we sometimes imagine it to be. It is a long journey, to be sure; but each person works his way along, not alone but in teamwork with others who encourage or discourage him, and they learn together by social experimentation how to love.

As we grow up, much of what we learn is antithetical to love. The infant who howls at 2 A.M. until he overcomes the patience of his family and gets attention and feeding is learning at a tender age to coerce others to give him what he wants when he wants it. The toddler who says, "Mine, mine," and seizes a toy away from a play-mate who is enjoying it is learning the lesson of taking property away from others. The schoolgirl who calls names to ridicule the unpopular classmate or scorns the Negro child in haughty disdain is learning lessons of caste snobbery and race prejudice. The schoolboy who smarts under the sting of taunts, knocks a chip off his enemy's shoulder, and pitches into a fight with all his might and anger is learning war and aggression. The boy who is "licked" in the fight and nurses his bruises in sullen resentment is learning how to hate and plot revenge.

Learning to love is no simple matter—first because human nature is so complex, and second because social relations are even more complex. Impulses to love are mingled with impulses to coerce, to possess, to ridicule and scorn, to taunt and provoke anger, to be aggressive and resent aggression with hate and revenge. Social responses are a mingled potpourri of moods and attitudes ranging the whole gamut of human emotions. Sensitive as each person is to the attitudes of his associates, he is like a series of tuning forks resounding the tones that vibrate his emotional life. So multiple and varied are the responses of others to him that he resounds with chords of consonance and dissonance changing in constant succession of moods. He calls the tune as well as responding to the tunes of others. To provide successful education in love for the growing child actually requires loving attitudes in the most significant persons and social groups that come within range of his sensitivity. And this is no partial task for part-time or grudging consent, but a far more complete program of social adjustment and character education than we have yet attempted.

When Harold was born, his world was one small room of a parsonage. Yet it was a busy little world that revolved about him as the center of interest. He was greeted by the hearty voice of the doctor, passed over to the waiting hands of the nurse who gently washed his squirming body, bundled him up, and placed him in his soft-lined crib. Then came his father, who lifted him up cautiously and put him in the curve of his mother's arm. He was not always comfortable, but no sooner did he break forth in lusty squalls than someone would come to his rescue to meet his needs in loving attention. Visitors who came to see him did not hide their interest; they played little games with him, and he was already learning to respond in the moods shown to him. It seemed as though everyone in his little world loved him, and he was learning to love everybody as best he knew how. As his world expanded later with the arrival of a baby brother and playmates, going to the church nursery and then to school, he learned to take kindly, hopeful attitudes toward other persons, to share with them, help them, and feel responsible for them in the spirit of the Christian family love he experienced.

In the first six years of his life Harold was prepared for Christian love by the following social conditions: (1) *Personal attention* that aroused his interest in other persons through their interest in him. By watching them he became aware of persons and developed you-me relations that led to mutual identification as like them, yet a different person himself.

2) *A hearty welcome* was given him by the family, who wanted him and felt that he belonged to them. This set up an empathy of harmonious social feeling in which by tones, gestures, and warmth of fellowship he was able to relax and be at ease with them.

3) *Favorable responses* were usually given him by his family and friends, who spoke kind words with encouraging tones and gestures. His associations with others were pleasant, exciting curiosity, stimulating social interest, and helping to facilitate his social activities. For

the most part he received approval, but at times he was reproved or forbidden, which aided his learning of "good" and "bad."

4) *Nourishing and supporting group membership* gave him security and stability because his family routine was regular. He was nourished by affection as well as food, by cuddling and caressing as a baby, by attention and approval at every age. His membership in a happy, integrated family group supported his ego needs and developed in him a basic confidence in persons which steadied his feeling tone with constant social satisfactions.

5) *Interpersonal activities* invited his response and participation in the social life shared by his family and playmates of neighborhood, church, and school. He developed more rapidly in a wide range of waking interests and skills by such interpersonal activity. He gained the tools and powers of social control to influence other persons, as well as the valuable lessons of teamwork and co-operation.

6) *Learning opportunities* increased his ability to learn with other persons. He had much to imitate in the actions, words, and attitudes of loving persons. His social adventures provided new interests, behavior patterns to observe, skills to experiment in by trial and error, symbols to perceive the meaning of, specific items to relate in larger generalities, competition of brother and playmates, intention to reach desired goals, and rewards of praise and punishment.

7) He tried *role playing* in dramatic methods, learning by taking the part of the person he wanted to become. At first he enjoyed the role of the baby of the family, whom everyone waited upon and exclaimed about. He took the role of mother and father in waving and saying, "Bye-bye." Then he played the role of an older brother in welcoming the new baby, loving him and helping him to learn what he liked to do. He took roles with other playmates in the church nursery of children who enjoyed each other in happy and kindly comradeship. In school he took the role that appealed to him, now the teacher's little angel and now a roguish little devil. At Sunday school he learned about a heavenly Father, sang and prayed, wondered about and tried to be like Jesus. In all these roles he tried himself out in social attitudes and skills of Christian love.

8) *Culture patterns* from his society were communicated to Harold in all these interactions. The culture of his family was demonstrated in countless ways by their doings, sayings, and feelings. He learned their codes by watching and participating in the behavior they approved. He felt the demands of their social expectancy, the guilt and shame of disobeying these demands. With playmates of his own age he met other codes and learned the rules by playing his part in their social activities. So the meanings and values of his culture seasoned with Christian ideals of love were mediated to him first in the family and then in larger circles of church, school, and community.

These motivating influences to love as one family of God are all interpersonal. Within himself every growing child has capacities to respond to other persons as they act toward him. He learns Christian love by actively participating in a loving circle of other persons who express Christian attitudes toward him. Beyond this inner family circle are concentric circles of other persons who have influenced one another in constant interaction. They represent the "cloud of witnesses" (Heb. 12:1) who have given their testimony and impetus to Christian love by loving. Above them the Christian acknowledges the activating spirit that Jesus calls "our heavenly Father." Learning to love is a social enterprise of living up to the expectations of other persons who belong with us in a loving community. Such motives are not reducible to words, though language is useful for interpretation and communication. They overflow in creative relationships that dramatize the meaning of love by action and develop the growth of love by responsible interaction.

If the soul is naturally Christian, as Tertullian said, then why do some fail and others succeed more in Christian love? The answer resides in the dynamics of motivation. Some persons are moved to love in the Christian sense in ways that others are not. What is it that moves a person to love other persons as members of one family of God? Not an inborn instinct that drives one mechanically and automatically to love; but rather a native capacity to respond, modified and developed by learning experiences in social relations. For learning is present from birth; and any human capacity, whether to love or to hate, is learned by seeking goals with other persons. Children learn to hate by receiving hateful treatment from other persons, such as blows and physical restraint, frightening noises, sudden loss of support, disapproval, scolding, ridicule, rejection, deprivation, fickle and unpredictable moods of anger or indifference. Children learn to love by receiving and participating in a family or group where Christian attitudes of kindness, tender care, faithful service, forgiving and reconciling, acceptance, unfailing interest, honest appreciation, and sustaining responsibility predominate.

Later events may counteract the effects of earlier experiences; as in the Hudson training school where kindness and free choices replaced coercion and punishment, or in the activity groups of the Jewish Board of Guardians where unconditional love replaced the hostile pressures of a careless society. From such changes in social relations and personal attitudes may come a conversion from one way of life to another. Then a delinquent boy may become an outstanding force for community progress, or a shy, self-centered girl may become an outgoing social worker or an unselfish mother. On the other hand many who grow up in loving homes are turned by later experiences into ruthless competitors and exploiters of their fellow men. The light of love may be overcome by bitterness in a darkness that comprehends not; yet always there are specific events and interpersonal causes for such effects.

Kathy had known the joy of family love, social success, and popularity at every turn of her seventeen years. It was easy for her to love life and every living person, for life had been good to her; she relished each new discovery and welcomed every social opportunity. Then after two weeks at college she was stricken quite unexpectedly with poliomyelitis and after days and nights of excruciating agony learned she could never run again. The shock of this crippling finality left her at first weak, then angry and petulantly bitter. She hated life that had cheated her out of her freedom, renounced God as quite unjust to permit this to happen to her, and felt alternately cold and hot with jealousy for all whose legs were normal. She resented the pity she saw in the eyes of friends, the loneliness of being left behind, and even the sacrifice of her family to care for her. For all was changed now; the good of life had turned to evil, the joy of youth to ashes of never again. She wanted to die.

But through the kindness of a few understanding friends she learned to laugh again, to gather inner resources to try the difficult exercises, and eventually to walk "with her stomach" and the heavy braces. She saw through the awkward efforts of her playboy lover to escape any further responsibility to her, but she came to rely on the steady, emotional support of a brother who helped her about again until she had the courage to return to college and live above her despair. Then she took a new interest in other people, a sympathetic concern for their disadvantages, and eased her own disappointment in helping them. Through such painful steps of growth in courage and understanding she at length discovered a new capacity to love and married a young man who had chosen a vocation in which to work for the poor and release the captives of injustice and sordid strife. Together they learned the meaning of Christian love each to the other, and in enlarging circles of unselfish regard for others in need of love.[8]

Social progress is at first personal, then interpersonal, and eventually group and intergroup achievements in learning how to love in larger ways.

[8] The biographical story told by Elsie Oakes Barber in *The Trembling Years* (New York: The Macmillan Co., 1949).

The Christian Family

1. THE FAMILY GENIUS OF CHRISTIANITY

The genius of Christianity is its family design of love. We have seen in Chapter II how the Christian dynamic extends family love to universal dimensions. God is the Father figure, the creator and sustainer of life. The human race is his family on earth, created to respond to God in filial love and to fellow men and women as brothers and sisters. A new society is created by Jesus and his disciples, where neighbors, strangers, and enemies are all regarded as members of one body, belonging together in the love and service of the family of God. In this way the local boundaries of blood relationship are transcended in the discovery of larger spiritual relationships binding all people together in one family.

How does the local family fare in this expanding Christian movement? Is it forgotten and slighted? Does the emphasis on the Christian community devalue the local family? Have the Gospels been good news for the family, the epistles love letters to strengthen or disputes to weaken the bonds of family life? Does love of God make it easier or more difficult for us to love those who live under the same roof and share our daily bread?

There can be no doubt that, in the main, Christian teachings have elevated the dignity and worth of the family. This has been evident first in the Graeco-Roman culture of the Mediterranean world, then in other countries and continents where its influence has come. For the Christian way of life has always accented the filial, fraternal, and paternal virtues of love, promoting devotion of children to parents, of parents to children, of brothers and sisters for each other. Likewise the Christian emphasis is to reject the negative traits destructive of family love, such as anger, lust, abstemious and acquisitive selfishness, rivalry for power and greatness, unforgiving resentment, hypocrisy, and favoritism. What have been the psychological and sociological effects of these teachings?

Christianity has made a new place for women in the family. In the Christian family the woman is no longer a slave or a victim of lust, treated scornfully and ruthlessly as an inferior, ignorant drudge or plaything. She is not a drone but a queen, to be honored and respected, to be admired and listened to as she brings her voice and hand to the guidance and growth of her family. Slowly but with increasing celerity women have risen to positions of equality, not yet entirely free and equal in man's jealous world but gaining ground steadily because their charter of freedom in the New Testament is acknowledged—not so much by what is said there about women as by the attitudes which Jesus and his followers show, and the confidence that every person is a child of God worthy of utmost dignity and respect.

Christianity likewise makes a new place for children in the family. In the Christian family they are no longer brats underfoot, interfering with male lusts and female freedom. They are not dwarf servants who labor long hours with neither pay nor thanks; they are not know-nothing ignoramuses to be kept out of sight or grudgingly seen and not heard. They have a central place of honor in the home. Did not Jesus set a child in the midst and say, "Of such is the kingdom of God" (Mark 10:14)? They are the chief interest of the entire family, the focus of attention and attraction to whom everyone turns with delight and serves with unselfish devotion. The child has become a person in his own right, the joy of the present, the climax of the past, the hope of the future. His responsibilities are as great as his privileges to grow and learn, to love and appreciate, to belong and co-operate in the family enterprises.

The man has a new place also in the Christian family. He is no longer the haughty master of the house, tyrant of his cave or castle who brooks no voice or will but his own. He is not the dominant possessive male who holds his family as chattels of his private property, who shouts commands and demands instant unquestioning obedience to his every caprice, who stays away like an absentee landlord when it suits him to pursue his pleasures elsewhere. In the Christian family he finds his greatness in becoming the servant of all, one who works, plans, and shares with his family, who faithfully loves and gently nourishes each member as the heavenly Father loves. As Christ is the head of the church, so the man is the head of his family, responsible for the religious and other interests of the family life. It is his place to lead the family in daily prayers at home and take part with the family in public worship and other church activities. For he is the mediator between God and his family (Eph. 5:23-33).

Ideals, you say, more honored than practiced. But these ideals have had an unbelievable influence in shaping the practices and customs of the Christian home. Not every one is perfect nor every home ideal, but the day-by-day level of family love is usually raised by the ideals its members hold. Many families who do not call themselves Christian are influenced by Christian ideals in the culture about them, and home life is thereby improved in standards of loving. It is like taking aim in any sport; the batting average or marksmanship is higher when there are targets to aim at. So in aiming at ideals of Christian love a family may often miss the mark and yet improve their average by aiming at such targets.

The Christian Church has made the family sacred. By the sacrament of marriage the church gives public approval, beauty, and sanctity to the wedding at the altar of the Most High. This ceremony brings families together in harmony (who might otherwise be in conflict, as in bride capture), gaining the consent of the parties concerned to the marriage and holding a festival in the spirit of uniting not only the bridal couple but two separate family clans into one. In the presence of God and the company of witnesses the vows are exchanged with symbols of eternal faithfulness in this union of marital love. Not always are the vows kept, but how commonplace marriage would otherwise be; how much more careless would be the keeping of a contract lightly entered into!

As the marriage culminates in the birth of each child, the church sanctions the new life by christening—the ceremony of giving a Christian name to identify, welcome, and dedicate him to God in expectation of what he is to become. As the child is presented to God for divine approval and blessing, the parents take vows to guide his religious growth by loving care, wise counsel, and holy example that he may be a true child of God. When he comes to the age of discretion, he is confirmed in his Christian development and received as a worthy member into the church fellowship to uphold it with his presence, his prayers, his gifts, and his service. This gives him a place with his family to participate in the larger religious community to which the family belongs. At Holy Communion the unity of the larger Christian fellowship is celebrated by spreading a family table of the Lord where the members may "break bread together on their knees" and receive divine blessing.

By the Christian ministry of worship, preaching, teaching, and pastoral services each family in the parish is brought within the concern and care of this love. Demonstrations of Christian love are given by unmarried priests who serve as "Father," "Sister," or "Brother" in the larger family fellowship; and in other churches where married pastors are privileged to show the pattern of love in the parsonage family. The pastor's wife and children may hesitate to be examples for the entire community, and it is unreasonable to ask of them a perfection other families are not willing to seek. But the parsonage family, in spite of its humility and reluctance, actually demonstrates the meaning of Christian love in the priceless lessons of practical living. It need not be wondered at that the demonstration of love in the parsonage can be more eloquent of the Christian life than sermons from the pulpit or chants from the choir. The members of the parsonage family become the unordained but none the less effective associate pastors who stand ready with the pastor to minister wherever may appear a family crisis of illness, death, trouble, or loneliness.

The genius of Christianity, as we have seen, is to make the family spirit inclusive. This larger Christian family includes and makes a place for single persons, the unattached and lonely, strangers, rivals, and even enemies who would otherwise be shut out. In this way the home walls of isolation and ingrowing loyalty open inside out as arms of love are extended in wider fellowship. A quatrain of Edwin Markham describes the strategy of Christian love.

> He drew a circle and shut me out—
> Heretic, rebel, a thing to flout.
> But Love and I had the wit to win:
> We drew a circle that took him in! [1]

As I record these words, the newspapers carry the story of Bishop Raymond A. Heron's narrow escape from death at the hand of a nineteen-year-old boy whom he had befriended. Paroled from a state prison, the boy had come to the bishop's home in Bolton, Massachusetts, in his absence and killed another boy, who was a ward of the bishop. Then waiting in ambush he fired two bullets at the bishop, demanded his purse, and escaped in the bishop's car. When taken by the police three hours later, he confessed to the murder of the one who stood in the way of his burglary, and said, "I meant to kill the bishop too. I had worked on that farm when I was twelve. The bishop worked me too hard. I never forgot it, and I planned to get even with him some day. Right now I'm not sorry for anything. Perhaps I'll change before it is all over."

When asked by the police an hour and a half later if he wanted to see the boy murderer "fry," the bishop replied: "I haven't changed my way of life because of this. My way is to see someone get another chance. . . . You ask have I lost my faith in such boys as he? No; I'd say no, frankly. Because of one boy all should not be condemned. When you give a boy a chance, you are doing the right thing. . . . I talked with the boy the best I could under the circumstances. All the time I complied with his demands, knowing his mood. . . . The boy

[1] From "Outwitted." Reprinted by permission of Virgil Markham.

asked, 'Do you think there is anyone above?' I told him I certainly did. I think I said it sure looks it." [2]

There is no denying the risks of Christian love. You may be killed, robbed, misunderstood, resented, and slandered by those you try to help. There is no guarantee that love will be returned. We may expect love to invite love even as anger provokes anger, for emotions are contagious and likely to be mutually responsive. And yet it would be naïve to deny that love is often unrequited. In this case the bishop did not lose his faith in boys; he did not draw a circle and shut out the murderer. He asked on his behalf another chance and drew a larger circle to take him again into the fellowship of Christian love.

The rich flavor of such love is often diluted by halfhearted belief and partial devotion, amid the rivalries, hostilities, and selfish ways of a somewhat pagan society. Yet Christian love is not in vain, for it raises the average level of love in our families and the standards of living, sharing, and service in our communities. Social responsibilities once the concern of none but the churches and religious movements are now taken up by public welfare agencies, hospitals and clinics, child guidance centers, and numerous humanitarian organizations supported by a majority of our citizens in efforts to relieve suffering and reconstruct society. These manifestations of family love on a community basis and world-wide front are developing further the outreach of Christian love by whatever names they may be called. Not that Christianity seeks the credit for these far-flung social services, but it is gratified to see the enlarging good that results from them.

2. Repression or Expression?

At the same time the church has repressed spontaneous impulses to love. Its repressive tendency has been most evident in dealing with sex. The conspiracy of silence to keep children in the dark about sex adds much to the uncertainty and insecurity of growing up. The sense of shame and embarrassment in which parents stammer and hang their heads when children ask about sex is not wholesome. Why

[2] Worcester, Mass., *Evening Gazette*, Aug. 7, 1948, p. 16.

should sex be treated so shamefully by well-meaning parents? Does not the Bible say that God created male and female? Why should aspersions and fears be cast upon what he pronounced good?

There is a long history behind our traditional prudery toward sex. Every generation has witnessed the debaucheries and abuses of sex and so feels impelled to warn the next generation away from them. But the tendency is to react so far against sex as to substitute repressions and crippling anxieties that are as dangerous as the impulses they seek to stamp out. This seems to have been the situation at the beginning of the Christian era and with varying emphasis to the present time. The New Testament is vigorous in its condemnation of adultery and fornication, an established prohibition as old as the Decalogue and the Code of Hammurabi (around 2000 B.C.). To this Jesus adds a new standard of inner purity. "Ye have heard that it was said by them of old time, Thou shalt not commit adultery: But I say unto you, That whosoever looketh upon a woman to lust after her hath committed adultery with her already in his heart." (Matt. 5:27-28.)

This is consistent with the emphasis of Jesus on inner motives as the source of good and evil. It sharpens the ethical focus by giving authority to the individual conscience, the power which every person has within limits to choose good or evil. And it adds considerable weight to the responsibility of each person to exercise self-control in his impulses and desires. Now, as everyone has lustful impulses, the burden of self-control is not easy, and the person who takes this rule of Jesus seriously will have his struggles with temptation and remorse. It is reported that one of the early church fathers was driven by these struggles to the desperate point of castrating himself to escape temptation.

The evils of sex were highlighted further by the practice of celibacy which the Roman Church has held as a mark of superior religious devotion. Neither Jesus nor Paul was married; Jesus called his disciples to leave their homes to follow him, and there is one occasion where he seems to renounce his own family for a larger loyalty to all who do the will of God (Mark 3:31-35). This might appear to compromise the family as the ideal home of Christian love and to give instead another pattern of community to replace the family. The Christian emphasis on purity has apparently set love on a pedestal as a heavenly spiritual ideal far removed from the entangling affections of this world. "Pure religion and undefiled is . . . to visit the fatherless and widows in their affliction, and to keep himself unspotted from the world." (Jas. 1:27.) Sex was considered unclean and sinful. "In sin did my mother conceive me." (Ps. 51:5.) The doctrine of the virgin birth of Jesus was thought necessary to uphold his sinlessness, and the doctrine of the immaculate conception of Mary was added later to protect the sinlessness of his mother.

Other natural impulses were grouped with carnal affections; the innocent pleasures of eating and lighthearted conversation, social participation in games and amusement, were suspected of evil temptations and condemned as too worldly for the Christian. Holy men became hermits to fast and endure self-inflicted pain. Others became monks to retire from the world, even from fellow martyrs by imposing the rule of silence at meals. In another epoch Puritanism came to rule out all pleasures as diverting the mind away from God and leading to worldly temptations. The stricter sects prohibited music in the churches, kissing one's wife or whistling on Sunday; banned theatres, social dances, circuses, card games, perfumery, and colorful variety in clothing.

Pursued by such a volley of prohibitions, these Christians felt their duty was to flee the world in a pilgrim's progress to heaven. The psychological effects were unhealthy repression, rigid self-denial, fear of temptation, and morbid dwelling upon one's sins. Guilt became an intolerable burden under the weight of such phobias, until the anxious conscience was haunted by ghosts and witches of abhorrent evil ready to pounce upon the unwary. Morbid guilt is a disease of unhealthy fears and repressions leading to exaggerated revolts and neurotic anxieties. This does not mean that all guilt feelings are unhealthy, for it is natural and normal to feel guilty in any event of failure to reach a desired goal.[3] Healthy guilt will spur one on to

[3] Johnson, *op. cit.*, pp. 214-21.

try again and achieve better the next time. In a dynamic relationship to a heavenly Father it is a sense of deep humility before divine expectations, seeking forgiveness and leading to a new dedication of life to God in the service of love. But morbid guilt obsessed by over-anxious fear of sin is a disabling and paralyzing restraint upon spontaneous freedom to do and be one's best.

We need to understand that Christian love is not something to suppress but to express. By fearing the evils of love Puritans almost forgot to express the goods of love. They cruelly punished minor offenses, held inquisitions for heretics who disagreed, and hesitated neither to kill nor drive into exile those who would not conform to their negative prohibitions. In this they failed to express the love they professed in their anxiety to avoid the lusts they repressed.

Love is not love unless it is expressed. It may be an idea about love, a memory of love in the past, or an intention to love in the future, but until it finds expression in attitudes and actions, it is not real love. For love as we have experienced it is affectionate interaction between persons, that is, interpersonal responsiveness to the good in another. The most prevalent failure of Christian love is the failure to express it. At church we repeat and approve Scripture, prayers, and sermons that advocate love. But Monday comes, and we fall back into the old familiar game of rivalry and resistance. This may look like hypocrisy from an external viewpoint, but viewed from within the motives of the churchgoer it is the cherishing of good intentions (with which some roads are known to be paved to withstand the heat) without going on to the more difficult steps of carrying them out in social acts of loving expression. Consequently the ideals of Christian love are often enshrined in the holy of holies of the temple as honest intentions of worship, without gaining the strength to walk out into the social world of effective interaction where lusty rivals hold sway.

There is a psychological law of use and disuse. Intentions unexpressed are useless because they are unused. The disuse of any intention is a dry rot that withers it away. Unexpressed love is a declining store of intentions that become feeble and futile by disuse. The Christian family is often declining for this same reason. Intentions to

105

love are crowded out and choked by other interests, fears, and defenses until it is quite out of the question to move out of the ruts of familiar habit, to take unexpected steps, or to use the dwindling supply of unexpressed love. In one of his rules for learning new habits William James suggests the need for a little gratuitous exercise of the new habit each day beyond the minimum required for its survival.[4] Habits of love also grow best by exercise, and to keep growing they need to go beyond the minimum required to survive the day before.

Religious and moral codes traditionally come in negative form, burdened with their woeful warning "Thou shalt not." Parents and teachers are often so anxious over the evils feared that they continue to say No, No until the positive impulses to act are repressed beyond the ability to say Yes even to the good. Rigidity of inhibitions and frigidity of sex impulses are the outcome of this negativism, often thwarting the success of marriage and damming back the free flow of love in the family. If we want Christian love, we shall need to release these repressions and guilt-ridden anxieties. For love is naturally a spontaneous expression of affection. Persons and families with such outgoing affection are wells of refreshing life in deserts of fearful dryness and ice fields of empty frigidity. When a person or family has the overflowing Christian experience of expressive love, it becomes attractive and often irresistible.

What does Christian love express that other loves do not? If studious theologians and hearty laymen are right, and at this point there is quite general agreement among them, Christian love is God's love (John 5:19; I John 3:1) working in and through us to others. It is a divine spirit of spontaneous love higher than the sordid passions of the flesh yet even more passionate in its desire to overflow in refreshing life to others. Psychology, by reason of its limitations as an empirical science, stops short of describing the nature of God. But psychology is well able to distinguish between higher and lower loves, to see in higher love a desire not for physical gratification but to appreciate and respond to the best, to take steps to save and develop the best in other persons.

[4] *Principles of Psychology*, I, 120-27.

The Christian purpose is to love in spite of every difficulty, to forgive every offense, to try again after each failure until eventually if possible (the possibilities we cannot always know) resistances are overcome and others are won over to the life of love. The enterprise of Christian love is not exclusive, as some loves are, but seeks to save one after another until it moves toward the ultimate goal which God seems to hold, the redeeming of all men in one family of love.

In the expression of this unfaltering Christian purpose to love the limitations of sex are outdistanced, for sex is then essentially a spiritual rather than a physical love. But Christian love has no reason to crush the legitimate desires of sex. Not all impulses, sexual or otherwise, are worthy of expression. But any persistent natural impulse can be sublimated and channeled into social values by a new perspective. Lust has been well described as a loss of perspective, choosing the part for the whole of life, the moment of pleasure instead of the eternally good purpose.[5] The sex urge in an unmarried teacher or social worker can with fair perspective be sublimated to an interest in other people's children and channeled into daily service to promote the growth of the best values in them. Bishop Heron has this devotion to underprivileged boys, and he keeps his Christian perspective to love and develop love in them in spite of murder, robbery, ingratitude, and revenge. The possibilities of utilizing all the powers of personality in Christian love are boundless. In the perspective of this purpose physical and spiritual energies are able to work together.

3. DEMOCRACY AT HOME

Repression is a dynamic reaction to autocracy in persons and society. In the sense that Freud uses it repression is the exclusion of painful or unacceptable impulses from consciousness and motor expression. The ego is the autocrat in personality that excludes unwelcome impulses of the id. Social opinions and moral authorities, such as parents and teachers, exert influence upon the superego (conscience) and exercise in this way control over the ego and id. The

---

[5] Ligon, *op. cit.*, p. 142, defines lust as "an intense emotional attachment of any sort which is not integrated with the total personality."

disorders of personality are seen as a civil war of these forces in which repressed impulses continue to fight against the ascendant purpose that keeps them under. Repression is therefore recognized as a cause of serious disturbances in personal and interpersonal life, usually an unsuccessful method of control, for the repressed tendencies continue to exert tensions and react in a spreading and unpredictable network of inner conflicts. One author compares repressed impulses to bad boys who for unruly conduct are put out of school but keep up the struggle by throwing stones at the windows. As boys rebel against the autocratic authority of a teacher, so excluded impulses are a constant threat of revolt against the unity and security of personality.

Wherever repression occurs, there is a dominating authority that prohibits and restrains instead of finding a constructive solution in a more acceptable expression. Frustration with its accompanying troupe of psychological disturbances is one price we pay for repressive authorities. Our typical social pattern is dominance and submission. It is astonishing to discover how nearly every situation in our society is of this kind. Someone dominates; others submit. Whether by election, appointment, or personal initiative someone gets himself on top and talks down to his associates. Like a gang of boys playing king of the hill they rush madly for the top until one at length succeeds in gaining the ascendant position by pushing the others below him. Then the others are unhappy and try again and again until one king after another is overthrown and the struggle to get on top goes endlessly on.

Is this pattern of dominance and submission inevitable? It almost seems like a law of social gravitation. The big potatoes shake to the top and the little ones to the bottom, as one agriculturist put it. But with human potatoes life is not so mechanical as jolting over a rough road, for some of us want to submit and others want to dominate. Not that we are born this way, but we are conditioned by satisfactions arising in interpersonal relations. There is enough security and comfort in dependence that a child may come to prefer submitting to a dominant mother rather than keeping up the struggle. Another child in the same family may discover the thrill of revolt in the struggle to assert his aggression, and want to keep up the struggle to dominate others.

In the typical family authority is vested in a leader who knows best and tells others what to do. And the family pattern is traditionally autocratic as parents hold authority over children. They are larger, stronger, and presumably wiser; they come first on the scene and hold the property of the home, not forgetting that possession is nine points of the law. They have their chosen occupation and interests; they have fixed habits of living according to their preferences. When the children come along, they are initiated into this established order, to accept it whether they like it or not, until the age when they can leave and become the authority in a home of their own founding. A father and mother may contend for ascending power in the struggle for home rule, or this may have been decided before the wedding day in trials of their strength of dominance. It has been observed that hens who associate together have their pecking order, from the most dominant to the lowliest who is pecked by all but dares not to peck back at any. In human societies this pecking order also obtains, from the most dominant down the line to the least. If the husband is henpecked, he can take it out on the children, who also have their order of pecking among themselves and their playmates, and so on down to dog and cat.

What has this to do with the Christian home? Jesus teaches the essence of democracy. He declares: (1) the unique worth of every person, (2) mutual respect for the rights of each person, and (3) responsibility of each for all and all for each. These three principles are the basic motivations in whatever democracy has been attained on this planet. Yet democracy is an ideal more than a fact, even in societies that proudly fly its banner. What we call democracy in government and community living is a very limited practice of these principles that falls far short of the full meaning they suggest. Even at our advanced stage of enlightenment midway in the twentieth century there are few who actually believe that full democracy is possible or practicable in church, school, business, and home life. As the family is our present interest, let us see what this means for democracy at home

Democracy at home falters because not many of us are ready to take the risk of trusting others to make their own decisions. We are slow to believe that other persons could possibly have the wisdom or at least the common sense to be right as often as we are. We are more readily aware of the mistakes of others than of our own mistakes, and we are not quite willing to let them, and thereby ourselves, suffer from these avoidable errors. Parents are especially reluctant, for children are so young and inexperienced, so impulsive and limited in knowledge, that we should only be inviting disaster to let them decide anything. Christian parents are even more reluctant, for they care so much; they have such high ideals and desire only the very best for their children. It is natural that the most conscientious parents are apt to be overanxious and fearful lest their children do wrong.

Yet Christian love requires democracy for its expression. Otherwise it is inconsistent with the principles of Jesus stated above, and contradictory to the fullest development of love in each member of the family. We have seen how autocratic control causes repressions and frustrations in those who submit to its domination. Children under such authoritarian domination may have to conform, but in so doing they are likely to deceive or rebel against their parents. Neither conformers, deceivers, nor rebels can contribute their fair share to democratic living.

Frustration prevents the growth of love by inciting anger, resentment, and revolt. Instead of promoting love the autocratic family promotes hatred and aggression or deceit and hypocrisy. Instead of enlarging the area of common interests and interaction it reduces the area of the life they share in common. Instead of growing in appreciation of their parents and the values they seek to impose by authority the children reject them as unwelcome intruders upon their freedom and self-chosen values. This is why love requires a democracy for its expression, because otherwise it is stifled and denied in bitter resentments to parental domination. Even the parents who think they should dominate by love for the good of the children are unwittingly changed by the role of authority into nagging, scolding, threatening, punishing agents of the laws they promulgate. Eventually the mutual irritations and conflicts fostered by authoritarian methods[6] result in mounting resentments that make them miserable enemies. This is illustrated by the boy who said when it was his turn to offer family grace, "Thou preparest a table before me in the presence of my enemies."

If Christian love comes to democratic expression in family life, it is not content to make youth dependent even upon a good authority but seeks to encourage trustworthy independence. It is not enough to foster growth in knowledge unless that growing comes to maturity in sound judgment and questions of value. For example, in budgeting family resources (time, energy, abilities, space, property, and money) there is opportunity for each member at whatever age above infancy to have a part in deciding what values are most important and to learn how to manage in sharing the goods that belong to all for the best advantage of each one. Such planning forces us to study our wants, to know what we want most, to discover our unappreciated resources for family living, and to develop them by developing ourselves in the wise use and sharing of them. When parents see themselves, not as lords of the exchequer who grant favors and allowances, but as trustees of goods belonging to all to be shared by all in joint decision, then democratic expressions of love are open to children as well as parents. For they grow to appreciate the values of family life and participate more freely in the responsibilities of love as members one of another.

A democratic expression of Christian love does not seek to hold power over others or struggle with others to gain such power. Leadership in such a family is shared, not only by joint decisions reached in family councils, but also by what we may call differential leadership No one has the right to be a leader in everything; it is not good either

[1] Authoritarian methods could have produced such resentment as the boy held against the bishop who made him work. If so, the senior partner in this work was doing what he thought was best for the boy's own good. But unless a boy shares that feeling or has some part in the decision to work, it is more likely to arouse aggression than love.

for him to hold such dominance or for others to be so dependent upon his domination. The aim of democracy is to develop as many leaders as possible by encouraging each person to use and enlarge his own skills. A mutually interdependent social organism has need of each member who in his way has a unique function to perform. So in a family democracy there is a division of labor and leadership. Each person has his particular tasks to perform, his ideas to contribute and plans to initiate. Each one is thereby a leader in his sphere, and the family will encourage him to improve his knowledge and skill in these ways until he is the authority in his field of specialization. There are many authorities, as in a college faculty or a laboratory of research associates. Each one chooses his field of interest and agrees to be responsible for the tasks in his domain. Each looks to the others for leadership in that area and defers to the expert for authority there.

To be specific, here is a family of six who co-operate in differential leadership, each one in different fields of interest. The father may be a physician who works every day in the field of medicine. He is the leader in diagnosis and treatment; the entire family refers to him in all questions of health. The mother chooses food as her special interest, having studied dietetics in college. She plans and prepares the meals, ready to accept suggestions and observing the tastes and desires of each member of the family; but in questions of food she is the leader who knows the calories and vitamins and how to balance well the family diet. The older daughter is majoring in English and drama; she entertains the family with accounts on the latest plays and books, and is consulted by every one of the family in questions of grammar, the best plays and movies, and what will be the most interesting reading. The older son is interested in science, has a laboratory in the basement, and keeps up with *Popular Mechanics;* he replaces electric lamps and fuses in sockets, repairs radios, phonographs, and electric doorbells, invents gadgets for the convenience of the family, does photography, and reports on new scientific discoveries to keep the family up to date, and the family relies on him for leadership in his area of interest. The next daughter is interested in nature, has flower and insect collections, keeps a bird log of when each new species is first seen, puts out water and feed for the birds; she also reads dog books and knows the last word in feeding and training the family dog. The younger son is an authority on sports and is up to the minute on the players and standings of the baseball teams, the football and basketball contests in their season; when anyone wants to know about sports, he is the expert, by his choice at first and before long by common consent. So in democratic families each member is a leader in a different way, and all recognize the authority of each in his field. Such diversity is the strength of a democracy, enlarging the variety of its resources and developing the leadership of the largest number in the service of all.

A democratic society has less need for coercion and violence. These are the weapons of an autocratic regime that needs secret police to spy and intimidate, storm troops to force obedience and liquidate minorities. Where democratic decisions are reached by common consent, there is naturally more willingness to carry out faithfully the enterprises which belong to all. Even where a minority is outvoted by a majority, there is no need for violent revolt because there is recourse in peaceful methods of social and political change for the minority to become a majority and win others to its program. There is a surprising amount of coercion and violence going on in family living. Why do parents so often command their children and punish them to compel obedience? Is it not because such families are autocratic? Decisions are made by parents without consulting the children, and coercion is needed to enforce the handed-down-from-above decisions upon the children.

It should be self-evident that coercion and violence defeat love and democracy in the home. Coercion is undemocratic in doing violence to the dignity and freedom of another person to choose his own values. It damages human relations by overriding voluntary consent with the weapon of superior might. It treats a person as a thing, pushing and pulling him by external pressures rather than inviting his consent and enlisting his co-operation. It is frustrating to be coerced, and almost never fails to promote hostility and counterviolent aggression rather than love and democratic teamwork. As it is impossible to hate and be completely healthy, it is a threat to health as well as to dignity, freedom, and love. Aggressors and their victims both indulge in anger that changes the chemistry of the blood, disturbs circulation and digestion, and upsets the vital rhythm of organic well-being. Anger also upsets the judgment, giving rise to prejudices and revenge motives that endanger the health of society by disturbing the fabric of interpersonal relations.

There are situations where coercion seems necessary for safety and welfare. A madman with murder or suicide in his eye needs to be restrained. An angry or alcohol-crazed father may harm his wife and children. A desperate criminal may shoot at anyone in the path of his cold unconcern for human life. Should they not be coerced to restrain their violence against innocent parties? From a psychological point of view it should be noted first that a great deal more violence is used than is necessary in the excitement and tensions of anger and aggressive hungers. Parents who punish their children in anger are more often giving release to their own internal pressures than reforming the errors of the children. The prevalent punishment of criminals is more effective in releasing the aggressive tendencies of society to get even and have revenge by giving them what is coming to them than it is in changing criminals into good citizens.

Again, it should be noted that punishment in the family or elsewhere projects the blame unfairly upon the culprit. It focuses attention only upon his evil deed and forgets to notice what caused him to act that way. It treats the symptom rather than the cause, and such treatment is always superficial if not futile. Furthermore it fails to consider the social causes of his misdeed, the interpersonal conditions that incited his revolt. A mother may punish one child for giggling when told to go to sleep, without seeing the tickling by her sister that caused the giggle. A teacher may punish one boy discovered in the act of striking a schoolmate without inquiring what teasing and provocation taunted him into the blow. Or she may overlook entirely her failure to provide an attractive recreation program to engage the boys in wholesome sports and team play. No parent can afford to blame a child without honestly blaming himself at the same time for failures in social planning and interaction that might successfully have moved around or ahead of the predicament the offender found himself in. Better than violence then is social intelligence to provide opportunities to learn together the lessons needed as shown by the offense.

Another psychological observation on violence is that it usually accomplishes the opposite result than was intended. In coercing a child the parent grits his teeth and says, "I'll make him do it and like it." But though the child is compelled to do it this time, he will certainly not like it or be likely to do it easily again of his own accord. Instead of providing incentive to wash behind his ears the parental insistence creates resistance to wanting to do it. In applying the rod the parent's aim is not to spoil the child; it is to discipline him so that he will feel sorry enough not to do it again. But sorry feelings do not often bring repentance to the point of his deciding to be a good boy. They rather deepen his determination not to be caught next time, to get his way by clever deceit, to have his cake without the punishment. In so doing the child is being spoiled more deeply than before, as he is forced by punishment to resent the hand that feeds him and to become a more clever criminal in evading the dictatorial authority of the law imposed upon him violently. The aims of discipline are better accomplished in other ways.

When I was seven years old, I was caught in a misdemeanor. I cut a piece off my father's rope to make a swing; and when I insisted I had not done the dastardly deed, he took me to match the piece with his rope until I could no longer deny his evidence. For some reason I did not then understand he did not swing the rope on my diminutive body with his muscular arms. I had committed three crimes in one—theft, destruction of property, and lying. I was a juvenile delinquent in the hands of the legal authority, and we both knew I had done wrong. But instead of bemoaning his loss of property and venting his wrath on the offender he called a family council. In the presence of the family the whole incident was talked over, and I came to see clearly that no one can trust a liar, that friends would always distrust me, and that I would be in one trap after another. At length I was invited to choose my own punishment. After careful deliberation my choice was to go without a birthday celebration. This meant no little sacrifice as birthdays were festive occasions in our family, with a bountiful dinner, a crown, a birthday song written for the event and sung as the family marched around the king for a day, gifts from each member of the family, and the warm glow of family enthusiasm for the fact that you were born. The choice was accepted as punishment enough, and by the time the birthday arrived I was unexpectedly hailed again before the family council and told that my conduct was so good I had evidently learned the needed lesson, and the birthday celebration could be restored. The important lesson of honesty was better learned in this democratic way than by violence.

It is of course to be expected that a family may not always agree on every question. There is a subtle coercion in the assumption that the family must always be unanimous. Then to hold a different opinion from others is taken in serious concern as a crime against the family unity and loyalty. We have heard a father say to a high-school son when they disagreed over the question of dancing, "That is contrary to the moral standards of our home. You may either live up to our standards or leave." The son did not leave, but his love for the father was somewhat strained by this authoritarian denial of democratic living. The ability to disagree pleasantly, to hold differences without emotional clashes or being a pariah in one's home, is a lesson worth learning. It may help this learning along to practice disagreeing in jolly table conversation over inconsequential items in preparation for the art of respecting each other's right to differ on more serious matters. The Chinese Christian Council was saved from a split over theological disputes when its secretary, T. T. Lew, arose and said, "Let us agree to differ but resolve to love."

When a husband and wife have not learned this lesson, the outcome is often divorce. The rising tide of divorces is threatening the stability of the American home. What shall we say of divorce from a psychological point of view? First it may be observed that divorce is always a tragedy, for it is the failure of a serious venture of love to weather the gales and reefs of family life. It is a failure of democracy as well if one party forces separation through the courts contrary to the desire of the other. Even when divorce is granted on mutual consent, there is the failure of family democracy to adjust differences peaceably and find ways of respecting and supporting each other's rights. Especially tragic are the effects of divorce on the children, who suffer most in their need for security and affection.

But is it not better to separate than to quarrel before the children? That is a complex question not to be answered with a simple yes or no. Harmonious family relations are better for the needs of children who are learning to grow in love. And yet quarrels are not so unhealthy psychologically as some other conditions, such as repressions, sullen resentments, or the separation of one parent from the home. Social interaction even by quarreling is healthier than isolation. For quarrels give vent to pent-up feelings, define social situations in frankly uttered words, and keep persons interacting on the basis of open responses to each other. The most important issue is whether the members of a family are trying to solve their differences and adjust their conflicts with intention to keep on loving. As long as this purpose to love continues, there is no reason to despair.

At this point it is evident why earnest Christian families are less often found in the divorce court than others. The earnest Christian who accepts the ideals of love as taught by his religion and sincerely tries to practice them is in a stream of continuing purpose to love. If disagreements arise between husband and wife, they are ripples in that stream whose main current sweeps on in the course of love. When quarrels arise, there is reason to face the issues honestly, for love must go on, and it is assumed an understanding will eventually be reached. When offenses are given or received, there is the expectation and requirement of forgiving again and again to the well-known number of seventy times seven. Where prayer is a daily practice, there is the opportunity in a melting mood of humility and reverence to ask God for a solution and seek to make a new start. Where the family are active in church, there is the weekly routine of going together and participating with other families who expect their love to succeed. In these ways the Christian fellowship upholds the family in the stresses of modern life and provides a larger reservoir of love to enrich the stream of family devotion.

4. A HOME FOR MENTAL HEALTH

The home is the best setting for mental health. In the warm affection and intimacy of family life emotional needs are most often satisfied. Here if anywhere a person can relax and be himself, try out his powers and grow. Within the family circle the infant receives his original impressions and learns to respond to other persons. His first lessons in living with others are here, and his self-knowledge is a reflection of the attitudes members of the family take toward him.

The mental-hygiene movement began in efforts to improve the care of the mentally ill in large institutions. Benjamin Rush (1745-1813) and Dorothea Dix (1802-87) were early pioneers in accomplishing notable reforms. In the twentieth century Clifford Beers wrote *A Mind That Found Itself*,[7] the story of his experiences as a patient in mental hospitals, which led to the forming of the National Committee for Mental Hygiene, of which he was the first secretary. In addition to effective education toward the prevention of mental illness, child guidance centers were established to aid in the wholesome development of children with special problems. It was soon discovered that children's problems most often arise from home conditions. Increasingly the focus in mental hygiene has turned to the family as the most influential source of mental health and illness. "Childhood represents the golden age of mental hygiene," said the psychiatrist William A. White.[8]

The family contains the major sources of human motivation. The mating interests culminating in marriage, the parental interests in children, the filial and sibling interests, the need for food, shelter, response, and security—all are met in family life. The family most of all makes the growing personality what it becomes; this is the conclusion of psychologists, sociologists, psychiatrists, and social workers.

[7] New York: Longmans, Green and Co., 1908.

[8] E. R. and Catherine Groves, *Dynamic Mental Hygiene* (Harrisburg, Pa.: Stackpole Sons, 1946), p. 6. This book is a convincing statement of the centrality of the family in mental hygiene.

No other social group has so many new beginnings and readjus
nowhere else do relationships have such emotional significance.
formed in the family are consequential in all the other successes and
failures of persons and societies. The specific relationships of husband
and wife, parents and children, brothers and sisters present the typical
problems of social adjustment. The four crises of life—birth, adolescence, the climacteric, and death—are all met in the family. And the
family shows additional strength in rising to the crisis. Progress in
mental hygiene can be seen to depend upon recognizing the primary
importance of the family in human relations.

The greatest hazards to mental health as shown by a large weight
of clinical evidence are (1) strong or frequent fear and anxiety, (2)
withdrawal from people and retreat into fantasy, (3) urgent feelings
of guilt or shame, and (4) intense and prolonged hostility.[9] Home
situations that foster these attitudes are unhealthy and need to be
corrected. How do Christian families rate on these traits? Obviously
no two homes are exactly alike in the social attitudes they produce or
fail to develop. No family, Christian or otherwise, is entirely free from
these attitudes. From church to church and community to community
religious attitudes vary according to the theological emphasis and
the cultural patterns. The preaching of Jonathan Edwards and more
recent hell-fire-and-brimstone evangelists has produced fear and
anxiety, guilt and shame. Ecstatic cults have encouraged withdrawal
from the people of the world and retreat at times into fantasy. Con-
troversial sects, like those of the tabernacle and fundamentalist persuasion, have shown intense and prolonged hostility to the "enemies
of the faith." In fairness it must be added that they are no more so
than many other social activities, secular movements, popular interests, and concerns in our civilization, as war, crime, sports, newspaper
headlines, movie and radio thrillers, fiction and magazine reading. But
it would be extravagant to claim that Christian families avoid the
hazards to mental health.

[9] T. A. Rennie and L. E. Woodward, *Mental Health in Modern Society* (New
York: Commonwealth Fund, 1948), p. 336.

It is a question of what kind of Christianity the family believes and practices. There is no guarantee that if a wave of emotional revivals should sweep a million converts down the sawdust trail to the mourners' bench, the families represented in those conversions would all take a new rightabout-face in mental health. To ascertain the effects of such a revival we would need to know what it meant to each person, how his emotional attitudes were changed for how long, how his social relations were reconstructed at home, and how his ideas, purposes, and habits continued to develop in the months and years following. I know persons who were so changed for the better by sudden conversion or gradual growth in Christian living that their family life was completely transformed. But I also know Christian persons whose religion has somehow not saved them or their families from emotional upsets and unhealthy mental attitudes. It takes more than exposure to Christian teachings to insure mental health.

Rennie and Woodward state it thus:

The primary goals of mental health in family living are the establishment of a basic sense of well-being and security and the progressive development of all the natural endowments and interests of children so that they can understand, accept, integrate, and use them with increasing satisfaction and social competence. To insure such growth the following secondary goals are likewise essential: (1) the consistent development of self-confidence and a genuine sense of adequacy; (2) the development of sociability and habits of co-operation which enable children to enter into the give-and-take of family life and prepare them to participate effectively in work, play, and citizenship; (3) the emotional and psychosexual maturing which is necessary for mental health and for successful marriage and parenthood.[10]

The Christian family as we see it aims at these goals. The family pattern of Christian love provides a basic security and progressive development of social competence. Christian faith and love at their best undergird each growing life with confidence and worth. They develop sociability and co-operation in the interaction of love. They

[10] *Ibid.*, p. 336. Used by permission.

challenge growth to maturity. "Be ye therefore mature." [11] "When I was a child, I spake as a child, I understood as a child, I thought as a child: but when I became a man, I put away childish things." (I Cor. 13:11.) Such love casts out fear (I John 4:18), withdrawal, shame, and hostility. It is wholesome and makes personality whole.

The home founded on faith and love is a training ground for social adjustments and skills. The family is an interacting unit of persons who learn to live together in varying conditions. It is a microcosm, a little world in which all the important issues of the larger society are represented. The major problems of timidity and aggression, dominance and submission, conflict and harmony, rivalry and teamwork, deceit and honesty, freedom and responsibility are all present in the dynamic interpersonal relationships of the family. Every family interest has social reference; every family activity is a training for social activities beyond the walls of home. The smiles and frowns, greetings and good-bys of family responses become the patterns of all social communications. The games played at home become the apprenticeship for the sports and recreations out in the community. Family conversations exchange ideas and report events that develop into public opinions, political debates, and moral codes. Home management trains for social administration of people and resources. Home decoration—the arrangement of space, color, and furniture—develops artistic taste. Music shared in the family becomes musical taste and appreciation for symphonies, operas, choirs, or dance rhythms. The budgeting of finances in the family is the business training for larger enterprises. The first discoveries of a heavenly Father are usually prayers at bedtime, mealtime, and family worship where little children sense the reverent attitudes of parents and share together in the exaltation of worship.

Not only skills are learned, but in each of these activities there is the emotional quality of what they mean to each person in his growing understanding and satisfactions. And what they mean is a complex

[11] W. J. Lowstuter's interpretation of Matt. 5:18. He is professor emeritus of New Testament literature in Boston University School of Theology. See also I Cor. 14:20 (R.S.V.): "Brethren, do not be children in your thinking; . . . be mature."

of social values, for each activity is in reference to other persons, each interest is shared or debated with others, each skill is a social adjustment in the constantly changing patterns of interpersonal relations. In the home there is or should be freedom enough for each person to express his individuality and withstand the pressures to conformity that the larger society brings to bear upon him. In so far as he learns to express individuality in the jolly and serious give and take of cooperation with other individuals of his family, he is learning to be a good citizen in a democratic society. A Christian family is also a colony of heaven where the vivid joys of invisible spiritual realities are experienced and God is felt to enter the family circle.

A few samples of how the home may provide training for social skills and adjustment are presented by Rosemary Lippitt. She employs psychodrama, that is, the acting out in spontaneous plays at home of the problems and social interests of the children, who are Larry (age five) and Carolyn (age two). Larry's fear of a fire when his parents go out in the evening was overcome by giving him the role of a fireman and dramatizing again and again his putting out the fire and saving the children. His emotional blocking against singing with his class at school was removed by playing school at home, singing together, and talking over the imaginary boy who did not sing. A number of psychodramas were given to improve social techniques, such as playing a birthday party, meeting the children and parents at the door, introducing them to the mother and sister until Larry learned to do and say the courtesies with ease and confidence. Carolyn learned to shake hands and find her way about socially in these plays too. Better social relationships were stimulated: a more understanding attitude toward pets, an understanding of miners on coal strike, preparation for an airplane ride, and general increase in spontaneity and creativity.

When he came home from school one day, Larry told about a newcomer, named Kate, who was crippled and who could not walk and run as others did. He imitated her and showed his mother how she walked upstairs. A few days later he made a remark that he and the boys thought Kate was a dope because she could not do the things he could do. That afternoon his mother suggested that they play a game in which he would get hurt by a car, go to the hospital, and then get better. He was interested at once and suggested that his sister be the nurse. A record of the play follows.

Larry, "Here I am in the street, and a car comes whizzing along and clips the tail of my bicycle so that I am thrown off on the street. Then my friend Jim (a much older and admired boy) comes along and trips over me so that I get hurt."

Mother, "Yes, he accidentally runs over your leg, perhaps."

Larry is delighted and lies kicking on the ground in supposed pain. Mother and nurse-sister come rushing along and put him in an ambulance and take him to the hospital.

Mother, "Now I am the doctor. Hello, little fellow. What happened to you? Oh, it is your leg. Say, it is pretty bad, and it will take a while to get well. You will have to walk stiff-legged for a few weeks."

Larry, "You mean I can't run and jump any more?"

Doctor, "No, you must take care of it for a long while. I guess you can get up now and try to walk." He lifts Larry onto his feet. "Oh no, you cannot move like that. You must not bend your knee except by lifting it up by your hand. See, when you want to go upstairs, you must raise the leg with the hand like this."

Larry, "Oh, that is difficult. It makes my back tired before I get up the first flight of stairs." He puts forth much effort and pulls each leg onto the next step. He gets to the landing and sits down. "Say, this is not fun. Why are we playing this? I want to get well soon."

The mother sits down a moment on the step too. "Well, Larry, did you ever think of what Kate has to do when she walks upstairs? She never complains but keeps right on trying. Don't you think she is brave and courageous?" . . .

Larry, "Say, she is. I never thought of that before."

Mother, "Do you know how you can make it easier for Kate and have more fun yourself?"

Larry, "No. How?"

Mother, "It makes Kate happy to have the boys and girls nice to her and not impatient with her when she is slow about getting places. Perhaps you can help the other children to be nice to her too. You know they think a lot of you, and if you showed them that you like Kate and think she is brave, they will not talk about her being a dope. That must make her feel pretty bad like it would make a soldier feel bad if you said he was a dope because he lost a leg fighting in the war." [12]

A few weeks later when the school had a visiting day the mothers had an opportunity to meet. Kate's mother approached Larry's mother and said, "It is amusing that Kate does not talk of any of the children at home except Larry. It is Larry this and Larry that all the time. She points out your home every time we pass it, and calls my attention to the fact that Larry lives there." Evidently Larry had learned to appreciate Kate and show kind and friendly attitudes toward her.

Florence Moreno has been bringing together children and parents in her neighborhood to put on spontaneous plays dealing with problems of name-calling, prejudices, and parents' refusal to let their children associate with others considered less desirable. In this way and by discussion stimulated by the plays a better neighborhood feeling has developed. This suggests how one family may socialize with other families until the neighborhood becomes a family of families.[13]

The Christian family has spiritual resources for mental health. Often they are undiscovered or undeveloped resources, but though hidden they are available to those who desire to use them. One of these resources is *emotional security through faith and love*. Faith in a heavenly Father gives a sense of security in his world among the members of his family. It leads to trusting attitudes toward others and peaceful serenity to overcome fears and anxieties. Love as received in the tender affection of parents and expressed toward each member of the family is conducive to emotional security. Karen Horney, as quoted in an earlier chapter, considers affection the most important condition of mental health.

Another health resource is *motivation to unselfish expressions of love*. The Christian is urged by teaching and demonstration to express his love to those about him. And the Christian emphasis is upon unselfish deeds and attitudes. This is the extroverted, outgoing style of

[12] Psychodrama in the Home," *Sociatry*, I (June, 1947), 148-67. Used by permission. The title of this journal has since been changed to *Group Psychotherapy*.

[13] F. B. Moreno, "Psychodrama in the Neighborhood," *Sociatry*, I (June, 1947), 168-78.

life that is just the opposite from the withdrawing attitudes that keep persons aloof in lonely and timid isolation. The unselfish expression of love invites responses in kind, reduces hostilities so that interpersonal relations become healthier. This prepares for marriage, parenthood, and social leadership.

There is in such a home *supportive companionship to meet crises.* An unfaltering sense of companionship in family living stabilizes each person with moral support. When a crisis comes in the life of one member or of the family as a whole, there is an unexpected increase of strength to meet it in the social support mutually given to each other. The crisis draws them more closely together, and even death or separation is less crushing because the sense of comradeship continues. This is deeply reinforced by the confidence a Christian has in his heavenly Father, who never forsakes him but sustains life with larger resources of companionship. Death is swallowed up in victory (I Cor. 15:15) because heaven is viewed as the Father's home where children return for eternal companionship. Psychiatrists have recently discovered how devastating bereavement can be as a cause of neurotic and psychosomatic disorders. The need for grief work to release this syndrome of tensions and establish new relationships is a task in which the pastor and church friends can be very helpful.[14]

Intimate family life also provides *educative guidance toward maturity.* This is encouraged by connection with a church that has a calendar of religious education for each week of the year in a graded series that leads from the nursery to adult lessons in Christian principles and action. Nominal Christians may be careless about this education, but families who take their religion seriously (as noted above in the Union College Character Research Project) have a genuine interest in such opportunities for learning at home and in the church school. Where the family keeps regular devotional periods, discusses daily experiences in the light of Christian ideals, and seeks to carry

[14] See articles by Erich Lindemann, Mass. General Hospital, Boston; also a Ph.D. thesis by William Rogers from the pastor's viewpoint on *The Place of Grief Work in Mental Health* (Boston University Graduate School, 1948). An abstract of this thesis is available from the dean of the Boston University Graduate School.

them out in practice, constant learning can be guided by a central purpose. Desired traits of character are loved into being as united aspiration and devotion give them spontaneous expression in creative adventures of Christian living at progressively mature levels of achievement.

A Christian home offers an *interacting fellowship of faith and work*. Family attitudes are more contagious than the measles. They multiply in the actions and reactions of family living, reflecting moods and arousing emotional responses that become characteristic of each family. Children not only look alike; they act alike and grow to be alike through constant interaction. Fears and anxieties are very "catching." Faith is also contagious and is communicated within a family by the empathy of unspoken attitudes even more than by words and argumentation. Faith without works is a dead faith (Jas. 2:17), but if there is vitality enough to be expressed in action, it is communicated to others. Faith produces actions as actions develop faith. The working faith of persons who believe in each other and work for each other results in a unifying fellowship that is healthy for all. It provides needed confidence and a sense of adequacy that arises only in close-knit fellowship.

There is also health in the *confessing and forgiving of faults*. Everyone has his faults and makes his full quota of mistakes. But no one likes to admit he is in the wrong as long as pride holds out the illusion that "I am better than you." In the close-fitting relations of family living personal faults and pride of superiority often become unbearable. The health of the group as well as the persons involved suffers no little anxiety, guilt, and hostility over these offenses. When no release is found for these feelings, they rise in mounting tensions that seriously threaten peace of mind. Unrelieved feelings of guilt may drive one to punish himself in numerous ways (accidents, illness, deprivations, inferiority, self-blame, overwork) that make life a dirge of misery. Or they may be projected outward to the ones we love most, holding length, resisting their advances, dwelling upon their erisms, hurting and disappointing them in subtle ways ghteous indignation. A Christian conscience may become so entangled with pride and blame that the meanest acts have an illusive glow of self-righteousness. Yet the Christian gospel has a way to save us from these stubborn resistances in the gracious acts of confession and forgiveness. He who confesses his faults is promised they will be forgiven (Matt. 6:14; I John 1:9). The honest admission of faults and mistakes clears away the fog of deceit, invites the forgiving reconciliation of the person wronged, and gives the humility needed to make a new start together in love. The family that readily and regularly confesses and forgives faults is saved from cumulating tensions and hostilities in the Christian way of restoring and renewing peace and love.

5. An Expanding Christian Family

The ancient Romans had a family religion that meant a good deal to them. The family hearth was the focus or bright spot of the home, the family altar where offerings were made to the gods of the family. Of these there were many, each with a separate function to perform in looking after the family welfare. There was Genius, the procreative spirit of the father; Juno, the procreative spirit of the mother; Vesta, goddess of the hearth; Lares and Penates, guardians of the storeroom and the granary; Terminus, guardian of the boundaries of the homestead; and the like. The duty of each little deity was to work for the good of the local family, and, like the domesticated animals and servants, he would be rewarded accordingly. Of course the next family had its gods too, and they worked only for the interests of that family. Consequently these puny deities were rivals one against another and joined with the local families in taking advantage and getting ahead of each other. Every force human and divine was working to keep families apart in opposition to each other. There were few if any forces to draw these rival contending families together in larger unity. In the spring of the year a group of families might join in raiding expeditions against more distant neighbors, but after returning home and dividing the spoils they separated into rival family units again. Later on as the Roman republic and empire arose, efforts were made to elevate the little gods to larger spheres of influence. But in spite of state decrees, a busy calendar of public festivals, the importing of numerous foreign gods, and deification of emperors, the religion of the Romans was a hodgepodge of confused and contradictory customs and deities that was never successful in uniting families or maintaining loyalties large enough for the social whole the people needed to achieve.

When the followers of Jesus united in a new religious movement, they too had a family religion. But instead of having many little deities to guard local families against each other they gave allegiance to one God, the Father of one family including all his children on earth. There were controversies in the early Christian community over this larger family pattern, but Peter won approval to the vision that he "should not call any man common or unclean" (Acts 10:28), and Paul gained support for open membership for all. "For ye are all the children of God by faith in Christ Jesus. . . . There is neither Jew nor Greek, there is neither bond nor free, there is neither male nor female; for ye are all one in Christ Jesus." (Gal. 3:26, 28.)

The effects of this discovery upon the Christian family have been far-reaching. In Jerusalem the enthusiasm for the larger family led the company of early Christians to hold all things in common, parting gladly with private possessions to share with each according to his need, breaking bread together daily from house to house (Acts 2:42-47). Missionary journeys were undertaken to carry the good news to all nations and bring as many as were willing to come into their expanding fellowship. In other lands and times homes have been maintained for the homeless, hospitals for the sick, schools for those who wanted to learn, churches for worship and the service of all who would accept that service.

There are still rivalries and separations among families, for self-centered interests are not easily dislodged. But the direction of Christian energies has been outward, and the thrust of these influences has been to expand the Christian family. You will reply that the size of the modern family is decreasing not only in the number of children but also in the space of its dwelling and the dimensions of time and activities the family spend together. This we have already noted among the changing patterns of family living in our urban culture. And yet the Christian family continues to expand in other ways. The interests of the family are outreaching into the community and the world at large. The radio, newspaper, and magazine bring the larger world into the home, so that no family needs to be out of touch with the adventures of the human race anywhere. There are world-wide interests and implications in almost every sermon and church-school lesson as in the discussion of youth fellowships and institutes. A Methodist youth institute recently held in the mountains of Montana was devoted to the theme "Our Hungry World," with classes, discussion groups, recreation, worship, and sacrificial offerings to send aid to the starving people of other continents. And this is but one of hundreds of church-sponsored meetings where the world family comes into focus.

There are degrees of social distance with Christians as among all other persons that make them feel closer to some than to others. We are naturally drawn to those who are most like ourselves, with whom we have the most to share in common. Within the family, ties are closest because social distance is the least. In the neighborhood and on the school ground children choose friends who are mutually akin in some way. Business, laboring, and professional men associate naturally with those who go through similar experiences and talk shop most readily. Cultural, racial, and national distances constitute major barriers to Christian love. Many nominal Christians follow the line of least resistance and stay at home with their native group. The effect of Christian expansion is to overcome social distance, not in every situation but surprisingly and persistently as this love moves outward.

The growing sense of responsibility for all God's children everywhere is what we mean by the expanding Christian family. The vital interest awakened in living as members of a local family is reaching out to a genuine interest in all people as potential members of a larger family. Will this expanding human interest undermine the loyalty which we feel to members of a local family? I think not. Rather will it enrich the meaning, joy, and responsibility of local family living as we discover the larger dimensions of Christian love and our responsibility to cherish and share the best that we have and are with others in unselfish service and unbroken fellowship.

Family worship motivates the extent and the intent of a Christian family. Worship is the ultimate outreach of love to God as the Father of every living creature. In worship a man feels his vital relatedness to God as his Father, by whom he is related to all men and women as brothers and sisters. There is no longer social distance in the spiritual unity of one family of God. Who can hate the enemy he prays for or be indifferent to the stranger he responds to as a brother? Worship expands the extent and deepens the intent to be one family of heaven and earth.

To neglect family worship tends to reduce the size of a family to the four walls of a single dwelling house. If the focus of attention is restricted to *my* house against all other houses in the world, it may then narrow to myself against the other members of my household in the struggle of the ego to assert its claims above all others. In that case we lose the intent to share all values in one family, and each person retreats into his own little world to vegetate in his egocentric paradise, which to his disgust becomes a private hell. The paradise is lost in the larger unity surrendered in anger or cold disdain when selves forget to pray together in a family. Little hope remains of expansive living in a world family if we retreat from each other in the local family.

To re-enact family worship at home is to discover our membership in the universal home of heaven and earth. The family that reaches out to a heavenly Father in the same act draws nearer to a family of the whole earth. The intent to pray to God for others changes the extent of family living. The extent of world family unity changes the intent of our local family living. In daily prayer the family grows daily in spiritual dimensions of higher aspiration upward, deeper inspiration inward, and broader expectation outward. The growing family finds enlarging appreciation and responsibilities through this exaltation of love.

VI

Sex and Marriage

1. ADVENTURES IN LOVE

Sex has two functions in human life. Procreation is the biological function, and it is usually deferred twenty years or more in our society until a new home is established and a married couple is ready to have children. Socialization is the psychological function, and it begins from birth into a world of other persons. Who can say which function is more important? Without procreation the human race would not survive; without socialization it would not be worth surviving. Christian love has an equal responsibility for each, and sex is therefore a major concern of Christianity.

The fact of infant sexuality cannot well be denied. For sex is not something we have; it is something we are. It is not added to a person later, though its potencies may require years to mature. The first report from the delivery room is: "It's a boy," or, "It's a girl." The sex of the infant is the first item to be reported because it is present from the first, and because it will make a significant difference all through life. It is not to be ignored, for it represents an essential characteristic of the new life that will become increasingly important as the boy or girl grows into manhood or womanhood. Sex traits are diffused throughout the entire range of the psychological life in ways that will be noted as we proceed. Psychological needs and satisfactions, in which sex has a natural part, draw persons together in social relations.

In infancy psychophysical desire (libido) centers in the mouth, which holds primary attention. Oral satisfactions invite nourishment and social interest in the mother first, then in others who share meals, becoming a lifelong social ceremony enjoyed by young and old, from lollipops and ice-cream cones to dining out, social teas, church suppers, smoking, and drinking beverages together. Speech is an oral activity which, according to Froeschl, develops from chewing, as lips, jaws, tongue, throat, and larynx co-ordinate rhythmically. The popular phrase "chewing the fat" suggests this relationship, though it is air we chew as voiced breath in talking. Conversation is a major social interest, a bridge of communication, an instrument of co-operation among persons. Thumb-sucking is often a substitute for social satisfactions. Stammering is a conflict of aggressive-repressive tendencies in interpersonal relations. Sudden weaning, strict feeding periods, rejection, lack of affection, and other deprivations disturb these oral-social satisfactions. Kissing is an expression of affection accepted in our culture as a social act that obviously brings people together.

Genital interest is at first solitary, as the baby discovers parts of its body. In childhood there may be a natural curiosity about genitals of playmates. Children in most families are punished for interest shown in the genitals. But scolding and punishment only drive a natural interest into secrecy, foster morbid feelings of guilt, and tend to make children withdraw as introverts when socially rejected. Toilet training may be too early and severe, causing tensions and anxieties, eventually coming at times to retention and constipation or other disorders of intestine and bladder. Rigid repression here at an early age may have repercussions later in life, accenting acquisition and restraint, sadistic tendencies, or guilt and frigidity in sex relations of married persons.

But sex is not entirely localized in these areas. It includes hormones and chemistry of the blood stream, bodily form and musculature, physiological energies, psychological interests and preferences, social attitudes, and cultural expressions. Sex is whatever makes a male masculine and a female feminine with the resources and potencies for developing in those directions. The difference between masculine and feminine traits, however, is not a bipolar set of opposites with a wide gulf between. Rather sex is a continuum of varying degrees of masculine and feminine traits that merge and overlap each other. Every man has some feminine traits and every woman some masculine traits. There are also many traits held in common between men and women as human beings.

Our culture expects and demands certain traits of women as feminine characteristics and other traits of men as masculine. These social expectations and conditionings seem to be as influential as heredity and hormones—if not more so. Of great influence also is the family constellation in which children may feel closer to the parent of the opposite sex (Oedipus complex) and develop masculine or feminine traits by this attachment and identification. The average man is not at the extreme of masculinity or the typical woman at the extreme of femininity; most of us are nearer the median. And this enables men and women to understand each other better and appreciate the common interests and responsibilities they need to share.

For example, the masculine role in our society is the dominant one of power and aggression; the feminine role is the submissive one of receptivity, pliable adjustability, and tender sympathy. When we insist that little boys don't cry and hold up heroic ideals of men who conquer and overcome enemies, we magnify the bully and perpetuate war. Men suffer neurotic ills by repressing emotions; they become criminals or ruthless exploiters to fulfill the role of the dominant aggressor; they lust for power to be the conquering hero in trying to live up to the he-man figure we expect them to be. How much more human, likeable, and socially useful men are when they manifest feminine traits of receptive adjustability and sympathy mingled with their masculine tendencies. On the other hand, submissive traits in a woman will make her a clinging vine of dependent weakness unless there are mingled with this the more masculine traits of initiative and independent resourcefulness. But a man who is overly feminine or a woman who wants to be a man and take a predominantly masculine role will suffer equal distortion of personality by overbalance in that direction. Each can best fulfill his own role in society with sympathy rather than scorn for or surrender to the role of the other. In these developments it is evident that sex has a social function to perform.

At first the infant is autoerotic. He discovers himself in learning to know other persons, and is so intrigued by the wonders and interests of self that others are used chiefly to bring satisfaction to himself. The mother is the lunch counter who serves in providing nourishment to satisfy the hunger for food, then the waitress who flirts with him when she brings the food and satisfies the hunger for attention and affection. The father is the professional entertainer, who is retained to amuse him with his antics and tricks, then the professional athlete whose main business is to be a good sport and play with him. Other persons, such as siblings, relatives, and friends, are as welcome as they are willing to satisfy his self-centered baby interests. These are social adventures of a rudimentary sort and altogether to be desired, for they meet the level of an infant's responsiveness and by playful exercise help to develop his social interests outward in broadening activities.

As he grows into childhood, his next social steps are apt to be homoerotic. He is attracted to those who are most like himself. The boy plays more with other boys; the girl associates more with other girls. The games of childhood reflect this division of interest. While girls play with dolls and dress up in trailing gowns for parties, boys are more likely to play competitive and aggressive games like "cops and robbers" or "cowboys and Indians." These are quite largely in the pattern of social expectations as children play what parents and older children suggest, but the social division of boys and girls is thereby demonstrated as a social development. For biosocial reasons it is easier to share social interests during midchildhood with others of similar age and sex. Gangs, clubs, and cliques take form along sex distinctions as boys are learning to live with boys and girls are trying out their budding social skills on other girls.

After this period the growing person is ready for the next social steps beyond self-interest. These will probably be heteroerotic interests in members of the other sex. Boys and girls now associate together more easily and learn to accept each other as human beings with common interests to share. The boy's exclusive world is not so firmly walled in by his gang; he is ready for games that bring boys and girls together on the playground or swimming pool as comrades in social activities. Boys eventually take risks and endure the awkward embarrassments of going to parties, folk singing, and dancing. Girls become aware of such honors as receiving admiring glances from boys and eventually having dates together.

The psychosexual development of life is a series of social adventures from one self to other selves and from one to both sexes. The attractions and interests that sex compounds are among the strongest forces available to socialize the human animal and refine his aggressive or evasive selfishness to courtesy, chivalry, and romantic awakening in the beauty of art, music, dance, and literature. By these social ventures outward in growing appreciation for other persons and the values of interpersonal relationships we come eventually in the normal course of maturity to desire the unselfish devotions of marriage and parenthood. Through these advancing stages of social development Christian love is enriched and finds sex not an enemy but a resourceful ally in awakening regard for others as it draws persons into closer, sturdier bonds of fellowship.

Love needs to be learned, as we have noted in Chapter IV. We are born hungry—for food and love. Hungers may be innate, but we must learn how to fulfill them and guide their development into socially desirable traits and attitudes. We learn by experimentation, by trying out how to approach and respond to other persons. From the first cry we are trying one social technique after another, noting results and modifying our behavior accordingly. Without social adventures no love. To produce love in growing children we must provide social adventures to interest and invite interpersonal responses.

Christianity as a religion of love is an endless series of adventures. If we grow too timid or forgetful to engage in social adventures, Christianity declines into a mere shell of empty words without the vitality of living expressions of love. Christian parents, teachers, and pastors are to be held responsible for the success or failure of love to grow in the rising generation. Unless they practice the art of loving and invite loving responses from each child, he will fail to grow up in social ways. In the home the first and most constant lessons of love are learned, as shown in Chapter V above. Parents need to be educated

135

in the art of teaching and evoking love, first in the family, then in out-reaching social activities.

In the church school learning to love is the primary aim, more important than all else. Keeping Johnny quiet or memorizing Bible verses is too passive and negative. To learn by doing we must have living adventures in loving one another as good friends who are find-ing better ways of expressing that love in kind deeds and unselfish service with growing understanding of what love means in our every-day life in everybody's world. Our church-school aims are too verbal; they need to be actual and practical experiments in love as the central program of the Christian faith and life. They need to be graded pro-gressively upward and outward with the enlarging social horizons of youth growing into love.

New learning activities are needed from the time of puberty. With adolescence life turns a corner. Latent sex powers awaken with physiological and psychological consequences. As sex unfolds, new insights and appreciations arise, unknown or dimly glimpsed before. Boy sees girl as for the first time to be a wholly new and marvelous creature. She is beautiful, graceful, and charming. To her he is strong, agile, and handsome. These are truly significant moments when the budding romantic interest opens in wonder to the glory of love. In such awakenings sex may appear as a ruthless lust or a shameful evil to be feared. It may become an honored potency to be cherished in wholesome social expression until the marriage prepares for procrea-tion. Information about sex is sought more earnestly than ever before, by deeper intimations of its powers and often perplexity as to its proper uses. It needs to be understood in a Christian perspective as a sacred gift shared by the Creator that we too may be creators of new life. Morbid guilt and ignorant or inaccurate misunderstandings need to be removed. Masturbation is better faced honestly with no exag-gerated horror or superstitious tales of its consequences. Freed of ex-cessive guilt and fear it will more readily vanish like thumb-sucking when not overemphasized or threatened but outgrown in wholesome social activities and sublimated in more mature satisfactions.

Social dating needs to be encouraged, for at the awkward stage of adolescence youth are insecure and self-conscious to the point where they hesitate and postpone these social steps. Parents have not always realized the dangers of fixation at childish levels of love and may indulge their own ungratified affections by holding children to them in dependent attachment. Adult men and women may fail to gain independence, to accept mate love, or to establish a marriage successfully because of a parental fixation. Autoerotic and homoerotic interests may become fixations also if a growing person fails to outgrow these earlier levels of satisfaction. To miss a social step outward at the typical age when one's fellow adolescents are attaining it is more serious than at first appears, for the older he becomes the more difficult it is to regain the ground he has lost or take the social steps more easily learned at an earlier stage before the rigidity of adult dignity has set in. Failing to progress in love does not exactly leave one standing still; it actually means slipping backward in regression to immature levels of social living. The girl who decides to take care of her father or win success in a career before accepting marriage is likely to remain a spinster or marry later in haste to escape from such a state. The boy who is jilted once and hesitates to try again for fear of being humiliated may remain a proud and lonely bachelor whose disappointments turn to bitter diatribes against women.

The church has a special responsibility to sponsor youth fellowships that will bring adolescent boys and girls together in Christian adventures. These adventures will include high moments of worship to express new aspirations, affirm larger social visions, and dedicate their lives to unselfish service in realizing the love of a heavenly Father. They will include discussion of important issues of mutual concern, not the least of which are the questions of what to do on social dates, how to choose a life mate and prepare for marriage and parenthood. Here are a few samples of questions asked by young people of high-school age in church youth group discussions:

What do you think about blind dates?
What will I do about differences with my family?
What privileges do you think a sixteen-year-old girl should be able to have beside going to *church* affairs?

Do you think a young girl should go steady (about sixteen years of age)?

What will I do—my beau thinks he likes my girl friend?

What is love?

In your opinion what is the difference between love and desire?

How can you know for certain that you are in love and not infatuated?

How does one know when he first really falls in love?

Mother always says, "Don't go steady," but if you don't go steady, how do you know if you are in love?

If a girl knows a boy likes her but is too shy to do anything, what can she do about it?

If a boy who jokes all the time shows me in class that he likes me, should I believe him?

How should we meet the right woman, and how will we know her?

What if you get a crush on an older man?

Because a girl is trying to forget Oscar, is it all right to go after Toby?

How late should a girl be allowed to stay out on a date?

I have been going with a girl for several months. I have a very bad case of inferiority complex and don't seem to be making any headway. Have you a solution?

Why is falling in love something for which a person can prepare? Does it happen at a certain time when you can be expecting it?

What are the stages of falling in love?

What if you're in love with someone you know you can't marry? What then? Would you go against your parents' wishes? Would you leave your circle of friends?

Suppose you want to marry, but you haven't enough money to start, what then?

In this world of chaos how can modern youth follow the straight and narrow path?

How can young Christians of today resist the restless spirit which invariably comes during an era such as the present?

Is it worth while to bring children into the world in its present state?

Do you have to prove your love by necking whenever out with a boy whom you are quite fond of?

How many times should a girl go out with a fellow before she lets him kiss her if she doesn't want him to think her fast?

Is a girl a prude if she won't give a good-night kiss to a boy she doesn't especially like?

What is wrong with petting if you know what you are doing?

What is the test of true love? Can you have it at seventeen?

Do you believe boys and girls of seventeen and eighteen can really fall in love? How far should people go in their relationships?

What qualities does a boy seek in a girl he would like to marry?

Should a girl marry a boy of a different race?

Should a boy and girl of different religions get *well acquainted?*

How about getting married in college?

Do you think a couple should wait until he is through with his education?

Does a difference in ages of say eight years make a lot of difference in successful marriage?

Should a girl marry a boy younger than herself?

Can a marriage succeed where the likes and dislikes of the two are not the same? Would it be wise to try to compromise and make a go of it?

Is it wise for people of opposite natures to marry? If, for example, one is the life-of-the-party type whereas the other is of a quieter nature?

Are the chances for love to last over a long period of time, say a year, without being together good or bad?

How young may a person be to make a happy marriage? Is it all right for a girl not yet graduated from high school to marry?

If a girl at college is engaged to a fellow at home but meets a fellow who gives her his pin not knowing she is already engaged, what should she do?

Questions like these buzz around the heads of adolescent young people quite frequently. Many times they do not feel free to talk with their parents or, when they ask, meet only firm and stern prejudices rather than sympathetic understanding. Even among themselves such questions often go unasked for fear of ridicule or raucous answers. If a Christian philosophy of life offers the answers needed, then occasion should be provided in which youth can talk freely with experienced counselors who are tolerant and sympathetic yet with a clear view of the values at stake and a sense of how youth can make their own decisions wisely.

There will also be a place for recreation in which youth may have good times together spontaneously, overcome their sense of awkwardness, gain social confidence, develop social skills, and grow in appreciation of each other. The freedom of interchanging friendships in a group of spontaneous fellowship is to be preferred in adolescence to steady dating and exclusive couple rights where no one dares to cut in. For steady dating at this age narrows the range of social experiences prematurely when youth need to try their social skills with many persons and learn from a variety of friends a breadth of viewpoints and attitudes in social adjustments. This is the age when group learning best promotes social development.

For adolescence is an exploratory stage in which every youth seeks to learn how to be an adult and develop by experimentation the social interests, conversational and behavioral exchanges that will be required of him in the future. The freedom which modern youth enjoy to conduct their social adventures without chaperones is likely to raise not a few eyebrows. And surely it is unwise to turn adolescents loose without guidance or resources for a constructive program of wholesome recreation. Petting parties are more dangerous and less useful socially than folk games, singing, sports, and social dances which provide larger fields of interest and activity to be explored together. In these social activities youth see others in the light of multiple relations and situations, hear their viewpoints, sense their reactions, and come to know their attitudes and traits of character. Psychological exploration is more revealing of personality than petting, and it stimulates a wider range of social techniques and interests worth sharing. There will also develop inner controls of ideals and purposes through these activities in youth fellowships that will provide a better guide for conduct and social attitudes than the weak and ineffective external safeguards of a censoring chaperone.

The Kinsey report [1] has touched off a chain reaction of discussion and no little consternation over the sex behavior of the males in our society. This is the first volume in a study which Kinsey plans to continue twenty years more until 100,000 persons have been interviewed on their sex history. From 5,300 confidential and carefully tabulated interviews with white males the authors report that over 12 per cent of thirteen-year-old American boys have already had sexual inter-

[1] A. C. Kinsey, W. B. Pomeroy, and C. E. Martin, *Sexual Behavior in the Human Male* (Philadelphia: W. B. Saunders Co., 1948).

course. At the age of fourteen one in every four has had such experience. By the age of twenty-eight over 86 per cent of American males have had premarital intercourse. They find a greater amount of sexual activity among boys in their adolescence than at any other time of life. The height of sexual capacity and activity the study finds to be in the late teens. By sampling different ages there appears to be no appreciable difference between the sex behavior of these adolescents and those of a generation ago.

There are several items of significance to our study of Christian love. (1) Sex activity shows more moderation among devoutly religious people. (2) Sexual activity is more moderate among those who attend high school and college than among those who do not. (3) Boys who will go to high school and college have less heterosexual intercourse and more masturbation than boys who do not go beyond grade school. (4) Sons who rise from lower to higher economic and cultural levels adopt the sex patterns of the higher level by the time they are fifteen. (5) Petting is on the increase and more prevalent among the higher than lower cultural levels. (6) The sex pattern of the American male is firmly established by the age of sixteen, and rarely do any circumstances of later life change it.

What are we to conclude from these observations? First, that sex is more active in adolescence than has generally been admitted. Second, that more adequate sex education is needed, not of the stern, repressive type but a sympathetic approach that will place the facts of sex in a meaningful framework of Christian values and be dedicated to these purposes. Third, a more attractive recreation program is needed to bring girls and boys together in wholesome social activities where their rising sex interests will be channeled and sublimated in co-educational group interaction and fellowship. Fourth, as youth reach the age of sixteen, parents and religious counselors may rely more upon trustworthy self-control due to well-established behavior patterns from earlier training, and may treat them more like adults who are responsible to make their own decisions. Fifth, early marriages may well be encouraged by counsel and financial assistance, so that in the late teens and early twenties sex activity may be invested in marital unity and love to strengthen the family.[2]

2. I Thee Wed

There are no more significant words in any language than "I thee wed." The unfathomable depth of meaning in these brief words baffles our utmost effort to understand or communicate it to each other. The "I" who stands at the altar is that mystery we have come to call a personality. He bears the hereditary traits of his ancestors plus the whole cultural heritage of the people with whom he has grown up from birth to manhood. The few things that he knows about himself are but a token of the far greater potentialities he has not yet realized. He recalls from early childhood his intimate dependence on his mother and in sturdy struggles to achieve independence his revolts against his father's authority. He feels a nostalgic warmth that draws him back to the protective nest of his parental home. Yet he sees the time has come for him to be a man, to stand up and look other men in the eye, to take up the responsibilities of strenuous vocational labor, to establish a home of his own as a world which, like Atlas, he will uphold with all his strength. Can he play the role of a man, equal to the demands of a husband and father? No time now to hesitate; he must give answer and dispel all doubts.

Beside him at the altar stands "Thee," in the beauty and vitality of her youth. She is just as great a mystery to herself and even more so to him. She also brings the hereditary traits of her ancestors and the heritage of a culture somewhat the same yet quite different from his. For she has been educated as a girl for womanhood, and she has selected from her culture the hopes and fears that represent a woman's viewpoint. She has been protected by the guardians of her virtue, saved all her life as if for this hour when she will present herself at the altar of marriage. Can it really be true; has the hour actually come? Will it be possible to step forth from the sheltering home of childhood where one's place was secure in the love of parents who always knew

---

[2] For a symposium on the Kinsey report by leaders in a dozen fields see *Sex Habits of American Men,* ed. Albert Deutsch (New York: Prentice-Hall, Inc., 1948).

best? Will she be able to get along without her mother, and will her parents now recognize her maturity and be willing to give her up? What does the future hold of wonder and surprise, of joy and sorrow? To be a wife and a mother is a very great responsibility, always faithful, unselfish, and self-giving. To make a new home where before others prepared and decided for her, to hold the love of a man who will have many interests, to devote all her life to her family yet not to be submerged or subdued by the family cares—this is no easy task. Did she actually want to come so far and so fast as these steps that have brought her to the altar? Anyhow, it is too late to turn back now; the die is cast and the decision is made. This is the wedding.

The two are to "wed." A simple Anglo-Saxon word, but we are not deceived by its brevity or the ease with which it slips off the tongue. For it is freighted with the emotion of memories and hopes of all who have entered into marriage. It is unique among all the relationships of life. To wed is to pledge and to join two beings into one. Yet it is unlike all other joinings of persons or things. It is a voluntary pledge in which each person is free to enter or not as he chooses. It is the most intimate of all human relationships, in which the privacy of each is shared in the mutual revelations of conjugal love. It is the most exciting of all relationships, for it invites the constant interchange of adventures between two unpredictable creatures, man and woman, capable of the most sensitive responses of satisfaction and disappointment. It is as far-reaching as any human relationship, joining husband and wife for as long as life lasts, and by their union starting a sequence of births that may extend beyond our ability to calculate. It is the most difficult and rewarding of all human relationships, with consequences productive of such values as to justify every investment.

In the wedding of two distinct and in some respects opposite persons we find the I-and-Thou relationship, noted in Chapter II, as indicating the true meaning of Christian love. To every thing our relationship is merely to *it*. But to another person I come to a *Thou*, and the relationship is heightened in significance: first by the values that each person bears, and second by the increase of values that comes in the creative expression of mutual giving and receiving. The more one gives in love the more one receives; each lives in larger ways by the life of the other. To wed is to bring not only our worldly goods but every potential capacity to create more values in living together. Each complements the other until both are more complete than otherwise possible. And each awakens responses in the other, unknown before, until he becomes a new creature in the developing love of marital union.

In becoming one these two create a new world that has never existed before. It is for this reason that lovers go apart and seek to be alone with each other; they are separating from others in order to spin a web of their own that will become a unique expression of growing meanings with constant reference to and interaction among their shared interests and values. This lovers' world has an entity and a sanctity that is their exclusive property, for it is created out of the experiences they have lived through and cherished together. In Christian perspective this world of love has religious significance. Our marriage was made in heaven; we were born for each other and destined to be drawn someday by a divine Providence into each other's arms. God has ordained and will bless our marriage as it fulfills his purpose and seeks to enact his love in our world. It is not easy for children to leave their parental home, and many fail to marry or fail in marriage because of unsevered fixations to parents with the undermining intention, "Well, if he isn't good to me, I can always go back home to mother." To release such a fixation the Bible gives divine authority to the new world of wedded independence. "Therefore shall a man leave his father and his mother, and shall cleave unto his wife; and they shall be one flesh." (Gen. 2:24.) Not that one loves his parents the less, but rather he enters into a new responsibility to create a home in which these potential parents are to discover afresh the meaning of heavenly love on earth.

If this new world of love is truly attained, there will be a sustained note of reverence in it. Whenever we hear the words "I thee wed," we are moved with a deepening sense of reverence. A wedding is an act of worship. In the Judaeo-Christian tradition the ceremony is held in a church or synagogue, at an altar or in a sanctuary, where the blessing of God is invoked by an ordained minister, priest, or rabbi. Worship means worth-ship, and the worth of the wedding represents every value they bring to each other multiplied in the sharing. There is reason enough to worship at such an occasion, for every value of life can be enhanced in this dedication of love.

Let us review the course of love to the altar. How do they come to this point where they are ready to enter marriage? Falling in love we have seen to be a misnomer; rather we climb into love by a series of steps in mutual appreciation and growing responsibility.

There is the discovery of *desired traits*, as attractive features, capacity to enjoy living, responsiveness to attentions, honest integrity, sympathy and understanding, and converging life purposes that measure up to character expectations. These traits call forth admiration and invite friendship with a sharing of experiences and interactive events that may deepen into love.

Mutual responses of interest arise in the give and take of conversation, the flashing smiles and sparkling eyes, the exchange of coquetries, the showing of admiration, the invitation to social dates, which when accepted provide activities to join interests and try each other out in a variety of social situations. In these shared activities new interests develop with memories of good times, feelings of at-homeness, and satisfactions that accumulate in going together.

Progressive idealization occurs in the romantic glow of admiration and the need to find all virtues in the "right one." There are illusions of beauty and grandeur which romantic love spins of its own excitement, aided by the beauticians and abetted by moonlight, sunsets, the glories of nature, and the glamour of artificial lighting, interior decorations, photography, flowers, music, good food, and entertainment. This may wear off or be punctured by sharp temper and quarrels until the realities of human nature are blended with the idealities. Nor should we underestimate the power of growth as new character traits develop in response to love and appreciation until we grow up to the expectations that we invest in each other.

Pair unity is another stage in developing love, in which the adventures and interests shared by a couple attain special meaning as belong-

145

ing to them together.[3] This is a process of relating two lives into one and creating a world of their own as noted above. The more values shared together in joint appreciation, the more unique and binding is their mutual interest in each other. As this snowballs, it becomes increasingly clear they have an investment in each other, and their love becomes incorporated in a joint enterprise of establishing their own home. One couple spoke affectionately of "their mountain"; they had so often looked at it together. Another couple shared an interest in antiques until they could not resist buying an antique dining set, and then it was urgent to marry at once in order to use it. Another couple came to think of their religious vocations until it became a joint purpose to carry them out together as man and wife.

Social support of friends and family is usually necessary to advance love to marriage. There are couples who fly in the face of public opinion and marry in spite of social disapproval, but they miss the support of family and friends who would otherwise give them a basic confidence that regardless of difficulties the marriage will succeed. Love at first sight may be spontaneous attraction, but it is not yet mature love. It takes a growing experience to bring love from the awkward and uncertain sorties of the first date to the sure understanding and confident interaction of mature lovers. The contagion of other couples moving on in love, of best friends who share double-dating together, along with family approval, serve to reinforce the security of love. Where this is lacking, marriages are apt to fail. The impulse to "build a sweet little nest" and "let the rest of the world go by" is a natural stage in pair unity. But it is not sufficient to weather the storms of home living unless there are strong and accessible community resources to uphold the family in larger social unity.

Tacit agreements precede and lay foundations for the contractual relationships of marriage. When a young couple start going together, they express likes and dislikes that if shared act as agreements. They may enjoy the same sports, prefer the same type of music or literature,

[3] See Willard Waller, *The Family; A Dynamic Interpretation* (New York: The Cordon Co., 1938), pp. 257-78, for this and other suggestions as to how courtship increasingly involves each in relation to the other.

and have good times together. These are reinforced by enlarging areas of common ground in work and play, in social, cultural, and religious interests. There are quarrels and stubborn differences which define situations, clarify what they may expect of each other, and strengthen relationships. There are absences and reunions to show how much the two have come to need each other in carrying on the activities they have learned to enjoy together. There are numerous forward steps in love, each of which is a tacit agreement which the two have reached together, such as going steady, sharing preferences, exchanging gifts, photographs, pins, and a ring to symbolize engagement. In these steps the progress is from secret to public declarations, from implicit to explicit agreements to cement their relationship.

As these two stand together at the altar, they take vows which culminate all previous steps they have taken. Each life history trailing its genealogy converges upon the life history of the other. Each step of truer understanding and appreciation adds up to the total gift of self to other self. The contributions of friends, symbolized by wedding gifts, become a supporting human wall of approval and encouragement. The Christian influences of family, church, and community activities all play their part in constituting the meaning of love and its responsibilities to be fulfilled in marriage. Far more than mating in the biological sense, it seeks a larger meeting of all the many powers and values of two persons creating together an interpersonal world of love.

The Christian wedding has multiple meanings for psychological analysis. To mention but a few, as the bride comes down the aisle, she is preceded by little flower girls and then bridesmaids who are not yet ready for marriage. They represent the girl she was in childhood and adolescence before she came to this threshold of maturity. For the younger attendants it anticipates the time they too will be ready to marry, thus indicating the unbroken continuity of love from immature childhood to the awakenings of adolescence to the coming of age in maturity. The bride enters leaning on the arm of her father, symbolizing her dependence heretofore upon her parents for economic and social support. At the appropriate time he steps back and gives her hand to the groom to indicate the severing of her dependent relationship to her father and the establishing of a new attachment to her husband.

The groom is also dependent upon his social relations and enters the church not alone in a false show of self-sufficiency but in the company of his best man friend, who stands shoulder to shoulder with him throughout the ceremony. The ushers are other close friends whom he has chosen to stand by him, often not yet ready to marry but loyal and ready to give him their moral support; and they close into the semicircle of the wedding party to show the strength of human comradeship in this hour of crisis. The entire families of the bride and groom are assembled in the front pews nearest the wedding party, and behind them row upon row of other friends who make up a congregation of love, married and unmarried, yet each from his own experience and by his presence witnessing to the worth of marriage and the family which they continue to uphold with the force of public opinion.

At the altar stands the minister, ordained by the church and entrusted by the state to officiate at the wedding. He represents the long tradition of Christian love and marriage as taught by the church and practiced by its members. He represents the organized community in the civic responsibility of seeing that marriage is entered into only by those who are worthy and prepared for it. In all probability he has known the bride or groom from childhood, or has known them together in their recent courtship and has been consulted by them about how to make the best preparation for the marriage. He deeply believes in marriage as a holy estate, recommends it from his own knowledge of its worth, and sanctifies it with the sacrament of vows publicly declared and witnessed. He represents the heavenly Father, who has created each person and whose love has drawn them together. In the sight of God this union is consummated, and as God joins them together, let no man put them asunder. In the prayers as well as in the vows the couple face not the congregation but the altar representing the presence of God. They may kneel, or not, but always the ceremony points them to God, the author and sustainer of

148

their love, whose blessing and purpose actuates the eternal creation of family love.

In the vows which these novitiates in love take there is foresight into the variable fortunes and risks of family living. They face the possibilities of sickness and health, of riches and poverty, of joys and sorrows, and promise to take each other for better or for worse. There will come death, but they promise to love as long as both shall live. They recognize together that love can fail, that marriage is serious business not to be entered into lightly but reverently and discreetly. They exchange rings in token and pledge of endless faith and abiding love. Thus they prepare in this dramatic enactment of the wedding to face the future unafraid whatever the difficulties, with love strong enough to overcome them.

The aisle of the church stands for the course of life. Every step along its straight and narrow way leads them to an altar where the love of two is consecrated by marriage into one family. Then with final "Amen" to pronounce the divine benediction and the bridal kiss to seal their love they turn and stride together up the aisle, signifying they will ever thereafter walk together along the road of life, in progress that leads to ongoing, outgrowing family love.

From this altar aisle will go far-reaching consequences. In their new world of love they will at first turn away from others in exclusive devotion to each other as they learn to attain the complete union they seek. When the honeymoon is over, they will re-establish social relations with others. They will invite friends and relatives to their new home to share the joys of hospitality. They will visit in other homes and participate in family reunions with parents and relatives. In due course a baby will arrive and then others, and their love will expand to family size. With their children they will go to church and participate in the religious, educational, recreational, and social activities there. They will be responsible citizens in the community and do their part to make a better neighborhood for all. Eventually their children will marry and grandchildren will come, who in their turn will marry, have children, and grandchildren.

The aisle of love is like an hourglass, broad at the top to represent

149

the many friends and influences that socialize the learning of love in the growing child and young person. At the center the stem is narrow to indicate the time when two persons arrive at mate love and devote themselves exclusively to each other. At the bottom is the broadening dimension of expanding love as the married couple have children and turn outward to share their love in unselfish social ways with ever larger circles of the human family. Pouring through the hourglass is the unfailing purpose of the heavenly Father, who gives time and impetus to develop love in persons and groups with dynamic overflowing generosity.

3. So Long as Both Shall Live

The wedding dedicates life for love and love for life. Together bride and groom face the prospect of everlasting love. The vows pledge it, and the lovers believe it is forever. The ceremony points out that difficulties will come; there are stresses and doubts to try their devotion, yet at the altar these are outvoted by faith in each other and the strength of their love. But every marriage is a venture. It has a full complement of risks. At the present rate of one divorce for every four marriages [4] it is evident that love does not always weather the gales of the family voyage.

The wedding ceremony refers to physical death as the termination of marriage, "until death us do part." There is a death of love that may precede physical death, not suddenly but a slow dying by inches. Divorce is the result of a long sequence of many causes. Love endures as long as both continue to live in love. How long will both live in that glowing radiance before decay and indifference set in? It is like the toast "May you live all the days of your life." The tragedy is that many of us live so little while we live. Or we plunge recklessly into the stream of life headfirst for a brief immersion, then stand on the bank and watch from a safe, dry place of inactivity. Love is such a

---

[4] In some cities during World War II there was one divorce for every two marriages, a figure that some sociologists predict for the country as a whole in 1960. See Hornell Hart and Henrietta Browne, "Divorce, Depression, and War," *Social Forces*, XXII (December, 1943), 191-94.

plunge for many in the exuberance of youth, and they go in all over. But in time they weary of the effort or become more interested in other things and leave the depths for shallow routine or the dry formalities of marriage. Recalling his wedding anniversary a weary husband observed, "It's not so long since we were married, dear; it just seems long." Marriage can be a slow drying up of the wellsprings of love. That is the line of least resistance if one or both forget to renew their devotion. As they live together, the life of love dies by neglect.

Why does marriage fail? The broken home is Public Enemy No. 1 in American life. For it does more damage to the growing children and their parents than any other social event. It has often been said that the home is the foundation of our whole society, and when it breaks down, society suffers accordingly. But divorce is itself a result of many previous causes. The time to prevent divorce is long before the suit comes to court. A great deal of misplaced emphasis is put upon high legal and religious barriers to divorce. But that is locking the barn door after the horse has been stolen. By the time love has departed, there is little to salvage. Rather than exhausting our efforts in fearing and condemning divorce we might well study the causes and put the emphasis on correcting them while there is yet time.

Marriage fails because it rests on a weak foundation. No house stands well on a poor foundation.

The basic and major cause of divorce is marriage, and we are not being flippant! The divorce rate is closely linked with the number of ill-advised and poorly mated pairs who pass through the engagement period without discovering their incompatibility. In striking at the conditions which produce divorce, we need to evaluate the factors which produce unhappy marriages, and to bring about conditions in which the marriages that do take place have a better chance at happiness. To make divorce more difficult does nothing to make marriage more tolerable. It doesn't strike at the heart of the matter at all.[5]

[5] Evelyn M. Duvall and Reuben L. Hill, *When You Marry* (Boston: D. C. Heath & Co., 1945), p. 249. The entire book is one of the most useful studies for young people and their counselors. The Roman Catholic point of view on courtship and marriage will be found in Winfrid Herbst, *The Catholic's Question Box* (St. Nazianz, Wis. The Society of the Divine Savior, 1938), pp. 168-99, 286-349.

In other cultures the parents have selected the mates for their children with certain standards held in calm perspective. A Chinese woman comparing the family-arranged marriage of China with the impulsive American plunge into love said, "We marry when love is cold and know it is our task to make it grow warm; you marry when love is hot and let it grow cold." This like most comparisons may overstate the advantages and disadvantages, but the contrast is worth considering. The present style of falling in love is largely impulsive and irrational, for love is taken as a romantic accident of fate that brings two lovers together with nothing to do but fall. In this helpless state of infatuation love is supposed to capture you against your better judgment; as long as you feel that way, there is no use trying to be reasonable about it. Parents who once guided the marital choices of their children are as helpless as the victims of love, for how can they understand what it means to *us* to be in love? What right have they to interfere with the imperious and unquestioned demand of love? Carried to its logical conclusion, this popular style of selecting a spouse by the test of excitement is a *reductio ad absurdum*, the victory of passion over sanity. Naturally many important questions that are decisive in the success of a marriage are overlooked in the irresistible sweep of let-love-have-its-way-with-me.

In recent years psychologists and sociologists have been making studies of what factors make for success in marriage. Ernest W. Burgess and Leonard S. Cottrell in Illinois selected 526 urban middle-class couples who varied widely in marital adjustment, and studied conditions of success and failure in marriage. About the same time Lewis M. Terman and his associates selected 796 middle-class couples in California and made a detailed analysis of their marital adjustment. The results of these studies correlate well, and the conclusions provide a scale for predicting happiness in marriage.[6] As synthesized by

[6] Burgess and Cottrell, *Predicting Success or Failure in Marriage* (New York: Prentice-Hall, 1939); and Terman, *Psychological Factors in Marital Happiness* (New York: McGraw-Hill Book Co., 1938). See also E. W. Burgess and Paul Wallin, "Predicting Adjustment in Marriage from Adjustment in Engagement," *American Journal of Sociology*, XLIX (January, 1944), 324-30.

the National Forum they make a list of seven factors conducive to successful marriage.

1. Happiness of parents' marriage
2. Balanced personality (happiness of one's childhood, congeniality with parents, type of home discipline)
3. Similarity of background (vitality of religious activity, standards of living)
4. Relative mental ability (educational level attained)
5. Attitude toward sex (premarital attitude to sex, parental frankness on sex)
6. Length of acquaintance (companionship vs. infatuation)
7. Desire of both for children.[7]

Unwise selection of a mate is usually a hasty or impulsive choice without honest consideration of what will make for marital harmony. These conditions listed above represent the American middle class and are not to be taken as final or invariable for everyone, but some such factors as these have been shown to be vitally related to success in marriage. In the glamorous parties, dances, movies, and sporting events so popular today young couples meet on parade and live on romantic illusions. They are apt to postpone working through to realities until after marriage and then find they are incompatible or, more frequently, unwilling to make the sacrifices and adjustments to come into actual partnership. Young people often mistake a fragment of interest for the whole content of love. In a legendary figure of speech Cupid has more than one arrow in his quiver, but many amorous youths are so easily wounded at the first dart that they give up the struggle and succumb without knowing the whole meaning of love's requirements. They mistake a thrill for love and marry the thrill. Others marry for convenience or money, to escape unhappy conditions at home, to get out of town, for social advantage, or not to be an old maid. Complete love involves the whole personality, which is more than sex desire or any other interest. Marriages smash because they are

[7] A poster available from the Association of Family Living, 209 South State St., Suite 1426, Chicago 4, Ill. Reproduced in *When You Marry*, p. 119. The complete marriage prediction scale of Burgess and Cottrell is given by Duvall and Hill in Appendix A, pp. 429-38.

cracked, fragmentary, or narrow from the start. Nothing less than the whole of life equals love. It must satisfy the unlimited needs of biological hungers, social approval, creative functions, moral ideals, religious aspirations, the sense of the beautiful, the desire to love and be loved for one's true worth.

Most couples enter marriage unprepared for its responsibilities. They may be encumbered by prejudice toward sex, fearful and ill-informed as to the art of conjugal love and the techniques of mutually gratifying coitus. They may have unsolved temperamental problems that will become mountains of anguish between them unless they learn to manage their emotions. Career conflicts may hang like a sword over their heads if the wife is unwilling to leave former friends behind to go where her husband's vocation may call him, or accept such absences and working hours as are required of him. Or career ambitions of the wife may demand expression at whatever cost to her family, pitting her as a rival against her husband, forgetting the responsibilities of the career she has chosen to be a wife and mother. Financial problems need also to be anticipated before marriage, an accurate accounting of probable income and costs of living, with heroic decisions to postpone many desires for such home and furniture, car and luxuries as the color advertisements assume brides must have. Budgetary problems involve one's whole standard of values, such as whether happiness consists in the abundance of things possessed, what comes first in importance for family needs, and how much we spend on ourselves or tithe for benevolent purposes to share with others. How many children and when to have them may be wisely agreed upon before marriage, lest such deep-lying differences become irreconcilable when intrenched in conflicting life purposes.

There are reefs ahead for couples who are unaware that love needs to grow in marriage. The chief romantic emphasis in our culture is upon love before marriage. Contemporary fiction and drama choose the scenes of first love, rival love, and courtship, until after hours of excruciating details elaborately spelled out they come into each other's arms to live happily ever after. Of course everyone knows that is the typical fairy story, but it makes us feel better to imagine a happy end-

154

ing. We need to be more realistic about marriage and honestly face well in advance the requirements of marital love. More attention should be given to the fact that love either grows or dies; there is no middle way. The popular view is that after you have hooked and landed each other in marriage, then it is time to "settle down like old married folks." But married folks can never afford to settle down, for inertia is the death of self-complacent love. It is dangerous to assume, as many couples do, that now we are married, we have proved to the world our love is sufficient; there is nothing more to do about it, and we just take it for granted the rest of our lives. In this way we forget the courtesies and surprises that meant so much in courtship; we assume the courting is over, as in fact it is when love becomes stagnant. In an earlier chapter love was defined as mutually growing appreciation and responsibility. Nowhere does this apply more than to marriage. For otherwise marital love declines, and love becomes a hollow façade that looks respectable to the passer-by but is a mausoleum within. Living love is a constant experiment, trying out the arts of loving in ever new ways and cherishing the results. Marriage has become the symbol of no more adventures. Having had their fling, burned out their flame, tied the knot of their freedom, and subdued their passions, the couple are bowed down with the burdens of a home. But monogamy need not be monotony. If every day is met with gratitude for the privilege of loving and growing in the joys and labors of family living, the home will be a shrine of ever more satisfying love. None but married lovers know how fulfilling a home can be for loving, or how dull it can be when love is spent. Those who continue to explore new ways to keep family love growing are the greatest lovers of any age, at any age.

Successful lovers will learn how to manage conflicts. There is something artificial about a human relationship with no conflicts. It may indicate the indifference of persons who do not care enough to bother or the top-heavy situation where one always submits to the domination of the other. Or there may be an outward show of harmony while underneath the surface resentments smolder. The home where a husband and wife sit silently through their hours together, eating together and doing the necessary chores but avoiding a meeting of glances, not responding to questions or taking part in conversation, is as frigid as the North Pole. The wife who resists her husband's advances or subsides into hurt silence rather than to talk over and work out the conflict is beginning the slow but sure alienation of love. Alienation is courtship reversed in which a series of little separations eventually add up to divorce. Beginning with the first mutually destructive quarrel, affectional responses are withheld, resistances develop, unkindnesses are shown to punish the other, the possibility of divorce is mentioned, others find it out, they move into separate bedrooms, break up housekeeping, and finally sue for divorce. How much better is it to quarrel openly and talk out heatedly the differences, thus releasing repressed tensions and defining situations more clearly. For quarrels need not be destructive; they may actually improve relations, get the anger off one's chest, then start over with new determination to make a go of it. The person who submits is just as much to blame as the aggressor. In wholesome relations each one has some resistance and does some of the yielding. Instead of giving up at the first blast of anger the resourceful person will guide the argument away from personal attacks to the issues which need to be clarified and can be solved when there is a will to do so.

Where love fails, it usually appears that religious resources have been neglected. However much it means to have a wedding at the altar or to have a religious service to dedicate a new home, no dose of inspiration will last without renewal. A family altar is not just a worship center of cross, Bible, or candles for interior decoration. It is a daily event in which the family unites in the act of worship. We are not in this psychological study considering the supernatural effects of worship. But humanly speaking the psychologist cannot deny the effects of sincerely praying together upon the unity and growing appreciation of those persons for each other and the values they hold sacred.

In Chapter V we observed how Christianity can affect the daily life of the family. Of course nominal Christians may not take their religion seriously enough to make any appreciable difference. But where re-

SEX AND MARRIAGE

ligious values are taken to heart enough to have family prayers daily, and where each one participates earnestly and intelligently applies the mood and teachings of religious devotion to family life, there is bound to be a difference in their attitudes toward each other. They will hold each other in higher esteem, seeing new qualities to appreciate, thinking of better ways to serve each other unselfishly, more ready to reconcile their affections following quarrels. The Burgess and Terman studies show that vital religious experience, frequency of attendance at church and Sunday school, and church weddings as an index of religious attitudes toward marriage correlate well with harmonious marriages. Not only is the rate of divorce less for active church members, but the dangers of inertia and conflict are both lessened by the growing aspirations and reconciliations of religious devotion.

4. Marital Counseling

From the first gropings of childish love and the exploratory awakenings of adolescence to the union of lovers in marriage and the growing needs of family living is a long, arduous journey. Fortunately no one needs to take that journey alone. Love is born in the family and develops outward by the constant interaction of persons in social relations. At every step we are guided and encouraged to love by the associates to whom we respond. But not all actions express love, for there are rival emotions and aims at work in the social scene. Not all acts that intend love are well chosen or wisely executed. Love is further complicated by the unpredictable moods and mistakes of others who leave us in quandaries of uncertainty, perplexity, or despair.

To cope with the tangles of love we need counselors. A counselor is a person who is able to share your emotional distress with responsive empathy and clarify your mental confusion by talking it over with you without robbing you of your freedom to decide or responsibility to carry out the steps needed for growth.[8] Counselors may be

[8] See Carl R. Rogers, *Counseling and Psychotherapy* (Boston: Houghton Mifflin Co., 1942); Seward Hiltner, *Pastoral Counseling* (New York and Nashville: Abingdon-Cokesbury Press, 1949); Paul E. Johnson, "Methods of Pastoral Counseling," *Journal of Pastoral Care*, I (September, 1947), 1-6.

to us as parents or teachers, pastors or physicians, psy-
or social workers, neighbors or friends. The list is apparently endless, and well it may be, for a counselor may come from
any profession or none, from our intimate friends or may be a stranger
into whose office we may step for the first time. His qualifications are
sympathy, understanding, and democratic respect for your responsibility as a free moral person. If he blames you, advises you, coerces
you, or decides for you, he is not a very useful counselor. But if
he listens patiently, responds to your feelings, sees the issues at
stake, upholds your best impulses, and affirms your awakening responsibilities, he may be of inestimable service to you.

Premarital counseling of this kind will aid young people in preparing for marriage. It will reduce the risks of the marriage venture
by facing honestly the problems of marriage, making needed adjustments promptly, and opening lanes of continuous growth thereafter.
The pastor is in a strategic position to become such a counselor.
He is usually acquainted with the families in which the young people
have grown up, and knows their backgrounds. He may have observed them come into adolescence, try out social techniques in
church recreation, and take turns dating around. He has listened
to their ideas and attitudes expressed at various stages of growth in
discussions at youth fellowships, or shared with them the leadership
of worship services. He has noted the progress of love until the
couple at length come to him to arrange a time for the wedding.

Unfortunately many young couples avoid every opportunity for
counseling. They may not know it is available or may not realize
it is for them; they may feel quite sufficient with no need to ask
questions of anyone; or they may have been advised so much by
parents that they revolt against the slightest suggestion that someone
is talking down to them, making them feel inferior, or violating their
freedom by telling them what to do. Other young people are shy
about sex and unwilling to talk face to face with another person
about the deeper feelings of love and marriage. Even those who
bluster the most and assume airs of sophistication are often using
defensive tactics to cover up an abysmal ignorance they cannot bear

to admit. Pride may consider it humiliating to reveal any inadequacy, and prefer to muddle through by awkward might and main. Or in the rush of many social events, shopping trips, and hectic excitement the young couple may postpone and not find time to arrange counseling hours.

States uphold legal requirements for marriage, such as minimum age, consent of parents for minors, unmarried status, responsible mentality, and so on. Recently they have been requiring blood tests for syphilis to protect health against disease, and a waiting period to prevent hasty marriages. In time public opinion may demand a less perfunctory legal access to marriage, a more thorough investigation and preparation for this event so crucial to human welfare. But for the present this responsibility rests almost entirely with the minister who joins the couple in marriage and invokes the blessing of God upon the union. He cannot take his responsibility so lightly as a generation ago when it was customary for the parson to marry on the spot any strange couple who appeared at the door with a license to wed. For conscience has been awakened, and public opinion expects more of the pastor today. Legal requirements represent a minimum standard of decency. Moral and religious standards for marriage go far beyond the law to fulfill the larger opportunities for happiness and creative living. The pastor stands for the best values attainable in family life, his church cherishes a tradition of glorious loving, and the community looks to him to unite couples in successful marriage. One pastor says with light touch but serious intent, "I guarantee this marriage, and if anything is not right with it, be sure to come and see me about it." This is a logical position for the pastor to take who recognizes that his responsibility is not merely to bring a couple together at the altar but to see that their marriage has the qualifications to succeed.

Churches are not yet entirely awake to the unique service pastors can give in marital counseling. Educational campaigns are needed to bring parents and young people to realize that after the engagement is announced, the next step is for the couple to call on the pastor. If people can be educated to see their physician once a year and their dentist every six months, to have chest X rays and donate blood to the Red Cross, they will also respond to the slogan "See your pastor as soon as you are engaged to marry." Together they will be able to think through what marriage can mean to them at best, to view the risks of marriage, face the issues needing to be decided, study the resources and techniques for marital harmony, and assess their own strengths and weaknesses for the success of their venture.

Roy A. Burkhart, pastor of the First Community Church, Columbus, Ohio, has a well-organized plan for premarital counseling. It is his practice not to marry a couple until they have gone through a process of study with him. Some ministers reply, "If you demand that of young couples, you won't have any weddings." But he has an average of one hundred weddings a year. He has written for them a little book, entitled *A Guide for a Man and Woman Looking Toward Marriage*,[9] which he gives them to read. The number of premarital interviews held with each couple depends upon their interest, their questions, and the insight they show. He usually holds three one-hour interviews with the couple in his study before marriage, and one in their home after marriage. He also refers them to a physician and when indicated to a neurologist or psychiatrist. All aspects of marital adjustment are considered, including what the church has to offer them. Frequently a couple is received into church membership at the time of the marriage ceremony.

Warren D. Bowman, pastor of the Washington City Church of the Brethren, also adapts his premarital counseling to the needs of each couple but has the following questions as a guide.

1. How long have you known each other?
2. Are you really in love?
3. What do your families think of the marriage?
4. How do your ages correspond?
5. Is there anything in the personality of either of you that might hinder marital happiness?

[9] Flushing, N. Y.: Hearthside Press, 1943. See also *Premarital Counseling: Manual of Suggestions for Ministers* (New York: Commission on Marriage and the Home of the Federal Council of Churches of Christ in America).

6. What are your plans for growth in love?
7. What attitudes will you take toward difficulties that arise?
8. What kind of friends will you have?
9. Have you had a physical examination?
10. What economic plans have you made?
11. What are your plans for living accommodations?
12. Have you discussed the matter of children?
13. Do you possess adequate information on physical adjustment in marriage?
14. What part will religion play in your marriage? [10]

Each couple receives a copy of Leland Foster Wood's book *Harmony in Marriage* as a gift, and Oliver M. Butterfield's book *Marriage and Sexual Harmony* is placed in their hands for study.[11]

For the pastor this will be a time-consuming service, but so is any job well done. And nothing he does is more important or will be more useful in building better homes, churches, and communities. Pastors will need special training for counseling, as well as ability to solve the problems of their own marital adjustment and release in themselves such tensions, embarrassments, and prejudices as distort the counseling relationship. Theological schools are now coming to offer courses in pastoral psychology, marriage, and counseling. Clinical training is also available to theological students and mature ministers in service. A summer invested in clinical training at a hospital under skillful supervision of a teaching chaplain and hospital staff is productive of new insights and skills in pastoral counseling.[12]

After the wedding the pastor is in a position to introduce the young couple to other couples their age in the church and offer a

[10] *Counseling with Couples Before Marriage* (Elgin, Ill.: Elgin Press, 1944). Used by permission.

[11] Wood and Dickinson, *Harmony in Marriage* (New York: Round Table Press, 1940); Butterfield, *Marriage and Sexual Harmony* (New York: Emerson Books, 1938). See also Helena Wright, *The Sex Factor in Marriage* (New York: The Vanguard Press, 1931); Abraham and Hannah Stone, *A Marriage Manual* (New York: Simon & Schuster, 1935).

[12] In addition to theological schools there are two incorporated agencies that provide facilities for clinical training of ministers in various centers over the United States. They are the Council for Clinical Training, 2 East 103rd Street, New York 29, N. Y., and the Institute for Pastoral Care, Andover Hall, Harvard University, Cambridge, Mass.

variety of social, recreational, educational, and religious advantages to them. As marriage is one of the major crises of life, a time for self-evaluation and new beginnings, it is a unique opportunity for spiritual growth. The church whose pastor is alert to the needs of young married couples will provide resources to nourish the new development. The newly wedded couple may be invited to the pastor's home, where the patterns for family living in the parsonage may suggest unspoken lessons. A wedding-bells reunion may bring together at a church dinner all couples married during the preceding year as special guests of honor. Anniversary greetings may renew the joy and significance of the wedding experience. Sermons on family and home may interpret the values Christians can achieve in living together in work and play, love and worship. Young married-couple classes in many churches meet each Sunday for discussion, and monthly for social fellowship. The birth of each child is welcomed as a matter of special moment by the pastor and church friends. Cradle rolls, nurseries, and graded classes for each age keep the growing family growing in religious experience and association. Attractive literature is also prepared for distribution in homes to continue education in Christian love and creative family living.

When trouble strikes the family, the pastor is ready to bring Christian resources to the needs of each member, while the church friends stand by to sustain them in the bonds of that communion. The pastor trained as a counselor is especially useful at such a time, and every pastor can enlarge his psychological understanding along with his pastoral skills by constant study and practice. It is evident that where premarital counseling has been well given, and the young couple are followed with pastoral interest and enfolded into the church life, it will be perfectly natural for them to turn to the pastor for help in time of need. Because the pastor is accessible at all times, charges no consulting fee, and sees the facts and problems of life in the perspective of spiritual values, he is a desirable counselor to seek. If he refrains from moral censure and traditional moralizing platitudes, listens earnestly and identifies himself with them in their predicament, moves with them into emerging solutions and practical steps, he will be a friend indeed.[13]

How does Christian love enrich marriage success? To conclude these two chapters on the family a summary of these resources is in order. Christian love (1) asks complete devotion—no less than all our love; (2) invites constant faithfulness forever; (3) promotes unfaltering growth of persons in mutual responsiveness; (4) accents unselfish attitudes; (5) relates sex to a larger perspective as a means to procreation, to social and spiritual values; (6) forgives mistakes or misunderstandings and starts again on a new basis; (7) keeps a central purpose to love as the greatest privilege of life, a divine commission to make a heaven here and now; (8) expands family horizons and loving interactions to community-wide fellowship; (9) expresses love in kindly motives and deeds of service; (10) worships a Father of love, aspires to ever-maturing devotion, and dedicates life energies to make human values more sacred and secure.

[13] See L. F. Wood, *Pastoral Counseling in Family Relationships* (New York: Commission on Marriage and the Home of the Federal Council of Churches of Christ in America, 1948).

VII

Explosives in Social Conflict

1. THE DEFEAT OF LOVE

Is all this talk about love in vain? Christian ideals of love have charmed us with their wistful beauty. The pattern of one family of God is a glorious vision; the life and teachings of Jesus appeal to our highest aspirations to love in a nobler way. For thousands of years men have been attracted to this heavenly love and hoped again and again it would redeem our sordid human clay. But will it work on this earth?

All things are possible, he said, if you can only believe (Mark 9:23). But this kind of love seems too impossible for us. How can we attain it? And in the stresses and strains of other impulses and forces in human life how can we believe it? Jesus was a pacifist who believed in nonviolence, nonresistance to evil, and forgiving love of enemies. But this love was too difficult for most of his disciples. The "sons of thunder" goaded by their rivalries and the ambition of their mother contended for places of honor on the right and left of Jesus in the new kingdom (Mark 10:37). Impulsive Peter wielded a sword in his master's defense until his hand was stayed by a word from Jesus that it was not their way to fight (John 18:10). Very few Christians out of the total number have taken the pacifist position. It does not seem to them practical, reasonable, or possible in our kind of world. If the whole society could be changed to one of peace and nonaggression, that would be

165

different, but in the face of threatening evil they feel impelled to resist violence with violence.[1]

In the early centuries of our era Christians refused military service until the time of Constantine, whose conquest in the sign of the Cross gave imperial blessing to their religion. Since then conscientious objectors to war have usually held a minority position in Christian ranks. When Saxon tribes were converted, it is told how their men entered the river with right arms held aloft, to baptize all but their fighting arms. It has often been so, as lusty pagans have reluctantly bowed to the Christian yoke, given lip service to its lofty ideals, and left its virtues to the women as more appropriate for feminine graces.

Actually Christians in two thousand years have done little to prevent war, class struggles, or industrial strife because they have insisted upon taking sides and joining ardently in the fray. The holy wars and bloody persecutions in which Christians have engaged add no small weight to the history of violence on our planet. The bitter quarrels and disputes, exiles and pilgrimages, separations and divisions within Christendom show the difficulty Christians have in keeping peace among themselves.

There is something in human nature that resists love. We have seen in Chapter III how love rises from deep motives within us. Impulses to love and cravings for love are as strong as any motives we have, unless it be the impulse to hate and resist love. Desperate as our need for love is, even to the point of life itself—for health, happiness, success, and survival depend upon it—the course of love is neither open nor smooth. There is another urge in our nature against life and love to death and destruction.

Freud saw love at first as the all-consuming passion of life that will not be denied but will find openings through every restraint, break around every repression, and sweep on to fulfillment. But in his later clinical studies of personality he revised that view to

[1] See G. J. Heering, *The Fall of Christianity; A Study of Christianity, the State and War*, tr. J. W. Thompson (New York: Fellowship Publications, 1943); A. C. Knudson, *The Philosophy of War and Peace* (New York and Nashville: Abingdon-Cokesbury Press, 1947).

EXPLOSIVES IN SOCIAL CONFLICT

include another drive equally strong which he called the death instinct (*thanatos*) in opposition to the life instinct (*eros*).[2] This was at first met by doubt among his followers but has gained increasing confirmation from the studies especially of Ferenczi, Alexander, and Menninger.[3] There is no lack of evidence for counterforces in human nature that drive against love toward hate.

Psychologists have found three basic emotions in the infant. By simple experiments in child behavior they have produced emotional responses of fear, love, and rage. The rage of a baby, as anyone can observe, is no weakling; it evidently expresses more energy than either fear or love, at least more violently. A baby in rage will scream, writhe, turn red with swollen circulation, and strike viciously with arms and legs, beating the air or any restraints savagely. Tantrums follow in childhood, and bursts of anger at every age may take quite destructive forms.

Any view of human nature or society is naïve and utopian that overlooks these aggressive trends. For every person is a complex unity of many impulses and motives. All is not sweetness and light, love and affection, in the souls of men. There are darker moods of sullen disdain and smoldering resentment. There are lurid explosions of blazing anger that lash out to destroy recklessly every value no matter how costly, how laboriously acquired, or how highly cherished to that moment. If love is to prevail or even to survive against these odds, it cannot do so by oversight that ignores the opposition. For love is a struggle to win a slight balance of power over opposing tendencies within us and our society. The cause of love is not won instantly and thereby settled forever. The contest of love against hate moves back and forth over the entire field of dynamic tendencies in every person. It produces one drama after another on the stage of history, and one act follows another in never-ending counterplay of conflicting and cohesive social forces.

[2] *Beyond the Pleasure Principle*, ed. C. J. M. Hubback (New York: Boni & Liveright, 1922), pp. 63-79; *The Ego and the Id*, tr. Joan Riviere (London: Hogarth Press, 1927).

[3] Menninger gives the most complete exposition in his valuable book *Man Against Himself* (New York: Harcourt, Brace & Co., 1938).

The defeat of love is an old story—as old as the story of love itself. The Old Testament brings from ancient times a moving account of these conflicting forces of love and hate, life and death. The first pair of brothers became rivals, and when Abel prospered more, Cain was angry; his love turned to hate until he rose up and killed his brother (Gen. 4:8). Abraham, who had longed for a son many years, felt impelled to kill his son, but with knife lifted in the air was prevented from heaven, so the practice of human sacrifice was in that instance set aside (Gen. 22:10). Jealousy between Sarah and Hagar, the wives of Abraham, twice led him to turn Hagar out into the desert, and the second time almost accomplished the death of her son Ishmael (Gen. 21:16). Twin brothers were caught in rival affections of their parents and fell into a conflict in which Jacob deceived, cheated, and fled his brother Esau until after long separation they were reconciled (Gen. 27: 19). Joseph with his grandiose dreams made his brothers angry, who plotted to slay him, but one saved his life by selling him as a slave, until eventually in Egypt Joseph forgave his brothers (Gen. 37:18). Moses was moved by anger to kill an Egyptian oppressor, fled, and later returned to lead his people through blood and battle toward a promised land (Exod. 2:12). After many tribal wars when the followers of Moses were in the land of Canaan, they elected judges and later kings to lead them in battle and promote the slaughter of enemies. Then followed the centuries of national intrigue and international warfare until the people were twice exiled, their nation destroyed, and they were dispersed around the world.

The struggles of love and hate continue in the records of the New Testament. Jesus, the Messiah of love, was rejected by the people, betrayed, arrested, accused of blasphemy, beaten, mocked, and crucified between two malefactors (Matt. 27:31). Stephen, while preaching his faith in Jesus, was seized, brought to the council, where he charged them with the murder of Jesus and the prophets, and was condemned to death by stoning (Acts 7:59). Paul on one of his journeys to persecute the Christians was converted (Acts

9:6) and became a missionary for the new faith, suffering many beatings, imprisonments and trials for the way of love. Peter, John, and other disciples boldly defied the authorities to preach this faith, and eventually gave their lives as martyrs to witness their devotion. Roman persecutions of Christians were a prelude to centuries of attacks by Christians upon their own dissenters.

During the long history of the ancient world every other civilization fell into strife and mutual destruction. Egyptian history is one long series of battles and oppressions. So also are the histories of Babylonia, Assyria, Syria, Persia, and the Greek and Roman states. History repeats similar conflicts in India, China, and Japan. Then new conquests belched forth from the barbarians of Europe and the Arabian armies of Mohammed and his successors. New empires in new worlds were discovered and conquered by Spain, France, Holland, England, Portugal, and Germany. As religious movements of love gained strength in monastic orders, missionary, and philanthropic enterprises, the secular forces of destruction broke out in new fury during the nineteenth and twentieth centuries. Sovereign states armed with the inventions of science and the frenzy of national violence led the way to the unprecedented wholesale slaughter of two world wars in a single generation.

Our tragic dilemma is heightened by the values at stake. Never has the human race accumulated such a store of values in such variety. The gains of human effort and ingenuity for centuries have gradually advanced the opportunities of mankind. Social organization, transportation and communication facilities, scientific inventions, industrial productions, utilization of natural resources, government and public services, the medical arts of healing, education, literature, and fine arts have enriched opportunities for living today beyond all yesterdays. All this is made possible by love—the desire to give and receive, to share and exchange, to co-operate and band together for the commonweal.

Yet never have human values been less secure. The abundance of our goods confuses us as to what we shall value most. The gains we have make us more frantic in our pursuit of other gains. The rush of working for gain leaves us little time to enjoy the fruit of our labors. The pressures of congested urban dwelling make us strangers to our neighbors and indifferent to the life that crowds upon us. The pride of race and nation has us drunk with lust for power and the baubles of political advantage. The overweight of military armament leads us in false security to trust yet distrust the safety of our defenses.

The fact is we are obsessed at this historical moment with the horror and fascination of another world war—this time with atomic and biological weapons too lethal to play with and escape from. As we totter on the brink of this destruction, we tremble in fear of what we will lose. Yet we are lured by an overpowering maniacal sense of necessity and destiny to kill before we are killed. Are we mad? "Whom the gods would destroy they first make mad."

At the very moment when we stand at the dawn of a new world of abundant life for all, with the greatest opportunities men have ever glimpsed, far beyond the dreams of our forefathers to imagine, we are held back. We hesitate to enter the promised land. For we are not of one mind, nor do we fully know our own desires. Instead of stepping forward, confidently with united purpose to claim and enjoy these advantages, we do not seem to free ourselves from inertia or bondage to the past. What holds us back is something within ourselves, a part of our own nature. As the proverb goes, a man is his own worst enemy. What is it that prevents our attainment of the larger values and security we are entitled to enjoy?

We have strange and seductive impulses to hate and to kill. We are somehow impelled to deprive others at our own expense, to have our revenge even if we all perish together, to break what we have built in a fiendish joy of destruction, and to die in the ruins of all we once cherished so dearly. This sounds dramatic, even melodramatic. Perhaps it is, but the facts speak for themselves; and if we hold our peace, the deeds of men will cry out in the exultant anguish of life struggling with death. The drama may be hidden under the weight of the repressions of our civilization. It may be a piecemeal war of attrition in which the slow gains of growth and

170

losses of decay are scarcely visible to the eye. But whatever the guise and however concealed, the endless contest of love and hate goes on playing for the stakes of life and death.

Aggressive impulses may be turned inward upon ourselves or outward upon others. This difference is worth noting as we shall see later, but in either case they are destructive and reap a harvest of dying love. The strange and fatal passions are no easier to understand than they are to curb. Are we possessed of demons, as the ancients were led by such events to believe? Is there a devil or a host of them who seek to tempt us into these follies of evil and destruction? Or as in contemporary philosophical interpretation shall we assign these uncanny tendencies and resistances to a Given, inherent in the structure of nature and human nature that neither God created nor man invented?

In psychological terms we are victims of inner conflicts that struggle within us. Every person has many impulses that play against each other, resisting and overpowering, canceling or uniting in actions for good and evil ends. Not that he is a helpless victim of his impulses, for he helps to strengthen or weaken them by his selective attention and interest, his responsive enforcing and enacting of them in behavior. They are potential attitudes that grow and decay by the way we cultivate or deny them. They have no power of their own apart from our use of them. They are not born with us or ready full-blown for human use—though it may be otherwise with the instinctive tendencies of animals. They are tendencies only in the tentative sense that they grow strong as we nourish them or weak as we neglect them.

Love and hate are not avowed enemies from the beginning. They mingle in the deeper sources of our motivations as energies to give and to receive gently or roughly interpersonal responses. Gentle giving and receiving is loving; rough giving and taking is aggression. Then why rough or gentle? That will come before us in a later section of the chapter. But now we are trying to see that we alternately love and hate even from infancy our parents, brothers and sisters, friends and lovers. We even love and hate at the same time in the mingling of these tendencies or the counterbalance of ambivalence. There is a mingling of these forces in the give and take of marital love, whose outcome is unpredictable and often surprising even to the couple themselves.

As the human race progresses in love, it also progresses in hostilities, and the capacity for either appears to be almost infinite. The impulses of individuals to love and hate other individuals is somehow socialized to the place where groups love and hate groups. From the multiplication of personal hostilities in interpersonal relationships there comes the organized social aggressions of group against group. Consequently the whole balance of human living, individual and social, is quite unstable. Without group security there is no individual security, and without the mutual confidence of individuals there is no security in our world.

This delineates anew how important love is to life on this planet. Every good we desire or cherish totters on the brink between love and hate. As love offers so much, who in his right mind will contend against it? But are we in our right minds? A mind where hate lingers cannot be a healthy mind. A society where hate festers and swells to aggression can scarcely be called a sound society. The forces of hate in our society are strong—enough perhaps to defeat love. Yet the forces of love in human nature are also strong—enough perhaps to defeat hate.

2 CONFLICTS AND THEIR CAUSES

Social conflicts arise wherever two or more persons are in a social situation to interact against each other. The number of such situations is beyond naming, and we can explore but a few of them. It should be noted from the beginning that every conflict situation provokes resistance and aggression. This may not be apparent to the casual observer, for personal attitudes are frequently well concealed. Yet incipient tendencies to resist and react against another are present wherever the social scene is set in a pattern of conflict. In sports and repartee it may be a good-humored exchange of blows,

172

but aggressive reactions are nevertheless called forth by the competitive social situation.

This does not mean that persons are helpless victims of external stimuli in a mechanistic social determinism. Persons create social situations fully as much as society creates persons. Neither is aggression the expression of an inborn, unlearned instinct that is bound to explode whatever you may do about it. The causes of conflict and aggression from our point of view are interpersonal. Nothing is finally fixed by either heredity or environment. What we are develops in the constant interaction of persons in a common environment. We inherit a responsive nature equipped with many growing potentialities which react to appropriate stimuli as they come into play. By the interaction of interpersonal stimuli and responses we become loving-hating persons and societies. We love one and hate another because of our specific responses to specific stimuli. We may love and hate the same person alternately if he stimulates us one way or another.

Consequently we can always do something about our conflicts. It is folly to fall into helpless apathy or give up in futile despair. We do not have to fight or work as enemies against each other. There are no fighting instincts that condemn us to an unbroken sequence of wars and suicidal destructions. Neither are we the hapless victims of social patterns which draw us irresistibly into endless conflicts. As we learn how to manage our social relations and decide what impulses we prefer to express, we can together come into control of the situation. Any one or all of us can be victims of circumstances if we do nothing but drift in currents of least resistance. But we need not be drifters, for we have motive power to redirect not only our own course but also by joint action the social currents in which we live.

What are the most typical social conflicts that bring persons into conflict with each other? As a brief sample let us consider the following. Relationships of *authority* produce aggressive conflicts. In a family husband and wife at first contest for authority to control the family decisions. This may be illustrated by the humorous passes at who "rules the roost," who "wears the pants," and the like. One husband after a year of marriage reported to a masculine friend, "We decided that she would make the little decisions and I would make the big ones, and we are getting along fine; no big decisions have come up so far." Then as the children are growing up, they come into repeated conflicts with the parents over authority. The boy may revolt against the father and win the mother to his side; the daughter may revolt against the mother and win the father to her side (Oedipus and Electra situations respectively). Conflicts of street gangs with policemen, of students with teachers, of workers with bosses, of revolutionists with autocrats or *status quo* make up a large stock of daily aggressions.

Conflicts arise at friction points of *ownership*. Children easily quarrel over toys, use of joint property, or the opportunity to occupy mutually desired space. Taking up homestead claims led to the motto, "Possession is nine tenths of the law." In our capitalistic economy the major incentive is to own as much as possible of what other people want. Success is measured by ownership, and the frantic, often ruthless, contest is to have more property and more and more. In the neighborhood and social circles the drive is to keep up with the rivals in finer homes, cars, gadgets, fur coats, and bank accounts. In the international scene the expansionist urge by conquest, diplomacy, or trade is to build an empire and have more possessions.

This leads to conflicting demands for *status and prestige*. Authority and ownership are valued for the prestige they bring. The man of authority or wealth is on top in his social scale. People look up to him, listen to him, and obey his wishes. This inflates his ego, and he relishes the position of ascendancy among his fellows. But they too crave ascendancy and are incensed by his advantages and airs; they strive to outdo him, overthrow and supplant him. The struggle for status goes on constantly in every society, whether in open combat (with the bully on the playground) or in subtle ways (as Mrs. Smith spreads a vicious rumor to gain prestige at the expense of a social rival).

Rivalry breeds conflict. More than any other sign rivalry is the epitome of conflict. For it sets one person or group against another in direct opposition as they struggle for a goal they both seek. It is present in all conflicts, therefore, and adds the zest of excitement to sports or the hostility of enmity to serious combat. The boy who raced the length of the skating pond with his playmate for the hand of a favorite girl to skate with was engaged in open rivalry, the aggressive drive of which was expressed in every vigorous stroke. When he stumbled and, falling flat, slid on his face to her feet in humility to claim her in temporary ownership, he suffered loss of status as a skater and loss of prestige in the eyes of all. Someone is bound to lose in every rivalry, and such humiliation renews aggressive impulses.

Gains and privileges are the goals sought in many conflicts. Whether in profits of economic gain or the privilege of prestige, the hunger for gain is insatiable. So it appears at least in our competitive society where progress is a fleeting goal and getting ahead is the way of making progress. Every goal attained is the start toward another goal beyond, and no one is expected to give up pushing on or ever be content with the already attained. This obligation to progress to new goals was to Kant a moral imperative and to Royce an argument for immortality, that there can be no last moral task. In the pressure of social competition, however, it has come to mean getting ahead of others, which makes for incessant strife in school for grades, on the playground for victory, in business for success, and in social circles to be better or more anything than another.

Beliefs and codes also eventuate in conflict. Theological controversies have divided men into bristling camps of furious opposition, separating every religion into rival sects and Christianity into some 250 denominations, while within each denomination fundamentalists consign the modernists to a fiery hell of everlasting torture. Political contestants, when sincerely expressing honest beliefs, have the heated temperature of righteous indignation as they debate disputed issues in public forum. Political mudslinging also releases aggression and adds fury to the conflict. Note the current orgy of Communist witch-hunting that prosecutes a man for what he believes in a democracy whose constitution guarantees freedom of speech and opinion. Temperatures rise even higher over moral codes, for they control conduct and lead to actions that threaten chosen and established ways of life. Public indignation aroused by differences in moral code was released in the past century upon the Mormons, whose belief in plural marriage set them at variance with those who just as stoutly held opposing views. A more recent example is the popular scorn and abuse heaped upon the conscientious objector in wartime, not because he is less but more determined to be conscientious.

Loyalties and prejudice result in conflicts. National loyalties for "my country right or wrong" accumulate explosives that are sensitive to national honor and pride, shout defiance at other nations, build armies and armaments, and prepare to the hair trigger when a slight border incident may release this gigantic load of aggression in wars of total destruction and unconditional surrender. Prejudice against other races has been described as "man's most dangerous myth."[4] Mingled as prejudice is with fear and frantic pride, it denies the ballot, segregates in slums, prevents eating together in public dining rooms, swimming at beaches and pools, or attending theaters, churches, and the concert halls together on the fictitious assumption that some blood is different from other blood, and that association will contaminate the "purity" of one race by proximity to the other. Repeated denials and affronts inevitably deepen conflicts and arouse aggressive exploits in retaliation.

Blame and punishment intensify conflicts by reinforcing all other resistances. The father who by his authority as a parent and his ownership of the home upholds his beliefs and codes, loyalties and prejudices, by whipping his fourteen-year-old son, who is now his rival in the family, will so reduce the boy's status and wound his prestige that he will sacrifice other privileges to gain revenge in subtle or bitter revolts against the father when opportunity permits.

[4] M. F. A. Montagu, *Man's Most Dangerous Myth: The Fallacy of Race* (New York: Columbia University Press, 1942).

To blame another is to accuse him of unworthiness, to reject him as an outcast temporarily at least (as when two brothers are confined to separate rooms and others sentenced to prison), to sever his bonds of fellowship in the community, to inflict denials and humiliations upon him that can only arouse poisonous resentment, callous indifference, or cruelty. How we expect to reform criminals by such treatment is a mystery; nor can we be surprised that prisons are schools of crime, sending their inmates forth more clever and more determined enemies of society. Blame and punishment serve better to release pent-up aggressions in the punisher than to reduce aggressions in the punished. Beliefs and codes, loyalties and prejudices, blame and punishment are invested in social institutions that confront the growing child and the adult with coercive authority.

These and other social situations are set for conflict. They naturally stimulate aggressive responses in persons who are caught in them. But it is persons who create these conflict situations. Why do people act this way? Let us now look at the inner impulses that issue in aggressive behavior. What drives or urges take aggressive turns, not as innate unlearned tendencies but as characteristic human responses to social patterns of conflict? In Chapter III I have called these impulses "needs" to indicate a dual role which they play, first in reference to nature within and second to nature without. We have seen that love is such a need arising from hunger within a person to respond to kindly gestures from a person who approaches him from without. Do we also have needs counter to love? At any rate we respond to conflict situations as aggressively as we do to kindly situations with love.

Let us explore this inner world by noting some of the typical human responses to conflict situations. The conflict situations are sociological causes of aggression; the responses are psychological causes. To be sure, they overlap, and it would be more accurate to call the former set of conflicts sociopsychological causes and the latter series of responses psychosociological causes. The former begins with a social situation calling for a response, the latter with a psychological tendency seeking a social conflict. The order is not significant, as they are too complex to classify in correlated pairs. Each situation may elicit a number of responses, and each tendency may issue in several conflict situations.

Feelings of *frustration and deprivation* are psychological causes of conflict. When the infant is hungry with no source of nourishment in sight, he will yell his rage to the world. When a boy has a date with a very particular girl and is denied the family car for the evening, he is quite apt to be upset and lift his voice in rash accusations. When factory workers at the end of a war are reduced severely in take-home pay, there follows a wave of angry strikes. When a nation as overcrowded as the population on Japanese islands is denied outlets for immigration and trade, they will naturally fight rather than starve. Who is the aggressor, the nation that contains and restrains with boycotts and exclusion acts or the one that fires the first shot? Research has demonstrated that frustration naturally incites aggression.[5]

Feelings of *inferiority and dependence* are painful for most persons to bear. Young children may enjoy a nest of dependence for a while or regress to it when unsuccessful at later stages of growth. But normally the growing child comes to a point where the dependent role is irksome and intolerable as an indication of his inferiority. In his struggles for independence the adolescent turns the free stream of his hostility against the parents who keep him under, and eventually he will divert that hostility to his teachers, employers, and other superiors who make him feel inferior. The radical movements against the authority of church, state, economic order, and social classes are likewise releasing aggression that boils up from springs of inferiority.

With this goes an even more violent desire to *revolt against coercion*. On request Watson produced rage from infants by holding them rigidly or restraining their freedom of movement. In Chapter V we have seen the lack of democracy in many families

[5] John Dollard and others, *Frustration and Aggression* (New Haven: Yale University Press, 1939).

and the resentments caused by coercive measures. Violence breeds violence, and wherever coercion bears down, there is bound to be an uprising against it. Coercion may be subtle, as when a silk glove conceals an iron will to dominate. And revolts may be just as subtle, in as many forms as the conscious and the unconscious minds of men can devise. The slowdown of workers in a factory is their revolt against the coercion of the assembly line and denials of ownership and status in the inferior position of a hired hand. The practice of malingering in the army is a revolt against regimentation and the futility of military routine. Disabling illness is often an unconscious revolt against pressures or neglect by loved ones. It may also be an inturning of aggression against oneself for reasons to be noted below.

Ego-striving for prestige often takes aggressive directions. For it is essentially an aggressive tendency to exhibit oneself and demand attention, to compel others to bring tribute to a hungry ego ever craving more recognition. It usually arises in one who feels neglected as a compensation for affection denied him. The demands of a starved ego may be insatiable, as in Napoleon for example. Ridiculed by his playmates as the puniest boy in his class, he developed an inexorable drive to conquer and rule over others. Hitler, Mussolini, and every other dictator reveal similar inferiority feelings inverted to terrific demands for prestige and glory. When such personal ambition is identified with a national ego, hell breaks loose in blood baths and annihilations of vast populations. So costly in aggression is ego-striving for prestige.

Related to this is the *power drive* to extend control over others. For the sake of prestige power is sought, but there is more than this in it. The lust for power is aggression naked or concealed; it is the insistent impulse to dominate, to push down and hold other persons under your might. There is an exhilaration in displaying one's might at the expense of others who are thereby compelled to yield tribute. There is often a sadistic delight in inflicting pain on others and watching them suffer. The sex component in this is also recognized, as the exercise of power over others magnifies the ego-

179

istic satisfaction of sensuous pleasure. In refined as well as crude ways the power hunger is expressed, by verbal aggressions, by identification with a powerful nation that flaunts superiority, or by the subtle ways in which a weak invalid can exact tribute and special favors from her family.

The *stress of competition* is another cause of conflict. Wherever rivalry exists, aggressive tendencies increase. Tests have repeatedly shown that students will exert themselves more and achieve higher scores when competition is introduced to learning or skill of performance. The champion miler does not set a world's record running alone, but when he is paced by four of his fastest rivals each running a quarter mile against him. The exciting power of competition releases aggression, and if a team is set to win at any cost, they will do anything to put their opponents under. Here is an interpersonal situation where one rival whips up another in violent efforts to outdo each other. Of course there are the losers as well as the winners, who are even more aggressive in their urge to win next time. The outcome is often a vicious circle of spiraling aggression that sacrifices every other value for an empty victory.

Retaliation is another impulse that takes aggressive forms. Tit for tat is a natural impulse that leads us to strike back without stopping to think or count the cost of what we are doing. This is like a flash of anger, an impulsive explosion that seems to release aggression in a passion of rough justice—"an eye for an eye, and a tooth for a tooth" (*lex talionis*). Only by dint of great self-control over long periods of education does one remember to count ten before he retaliates. It is natural to retaliate, while self-control is a difficult lesson to learn. Retaliation is so prevalent in interpersonal relations, and so instant in striking back without warning, that aggression multiplies blow for blow. A fight once started is hard to stop; for getting even never comes to a balance, and there is always a margin of hostility to return.

Defensive reactions are more elaborate efforts to retaliate. We have impulses to defend ourselves against attack or threat, but defense may become a studied plan or strategy. Whether impulsive or considered, defense reactions are composed somewhat of fear and somewhat of protective tendencies. Because we are threatened and fear the evils of being attacked, we seek to protect ourselves. This is a well-known parental trait in animals, who exert extraordinary aggression to protect their young. As social ties are strong among human kin, they may take elaborate precautions to protect their families. National defense has become an obsession with us after two world wars, and nations are arming in frantic acceleration against possible attacks from potential enemies. Unfortunately most national leaders are blind to the folly of weakening their resources in a military defense program that does not defend. So better defenses such as a sound economy, a working democracy, effective good will, and co-operation in a United Nations with added resources for world government are overlooked as of slight consequence.

Guilt feelings are as painful as any human experience. They reduce self-esteem and deflate our sense of well-being and social approval. We feel inferior, frustrated in aspiration, and deprived of personal worth. When others blame us, we show defensive reactions, deny accusations, retaliate with countercharges, and resist self-righteously the unwelcome guilt forced upon us. In these reactions we lash out aggressively at other persons or society for taking us to task so painfully. When guilt is self-given disapproval in which one comes to blame himself, he turns his aggression inward and hates, rejects, or punishes himself. He may violently commit suicide in one terrible effort, or he may take the ascetic way of martyrdom, the helpless way of neurotic invalidism, or the reckless way of alcohol addiction. He may punish himself with mutilations and needless surgery, purposive accidents, impotence or frigidity, organic disease and fatal illness.[6]

Hunger for love we have met before. We began with the need for love and then started off to explore tendencies that defeat love. That cycle of destructive impulses now brings us back to love.

---

[6] Menninger, *Man Against Himself*, gives an extended analysis of these punitive tendencies.

Does this mean that love causes hate? That would be a paradox indeed. Unwise love, such as the dominating love that holds another dependent, or selfish love that clasps and smothers another in self-gratification, or jealous love that is obsessed with rivalries, or defensive love that is fearfully and anxiously protective, may provoke hatred. But here we are concerned rather with lack of love and its effects upon personality. When a child is unwanted in a home, he soon makes that discovery and retaliates with aggression toward those who rejected him. It is clear from the overwhelming evidence of case studies in delinquent and neurotic children that broken homes produce broken and bitter personalities. Every situation where love is denied is a source of trouble in maladjusted lives and a variety of aggressive distortions. No other source is more prolific of aggression than unfulfilled hunger for love. A glance at the millions of children in Europe and Asia homeless because of war, starving for love as much as for food, is a foreboding picture for the peace and health of the next generation. Even in well-fed America there is cause for dismay in the mounting number of broken homes and the denial of secure love to growing children.

Do we know enough and care enough to prevent the bitter harvest of greater hostilities whose seeds of neglect and despair have already been sown? If not, are we wise and social-minded enough to cease sowing more seeds of hostility in our homes and communities? If we are, can each do this work of love alone, or will we need to organize a united front of social co-operation to reduce hostility with love?

3. The Power to Destroy

As a lad of six I witnessed a scene that impressed me deeply. It was among the trees along a dry run near our home that I came upon a larger boy with a slingshot, whose aim brought down a robin. In the face of my protests he continued to pelt the wounded and mangled bird. The horror which I felt for the needless murder of the bird was heightened by the fury of the onslaught with epithets of raging hatred and savage expression of unmistakable glee. I wondered then as I do now why he was so gleeful in the act of killing.

It is a long way from the slingshot to the atomic bomb dropped on Hiroshima, perhaps six thousand years in the progress of weapons for destruction. Many hands and minds along that way have contributed their ingenuity and science to the history of weapons. Yet each according to his capacity was using his power to destroy. The power to destroy has increased vastly and is strangely equivalent to man's power to create. As man invents tools to build, he also invents weapons to destroy what he builds. And the more man builds, the greater is his opportunity to destroy. The primitive man is a weakling; he builds a hut and kills only one life at a time. Modern man is a giant; he builds cities and kills a hundred thousand people in one explosion, all life and all that life has created in the culture of a city.

The more values a person cherishes, the more vulnerable he is to attack. If an Indian has one loincloth, one bow and set of arrows, he has not many things to lose as compared with a modern city dweller whose house and office are full of heirlooms and gadgets in varied assortment. The wider his range of values and appreciations, the more refined are the instrumentalities by which they can be attacked.

We shudder at the power of atomic bombs, and yet their explosion is crude as compared with the subtle ways in which a wife can torture a husband. She can of course wield the rolling pin, but that is too old-fashioned. She can nag at his faults and mannerisms, but that is not subtle enough either. To be cruel with finesse she will discover one after another his dearest delights and vanities, then puncture them neatly after inflating them. She will recall how handsome he was before his bald spot appeared, or how courteous he was before he got involved in business. Or she will receive him passively without meeting him at the door, kiss him absent-mindedly, decline his invitation to go out for the evening, and show the mildest disdain for his enthusiasms. Passive resistance can be quite as aggressive as open attack; it has power to kill love more steadily and surely than blows ever do. The martyr role of injured innocence or helpless invalidism can accumulate a heavier burden of suffering upon a family than outspoken accusations. Such aggression is more destructive by its studied deception, apparently sweet and gracious, devoted and righteous, yet all the time piercing the tenderest emotions with unerring aim and unrelenting cruelty.

The husband is not usually one to take punishment lying down. Goaded by a multitude of invisible stings, he is apt to throw his weight around like a bull in a china shop. But his snorting rage and charging violence are futile; they make a loud noise and beat the air with little effect. Awkward strength is no match for supple grace and deft thrusts. Not until he learns the art of indirection will he wound the inner heart of love. When he is repeatedly late for dinner, though protesting he was unavoidably detained at the golf course; or hides behind the newspaper, responding to queries with reluctant grunts; or spends most evenings away at his clubs and civic responsibilities; or goes on camping trips with his cronies instead of his family, the absence treatment accomplishes its purpose. However generous his material gifts to keep the wife clothed in splendor, he is only decorating a corpse of the love he has found decorous ways to kill.

A mother who does not welcome a child may have a miserable pregnancy with vomiting spells symbolic of violent rejection. At childbirth she and the baby will suffer severe labor pains in the muscular tensions and struggles of her unwilling desire to release the child to birth. In nursing she will hold him rigidly, take away the nipple suddenly, and put him down abruptly without the cuddling and nestling that spell tender, loving care. She will keep him sternly on an inflexible feeding schedule, not heeding his wails of loneliness, disregarding the rhythm of his hunger, and leaving him alone to cry uncomforted on the stoical theory it would spoil him to pick him up and give him attention. In bathing and dressing him her aggressive mood handles him roughly, with heavy hand scrubbing his tender skin fiercely, holding him tightly, and moving him with jolting pickups and letdowns. In toilet training she begins too early, expects too much of his tender age, scolds and spanks him for his errors, or leaves him on the stool for long waiting periods. She weans him abruptly, with no patience for his cries or thumb-sucking, demanding that he eat like an adult with no favors asked or given. At the table, with the vocal assaults and angry insistence of her male accomplice, she demands that he eat everything on his plate whether he likes it or not before he can leave the table. When he learns to walk, there are few kisses for his bumps and bruises but sharp words and blows when he walks out the front door, slips in the mud, and soils his clean clothes. When company comes or he goes visiting, he must be a model boy, not touch anything but sit still without wriggling or interrupting and not be a bother to anybody.

On his part he is miserable enough to return blow for blow. At birth he greets the world with a wail of anger for its cold and unaccustomed discomforts. He bites the nipple with toothless gums, roots with his head, strikes out with arms and legs, arches his back against his mother's arms, has colic and keeps his parents awake at night, refuses to eat at the table, messes his food with his fingers and, if forced to eat what he does not want, regurgitates it. As he grows in comprehension of the family situation, he sees his parents doting upon his older sister, who is the apple of their eyes. Even as he resents the favors shown her, he observes the tricks of coy smiles and coquettish manners, hugs and kisses, ready submission and sweet assent by which she wins her way. At length he tries these techniques himself and gains by stealth what he could not take by force. He learns the language of persuasion and the gestures of submission until he finally becomes mama's darling and papa's little man. The open warfare yields to a strategy of trading favors—this for you and that for me. Outwardly he gets along better with his parents—he minds them and pleases them more; they tolerate and put up with him as somewhat less of a nuisance. Hostility is repressed beneath a smooth exterior of respectability, but he is uncertain whether this is love or just endurance. He is insecure and so dependent on his parents in comforting discomforts that he resents this bondage to his freedom that cripples his initiative. He identifies his cramped ego with his father, who is strong, and his mother, who has her own way. Fixated through fear and cunning at a childish level of dependence, he awaits the day when he will supplant and overthrow them. With impatient patience his anger stores up energy against those he loves, until he is strong enough to revolt and strike for freedom.

Whether active or passive, aggression is desire to hurt or harm. The boy who resents his dependent relation to parents who coerce and deprive him may play a waiting game of submission for aggressive ends. The husband who gives his wife the absence treatment may not lift a finger against her and yet hurt her far more deeply by his cruel indifference. The wife who harbors aggressive impulses toward her husband may not say an unkind word yet gain a victory for revenge by a martyr's attitude that displays in silent eloquence the message to the world, "See how he makes me suffer!"

The most subtle aggression of all is to withdraw emotional support. We all live and flourish in the atmosphere of social approval, moral support, and sustaining affection. When that emotional support is withdrawn, the downfall is sure and swift. The "bad boy" at school who alienates his classmates and the teacher is headed for more destructive tactics by their aggressive disapproval. The ex-convict who tries to come back and succeeds in making good is rare, because he has lost public confidence and knows society is against him. He is made an outlaw by the act of society in locking him up and branding him a criminal. Within the family such aggressions are equally disastrous. The irate father who casts off his son for some disobedience, the mother who gets discouraged and doubts if the unregenerate child is worth trying to help, or the wife who gives up her alcoholic husband and ceases to hope for his recovery or wish for his return—these rejections kill love and destroy character.

After the suicide of her husband a woman confessed to her physician the anguish of a tortured conscience.

It has been over a year, and I still cannot sleep or eat or work. Our years together had been so wonderful! They were the happiest of my life, and of his too, I am sure. Why should he have ended them in this way? Was it something that I did? Or something I didn't do? He was always inclined to be a little melancholy and he would get discouraged so easily. I used to have to urge him on and pump him full of courage and reassurance every day, and tell him I knew he was going to succeed. I am afraid I got a little tired of this and let up on it. Sometimes I used to wish he would give *me* a little encouragement—but that was selfish of me. I just let him down. So now I blame myself. I feel as if I were responsible for his death.[7]

Why do we have impulses to destroy? There may be a natural tendency in all life to destroy. This is the conviction of the psychiatrist Karl Menninger, arising from extensive clinical experience and observation of human behavior. He follows Freud in holding that there are two basic and opposite drives, one the life instinct and the other the death instinct, that struggle against each other. In his two books referred to in this chapter he gives a wealth of evidence and interpretation of these urges. He calls this to our attention in the hope that if we realize how human nature is loaded for death, we will know our danger and unite the energies of life to save life. And, instinct or not, there is wisdom in what he says, for destruction is altogether too easy, and the threat of death is not far from any one of us.

There is a proverb: "Power tends to corrupt; absolute power corrupts absolutely." This is probably an overstatement of a half-truth. It would be truer to say all power tempts. To have power of any kind is a temptation to use it. The healthy colt or boy is tempted to kick up his heels and run for all he is worth. The man at the wheel of a high-powered motor is tempted to "let her out and see what she will do." The boy with a slingshot or the man with a shotgun is tempted to "let her go," try his aim at a bird and see if he has power and skill to bring it down. The boy with firecrackers, regardless of the law, can hardly wait until the Fourth

[7] Menninger, *Love Against Hate* (New York: Harcourt, Brace & Co., 1942), p. 110. Used by permission.

of July to shoot them off. It is no light responsibility for a nation to manufacture a stock pile of atomic bombs, for the temptation to use them may easily overcome better judgment when a crisis arises in international relations. To have power, to know it is there, to feel it tingling in nerves and imagination, is to want to use that power. Life has the power to destroy life or love—and we know it. Consequently there are many explosions of these powerful impulses.

Another answer is that we learn to respond to aggression with aggression. Love is learned by example and invitation in response to being loved. Hate is just as contagious as love, and we learn to hate in returning hate. Menninger in *Love Against Hate* has shown how love and hate mingle and struggle together in family life. Parents foster aggressions in their children as they were restrained, intimidated, and coerced by their own parents. The father and mother carry unconscious aggressive impulses from the repressions inflicted on their childhood. They suffer additional pressures and conflicts in our competitive and aggressive society. In countless ways they irritate and punish each other. When children are born to them, they naturally and to quite a large extent unintentionally displace their anger and resentments upon their children. The first two years of infancy are especially significant in the formation of character; and during these impressionable years the careless ways in which parents frustrate, deny, and force their children into anger provide seeds enough to continue the circling harvests of fatal aggressions in our society.

A third answer is that we fear our power to destroy. To sense a throbbing impulse to do a terrible deed is a frightening experience. Much as we fear others who have power to punish or destroy us, and even because we fear them, we are more afraid of our own impulses to destroy. When Moses killed the provocative Egyptian, he looked this way and that to see if anyone saw his murder; then he hid him in the sand and fled far beyond the land of the Nile (Exod. 2:12). "Intendest thou to kill me, as thou killedst the Egyptian?" was not only the voice of a fellow Hebrew; it was the voice

188

of his own conscience, and he feared others no less than his own impulses.

Fear is a powerful motive that has a double action in two directions. It lures us to the fearful thing it drives us away from. The power to destroy is fixated by fear with a strange fascination that holds us more tightly in its grip. At the same time the fear of our aggression makes us overcautious and overanxious to do the opposite. By this fearful inhibition we reject the fierce impulse and repress it to the unconscious where it continues to exert its pressure against our peace of mind and unity of purpose. To submerge such impulses we exert ourselves to love the more, and submit with painful patience and miserable dependence, or suffer disorders of inner conflicts and tensions. When unexpectedly a child has a death wish toward his mother, or toward any loved one who irritates him sufficiently, he is struck with guilty remorse. Then as guilt grows through years of self-condemnation, he must punish himself in one of several ways that aggression may be turned inward, such as accident, neurotic disease, obvious misdeeds that cry for punishment, failure again and again in conspicuous ways, self-pitying feelings of inferiority, compulsive toil and asceticism, or suicide. We seldom realize how many of the misfortunes we bear are the fruit of aggressive impulses expressed and repressed, feared and repented of.

4. Is War Curable?

War is a disease that may prove to be more fatal than any other human disease. By the number of its fatalities it will rank high in devastation of life, plus all values life has created in the slow march of civilization. Like cancer war multiplies its rapacious cells at the expense of all healthy cells in our society. More striking is the resemblance of war to mental disease. In fact the behavior of whole populations in war is so parallel to the symptoms of paranoia that it takes on the character of a mass psychosis. Ideas of grandeur and persecution release ungovernable impulses to violence and destruction.

Little progress has been made in six thousand years toward curing war. Rather than toward curbing it the tendency has been for war to spread until increasingly more people are drawn into increasingly violent orgies of destruction. Rather than being put out or localized to confined areas these fires spread irresistibly into world wars in which it appears next to impossible for any nation to remain neutral or unscathed by the holocaust. Is war man's incurable affliction that he must bear grimly and hopelessly, forever a victim of his explosive passions and the circumstances that ignite them? Or is a cure for war possible?

There is no panacea for war, no one remedy that will be a cure-all, for war is the result of many complex causes. There are *economic* causes of scarcity and inequality among the "have and have-not" nations, ambition to possess, competition for trade and higher standards of living, exploitation of resources and markets. Most people prefer fighting to starving, and economic demands are as insatiable as they are aggressive. There are *political* causes in efforts to gain power over others, crying "enemy abroad" to whip up popular support at home, provoking international crises to win desired legislation and budgets for gigantic military machines. Patterns of diplomacy follow well-known political devices of threat, negotiation, and expansion to maintain a balance of power. There are *national* causes of sovereignty, aggrandizement, patriotic fervor, pride and superiority, authoritarian statism with its denial of democracy, military preparedness with its phobias and compulsions of frantic defense.

There are *historical* causes of previous events that provoke hostility, cry for vengeance and retaliation, seek to regain losses suffered and overtake rivals feared, bound to traditions and gaining aggressive ends otherwise unobtainable. History shows that instead of ending wars each war causes other wars in widening circles of destruction. There are *educational* causes of nationalistic history books playing up the evil designs of other nations, hymns of hate fomenting bitterness and impatience for the day when victory will settle old scores, pledges of fanatic allegiance to nations whose chief function is death, military training, and indoctrination for war. There are *religious*, *cultural*, and *ideological* causes in their divisive loyalty to conflicting ideals and codes of living with dogmatic intolerance for arch-enemies whose destiny requires human sacrifice on the altar of uncompromising hatred.

These causes contribute no little to the wars of nations and classes against each other. Yet all of these visible causes for war have back of them the invisible forces of psychological causes. They each rise from the dynamic urges of human nature, the actions and interactions of needs and impulses, hopes and fears, desires and ego-strivings. Here we come upon the original causes for war in the inner motives by which individual persons join their frustrations into aggressions to gain the ambitions they so urgently, though blindly, strive for. Most of the cures for war are mustard plasters, external in application and irritating in effect. Like other superficial attempts to treat the patient with artificial remedies he neither wants nor needs, they are doomed to fail. No external measures can cure the war sickness of our humanity until we turn from surface symptoms to deeper causes of inner motivations. There our task will be to redirect the violent impulses of aggression toward peaceful attainments.

Then we discover that the wars of nations are grandiose manifestations of the wars of impulses within persons. Some of these inner battles we have noted above as conflicts and their causes. There we have seen that human nature is loaded with high explosives by the interplay of conflicts within and between persons. When other persons, from parents on, frustrate and provoke us to relieve their aggressive feelings, we respond in kind by taking out aggressions in our own ways. Or if taking them out is not convenient, we turn them in and dam them up by repression until their pressure is more explosive. By that time a convenient enemy or scapegoat is found, and the individual tensions join by chain reaction in the larger explosions of war. If we are to reach the basic causes of war, we will need to work with these psychological causes.

We do not want to discount other causes or other efforts to cure war. Every attempt is worth trying as a fruitful experiment. By our mistakes as well as our successes we learn much from these experiments. Pacts to renounce war, associations and leagues of nations, international laws and courts of justice, political and economic treaties have failed. Not always and not entirely, but they teach us we must work with deeper causes if we want better results. They are worth trying again if we profit by previous mistakes and build more truly upon the psychological causes of human motivation. Next time they will work better if the sociopsychological conditions are better fulfilled.

Every true reform is an inner reform. Every real cure works from within human nature, for healing is a growth of new life to meet the actual needs more effectively. Every social change that finds continuing success is a change in the desires of individual persons. The mind that masters nature, splits the atom and harnesses it for his use, has a greater task and more urgent—to master his own impulses and harness them to life rather than to death. To cure war we must change the minds of men from aggression to love. This is clearly understood by the framers of the constitution of the United Nations Educational, Scientific, and Cultural Organization (UNESCO), in whose preamble they declare: "Since wars begin in the minds of men, it is in the minds of men that the defences of peace must be constructed." [8]

We cannot save the world from war without saving man from war, and we cannot save man from war without saving his soul. By soul I mean what theologians and philosophers have always meant, the very essence of the real man where his decisions are made and his destiny wrought. In psychology the soul will be stripped of metaphysical presuppositions, the more clearly to reveal the nature of his motives by which he moves his world. The inner motivations of the soul are the original battleground of war. It is likewise the ground of peace as we learn and use the science of making peace within and among men, women, and children.

In 1944 American psychologists issued a manifesto entitled *Human Nature and Enduring Peace*, which declared, "War can be avoided."

No race, nation, or social group is inevitably warlike. The frustrations and conflicting interests which lie at the root of aggressive wars can be reduced and redirected by social engineering. Men can realize their

[8] *UNESCO and the National Commission: Basic Documents,* Department of State Publication 3082 (Washington, D.C.: U.S. Govt. Printing Office, March, 1948), p. 1.

ambitions within the framework of human co-operation and direct their aggressions against those natural obstacles that thwart them in the attainment of their goals.[9]

This is no time for defeatism, when the issues of war and peace, life and death, are hanging in delicate balance. Defeatism about the inevitability of war and the incorrigibility of human nature will do more than any other thing to draw us into endless series of destructive wars. Human nature is what we make it by our desires and fears. Fears distort our desires until we are apt to choose the lesser of imagined evils because we have not the faith and courage to choose the greater of possible goods. If we desire a better human nature or a better world, we will need both to believe in it and to work wisely for it.

As war is a contagious disease of emotional attitudes, insatiable desires, obsessive fears, and competitive aggressions, we need to find sociopsychological solutions to cure it. Interpersonal psychology has tools to analyze dynamic human needs and find ways of meeting them in growing harmony and mutuality. Not that psychologists alone can bring about these changes; but if their research is devoted to curing man's destructive aggressions, together with the research of other social scientists in their respective fields, there will be clearer blueprints of how to proceed.

Social planning is needed on a world scale to diagnose human needs and provide constructive ways of meeting them. We are beginning to do this in the political realm with the United Nations. We shall also need to diagnose the psychological needs of people around the world, and to develop resources to meet those needs more effectively. Within each nation mental health programs are making a good beginning, but there is need for more public support and popular interest. Within each community there is need for larger mutual appreciation and more continuous co-operation. Within each family and school nonaggressive emotional education of children is needed; and to provide this parents, teachers, and youth leaders must be emotionally

[9] Third Yearbook of the Society for the Psychological Study of Social Issues, Ed. Gardner Murphy (Boston: Houghton Mifflin Co., 1945), p. 455.

prepared to show children how to grow in peaceful and wholesome expression of their impulses.

Somehow we must get beyond the planning stage, for the best blueprints in the world will not usher in the peaceful society we so desire. More average people will need to catch the urgency of our social task and volunteer to learn and practice and teach mental health with unfaltering enthusiasm until it becomes the vogue, the popular style of living that is irresistibly attractive and justly desired by the flavor of its fruits in gracious, healthful, harmonious social love.

5. Social Channels for Aggression

Why not be aggressive? you may well ask. If aggressive impulses are natural, then why object? If people are happier quarreling and attacking, why interfere with a good fight? Is this effort to curb aggression just another moralistic prejudice? Perhaps the end justifies the means, as many have said in reference to war.

There is no easy answer to these questions. The most conscientious minds have not been able to agree. In this discussion we are considering causes and effects of human behavior; our point of view is consequential. "Ye shall know them by their fruits." (Matt. 7:16.) Ends cannot be separated from means or fruits from roots, because they are involved in each other. The law of growth is that a good tree brings forth good fruit according to its nature and kind. Many fruits of aggressive impulses are bitter and poisonous. In the family and community the intense sufferings that result from aggression are as tragic to the aggressor in the anguish of guilt as to the one attacked in the pangs of punishment. In the world at large the extent of human destruction is becoming a total war of all against all, spreading like a raging forest fire beyond control and threatening to engulf the human race in calamity.

Aggression does a large amount of damage. It breaks hearts and homes; it strains the ties of family and friendship. It has devastating consequences in war, crime, strikes, mob fury, as well as in the silent enmities and resentments that pollute the wells of human kindness and happiness. Explosives are dangerous, yet they are also useful when wisely controlled and released in constructive ways. For aggression is energy that may be constructive or destructive depending upon how it is used. Like electricity and other energies human impulses may carry high or low voltage and be stepped up to more or down to less dangerous potential. Aggressive energy can be a priceless asset in human life, providing motivation and expressive dynamics for action.

The question is how to use this energy. Direct attack on other persons is divisive and destructive. But attack on things for a constructive purpose is production; attack on ideas and figures is problem solving and creative thinking; attack on social evils is reform and reconstruction. Repression of aggressive impulses is damaging in two senses. It blocks the flow of energy, raising the level of pressure to more dangerous potential like water in a power stream or high tension electricity built up by resistance. It also dams the good with the evil in holding back expression of useful energy and distorting personality by hypertensions.

What we need is well-directed aggression that will conserve and release this energy in socially useful ways. There are risks at any rate, for every power has its risk of misuse. But the alternative is futility in the constraint and misery of impotence. The risks can be reduced by intelligent moral control of our powers. William James once urged us to seek "a moral equivalent to war" with socially useful activities in which the aggressive and heroic impulses can be turned to constructive enterprises.[10] What are some of the social channels for useful aggression?

Work is one of the most productive social channels for aggression. Work builds men, and it builds society in the enlarging human achievements we call civilization. Into our work we can throw all the energy we have until tensions are released and we can relax. By working we learn skills and gain satisfactions in the rewards of labor. A large share of work requires co-operation in which we have the comradeship of associating together in common tasks for mutual benefits.

[10] "The Moral Equivalent of War," first published in *McClure's Magazine* (August, 1910); then in the volume *Memories and Studies* (New York: Longmans, Green & Co., 1911), pp. 267-96.

"Blessed is he who has found his work," said Carlyle; "let him ask no other blessedness." The value of work is evident to anyone forced by disability or unemployment to endure idleness with its restless and frustrating futility. It is apparent in the delinquencies of boys who have nothing to do; they are "spoiling for a good fight" and "dying" of a boredom that demands excitement. Occupational therapy is a saving health for convalescents and no less for the well whose jobs keep them going. For without regular work to express aggressive energies life gets snarled up in its own conflicts.

Play is another social outlet for aggression that has long been underestimated but is now coming into increasing popularity. Competitive sports are good-natured aggression according to the rules agreed upon to keep it in bounds. Friends take the position of rivals and violently toss their energies into winning harmless victories. The strife is real and the enthusiasm hilarious, but the players hit, kick, or throw a ball instead of attacking each other. Table games and social games take aggressive positions in symbolic ways that have the gestures of challenge and capture. Drama portrays on stage or screen the adventures and exploits of human aggression and love. Music, dance, fine arts, and fiction offer stimulating invitations to release aggression vicariously. The psychology of identification permits the spectator to enter into the action of the players emotionally and live through their experiences with the cathartic release and purgation that Aristotle first described.[11] Psychodrama is proving a significant medium for catharsis of aggressions and learning of roles to take in social activities of real life. Juvenile delinquency is headed off by recreation, and communities are finding what a good investment playgrounds and recreational facilities are in healthy social living.

Education provides a channel for aggressive impulses, not only in schools, but wherever one seeks to influence the mind of another. Teachers, though traditionally mild-mannered, are aggressive in expressing ideas, assigning learning tasks, and directing the growth of students. Salesmen, advertisers, and public relations people, who persuade others to buy and to believe, are obviously aggressive, as are

[11] *Poetics* VI. 1449 *b*. 23.

preachers, evangelists, and orators. Authoritarian methods of education are overaggressive in forcing learning upon others. But democratic methods of discussion and full expression of differing opinions are mutually releasing for all. When the lid of domination is off, a class or group of persons of any age will talk out aggressions in vigorous exchange of verbal explosions. This stimulates thinking, clarifies issues, and promotes growth in understanding.

Leadership and organization is an aggressive channel of large social usefulness. Before they organize, people are isolated and indifferent, weak and chaotic, each following or inhibiting his impulses ineffectually. As soon as two or three organize a committee or a club, they begin to make plans, unite their purposes, and work together for mutual goals. Impulses repressed before are now released in plans and their execution. Each person who participates in organizing activity is to that extent a leader. He takes the initiative to suggest ideas, to persuade others, and to take a share of the joint responsibility for carrying out the plans agreed upon. We sometimes smile at the American tendency to multiply organizations, but this is because we are an energetic people and need to express our aggressive energies in social interaction. The authoritarian leader is overaggressive in demanding that others submit to him. But the democratic leader invites free expression of initiative from all in a mutual interchange of leadership where each person gives forth his impulses to be met by the impulses of others in a dynamic equilibrium of social achievement.

Social action is more than organization, though it cannot be less. It is the united energy of a group of persons who act together. Each person has a share of leadership in organizing, extending, and promoting the cause they work for together. The like-minded who unite for social action may become a political party or a legislative committee working to gain public support, get out the votes, roll up a majority of those who demand a social change. They may become a labor union and organize to have their needs more effectively represented in collective bargaining. They may form other occupational groups and service clubs to identify their interests and work for social gains. They become churches who associate for worship, discussion, and the developing of programs of religious service at home and abroad. They form community welfare agencies, participate in the International Red Cross or the Friends Service Committee to raise funds to administer relief to those in special need anywhere in the world. Aggressive energies are put to good use in these ways.

Love is the sublimation of aggression. This may come as a surprise to those who have seen love as the antithesis of aggression. But psychologically we have noted that love and hate mingle together in the deepest motivations of human impulses. It is well known that sex play is an interchange of aggression and submission. It is also evident that parental love may take an aggressive turn in protecting the young, guiding their growth, and controlling their behavior.

Love can be dominating and demanding when the lover or parent is a tyrant. Authoritarian love is overaggressive and has repercussions in neurotic repressions and revolts of those who are held in submission by oppressive attachment. But there is also the love of self-sacrifice for the larger good of others, in which a person disciplines himself aggressively in unselfish ways. Because love and hate are mingled so closely together, nothing has the power that love has to overcome hate. Not by hating hate is this accomplished, for that only increases the hateful energy; but by loving in the midst of hate until the hating impulses are dissolved in the more aggressive love. Without love sublimation is impossible, for nothing else has the buoyance to do this. Love is so intrinsically satisfying that it provides the best therapies by which to cure the evils and encourage the good potentialities of aggression. To love is a social expression that is able to enlist all impulses and resources in dynamic realization of human values.

The Beloved Community

1. Is Society Ill?

The individual person owes much to society; for no life stands alone, and isolation means not only misery but death. Society arises in creative interpersonal relations that multiply human values by mutual production and distribution. It undergirds security, peace, and confident living; at the same time it invites exploratory adventures and ever-new inventions. The verdict of all religions and social sciences is unanimous that life is essentially social, and the interests of each person are inextricably bound up with the welfare of all.

But no society is altogether healthy. The ills of our society are serious enough, as we have seen, to call for emergency measures. Wherever living creatures interact, they spread disease and suffering, rivalry and exploitation, domination and deprivation. In society we learn to hate as well as to love, to intimidate and extort as often as we encourage and support. Social assets and liabilities teeter back and forth until we wonder which is after all ascendant. Can we have social goods without social evils? Evidently not, for much of evil seems to be inherent either in social structures or in the ways in which people naturally act toward each other. Social evils may be reduced, but they do not appear to be entirely preventable.

Yet it may be possible by good will and social ingenuity to decrease needless evils and increase needed goods. If our society is ill, it concerns every one of us and requires immediate action to restore its health. We may be willing to leave society to the experts, and surely we cannot proceed wisely without expert diagnosis and appropriate

199

remedies skillfully employed. Yet no expert can practice without the consent of the patient or carry out reforms without the co-operation of the people who are most affected by them. We are the patients who need to be healed; we are the people who will accomplish or neglect the needed reforms. For society is no lump of clay or mass of humanity apart from us who are its members. We are the constituents of society, and if society is to be healed of its conflicts, we are the ones to partake of the healing. The physician may diagnose and prescribe, but the healing is wrought within the patient by mobilizing his neglected health resources and learning how to live in more wholesome ways. Whatever may be done for us is external and superficial; only what we do for ourselves with others has the inner strength to endure. Not that we are self-sufficient, for we live by the grace of an unfailing creative Activity from above; but each person decides whether to obstruct and defeat the health that is in him or to accept it joyously and share it generously in open relationships of love.

How can the person who desires health cope with the ills of society? There are three possibilities. (1) He may yield to society as it is, a helpless victim or a willing conformist to the *status quo*. But this is to accept the evils of society supinely and perpetuate them. (2) He may withdraw from society to save himself from social contamination or to criticize it from a distance by his departure and protest. (3) He may remain within society in order to change society, not to conform but to reform and transform what is evil into good. This is the most difficult but the most hopeful way, in which the individual identifies himself with the group as a responsible citizen who works with others in unfaltering co-operation to make life better for all.

In the long two thousand years of Christian history these three ways of coping with the social world have been thoroughly explored. The line of least resistance followed by a majority of the people is to yield to the customs of the world in which they live. Christians have been uneasy about this yielding, however, as the New Testament emphasizes the dangers of social conformity. But no society is altogether evil, and when one accepts this and that good custom, the distinctions

and separations gradually merge in identification until it is not easy
to tell the Christian from the non-Christian as they mingle in the
common life of the world as neighbors and associates. A Christian may
give an hour or two a week to church activities, but otherwise what
distinguishes his daily activities from others about him who do not
claim to be Christians? Perhaps he may refrain from one or two "social vices" which his church prohibits, but beyond negative restraints
what does the Christian do that is distinctly and uniquely health-
giving?

This persistent question has led a number of Christians to be sepa-
ratists who step out of the common life into another world distant
enough to be unmistakably different. Unlike Jesus, who went apart
at intervals to prepare to return with renewed compassion and resources to heal others, a hermit is unwilling to return but from his un-
yielding seclusion insists upon standing dramatically alone in protest
against society. The most determined of these hermits have been fa-
mous for their endurance in refusing to return to the society they
conspicuously renounce. They have their reward in gaining revenge
on society for misusing them, or releasing aggression in punitive
ways against themselves and others in the severity of unforgiving
condemnation. With obsessive attention to the one issue in which they
invest compulsive energy they reject all else to invite a martyr's
anguish. It is doubtful whether the individual or society can ever be
saved by protest alone.

Other separatist movements are social. A group of like-minded individuals may go apart together to form a new society nearer to their
hearts' desire. Monastic orders arise in many religions, departing from
the world to form a new society as a social experiment in brotherhood and constant devotion. There are also colonies of families who,
like the pilgrims of Plymouth, migrate to a new world to have freedom to create a society on new foundations and idealistic principles.
Such ventures have proved fruitful experiments with lessons to learn
and demonstrate in social resourcefulness.

The third alternative of remaining in the world yet organizing
societies to change the world is the main stream of Christian history.

This was the desire of the first Christian community in Jerusalem as related in the Acts of the Apostles. It was the direction of missionary enterprises, as shown in the letters of Paul, to establish Christian churches within the pagan cities of the Roman empire. From that time to this the Christian Church has become a society within the larger society dedicated to serve individuals and families by surrounding them with a loving community whose fellowship and group activities are to provide dynamic energies and influences to create new social life—a colony of heaven on earth.

2. THE GENIUS OF CHRISTIAN COMMUNITIES

Christian communities have something—though it is not always clear exactly what they have—to change the lives and interpersonal relations of their members. What is the genius of a Christian community? Where does it gain its dynamic energies, and how does it transact its causes into effects? A theologian will turn to supernatural causes—such as divine Grace—for his explanations. A psychologist may share the beliefs of a theologian but in seeking psychological causes will limit his investigation to human motivation. Our question in the framework of psychological analysis is, What human motives make up the genius of a Christian community?

Social enthusiasm was the most obvious trait of the early Christian community as described in Acts. When Jesus was crucified, his followers were defeated and scattered into hiding for their own safety. In the next forty days events transpired that brought them together with new hope and confidence. A change of spirit or morale occurred that turned their despair and defeat into a sense of victory. We often observe the power of group spirit in athletic, political, and other contests when something mysteriously happens to a losing team, and they rise up in unexpected strength to win with irresistible momentum. In the followers of Jesus the change was electrifying. On the day of Pentecost they were "all with one accord in one place" (Acts 2:1) when a unison spirit of enthusiasm caught them up like a tide or "a rushing mighty wind" (Acts 2:2), kindling them into flaming utterance in tongues of eloquence. They preached boldly in the capital of their enemies, refusing to stop even when arrested and warned by the authorities or persecuted and attacked by mobs. They sang hymns of praise, gathered together daily in prayer and fellowship, and attracted new members in large numbers. They went forth to other cities and countries with a dynamic message and mission to spread the good news to every creature.

A second motive in this community was a *social desire to share*. They shared what they valued most, the good news of Jesus, the Kingdom of God, and eternal life. They were steadfast in doctrine and fellowship, breaking bread together, testifying and sharing personal experiences. They sold their goods and possessions gladly to have all things in common and distribute to every man according to his need (Acts 2:44-45). Caste and class lines disappeared, special privileges were given up, superiorities of race, nation, or position were dissolved in repentance and brotherhood. In Christ there were no aliens or slaves, no rich or poor, no preferences of age or sex, no ambition to rise above or lord it over others. All were voluntary servants of all, and none asked for gain, for each wanted to give his best in the comradeship of sharing.

A third motive undergirding both the social enthusiasm and social sharing was a sense of *social destiny and resources*. They believed God had sent his son to call them into his service to establish a divine kingdom. All that came before was preparation for this new day; history was but a prelude to usher in the greater future now ready to dawn. They were chosen for this special work, to fulfill the purpose of a larger destiny. Irresistible energies they believed were at their disposal, with adequate resources to meet every need. All things would work together for good; the whole creation was in travail to bring a new era to birth. Nothing could stop the onward course of this movement, for it was the unfolding of an inevitable design.

The reader will note to this point in our description a rather striking parallel with Marxian Communism. So far these two gospels have common interests. Both have generated social enthusiasm leading to social sharing—though not always voluntary in communist societies—upheld by a sense of social destiny and resources. The dynamic expansion and power of each movement is a result of social enthusiasm, sharing, and destiny. But here we come to a fork beyond which the Christian and Marxian ways diverge.

Faith in a divine leader was the fourth motive in the Christian community. Jesus, at first unknown, was to become the Christ, sent of God as a Messiah to save his people by forming a new society on earth based on heavenly principles—the Kingdom of Heaven. At first they envisioned an earthly empire of pomp and glory upheld by military successes. As Jesus dissuaded them of this idea, they were reluctant to believe until the rude shock of his sudden capture and death by the powers of this world. In their experiences of his resurrection and ascension they were finally convinced he was truly the Son of God, whose vocation it was to suffer these things, reveal these truths, initiate this new society, and return to heaven to inaugurate a new age of peace, love, and service. It may be suggested that Russian Communism has uplifted Lenin to divine status and given apostolic succession to Stalin and other leaders to inaugurate a new era. But not from heaven, it is rather to rise from earth by man's effort, with stern rejection of heavenly assistance.

Supremacy of spiritual interests was the fifth trait in the Christian community. Unlike the economic determinism of Marx and the emphasis of his followers upon material gains, the Christian motive is to hold spiritual interests above other matters. The first Christians sold their possessions and distributed them to the poor because they held them of lesser value than spiritual growth in a fellowship of sharing. To them "real estate" was not such property as land and houses or economic goods and chattels but the building of a community of love. They came to see that economic goods have their place as instrumental to spiritual values. They appointed stewards to look after the economic goods; they labored with their own hands—Paul in tentmaking—to meet the necessities of life. They took up offerings to send to those in need in other cities as well as their own; but economic goods were dethroned, no longer to be the chief end of living, rather to be used and shared as means to the enlargement of the loving spirit in persons and society. To give up or give away goods was consequently no sacrifice but a privilege to free one of bondage to things, to enrich community life by sharing, and to elevate the lowest to equal respect and concern with the others in a family of mutual aid and care.

Returning good for evil was a sixth trait in the Christian community. This desire arose from the example and teaching of Jesus as he showed them how to use nonviolent methods, not resisting evil but surrounding it with creative good. By unswerving good will and disarming kindness he sought to reconcile enemies. As he hung upon the cross, it looked like the triumph not merely of his enemies but of their way of violence. Was he not defenseless when they came with swords and staves to take him, to mock him at the trial and turn him over to the Roman soldiers whose military power could not be disputed? Yet on the cross he forgave them, spoke a word of hope to the dying criminal, asked John to care for his mother, and came through the agony of torture to calm trust in his heavenly Father. His followers came to see that returning evil for evil is a vicious circle of perpetual enmity and mutual destruction. They saw that one can give his life without bitterness and accept the worst men can do with forgiveness and good will. Here is a way of breaking the vicious circle of hatred and revenge by paying the whole cost and going the whole way in returning good for evil.

Redemptive love was the seventh motive in the Christian community. Such love, as his followers learned from Jesus, was concerned for each person no matter what his social position or condition might be. The sinner was to be as precious in the sight of God as the righteous man, the unjust as significant as the just. The enemy was to be loved as much as the neighbor; the evil person was not to be condemned and rejected, but accepted and loved into the family of God. This love is not sentimentalism that sees only the bright side and overlooks the recalcitrant evil. It is full of compassion for the afflicted or tempted; it is full of determination that nothing shall prevent our doing our utmost to help and save them. The greater the need, the more urgent the service to meet that need; the greater the evil, the more patient and persistent the love to redeem persons from their evil tendencies. Such love never gives up, no matter how many the offenses or how hopeless the outcome appears to be. For the Christian finds God's love inexhaustible, and seeks to mediate this unfailing divine love to all, even to those who resist it most. In this perspective every person has infinite value and regardless of his misdeeds or unrelenting evil intentions is worth infinite cost to be redeemed. Redemptive love is never discouraged, never gives up, is never defeated. It keeps on loving in the face of every rebuff with an unselfish love as deathless as immortal life.

Universal loyalty was the eighth motive in the Christian community. Most loyalties are limited to the preferred few, to the members of our group, to the nation or people on our side who will be loyal to us. Communism is loyal to communists, capitalism is loyal to capitalists, labor is loyal to labor, nations are loyal to friendly powers in a rapidly shifting balance of power politics to hold the advantage over others who are assumed to be seeking to gain advantage over them. But a Christian community is not a closed society with interest in the selected few. There had been traditions of chosen people, elected by divine favor or called for service in the Kingdom of Heaven. But the call of Jesus was for all who would respond, take up their cross of self-sacrifice, and follow him. Even those who did not realize whom they were serving when they "did it to one of the least of these" were accepted. No one is outside the Father's love and care; even the shabby little sparrow is of value to God. Christian loyalty therefore reaches out to everyone everywhere. This has prompted evangelistic social service, hospital and educational missions to all people in every land. A Christian community is open to all and dedicated to the service of all. There can be no parties or enemies in set lines of determined opposition whom we are free to give up as beyond our province or concern. If they consider themselves enemies, they are potential friends worthy of redemptive love. If they renounce us, we are not to renounce them but continue faithfully in loyalty that never falters.

A society of this character Josiah Royce called the "Beloved Community." [1] Every other society teaches us by comparison with other

[1] *The Problem of Christianity* (New York: The Macmillan Co., 1931), I, 172-213.

persons who are better or worse, until we suffer the disease of self-consciousness. We learn how to behave by mutual criticism in competitive social situations. Moral thinking proceeds by comparing and criticizing the individual who is urged to struggle to improve himself to become like or better than others. These social tensions pit us against each other whether we revolt or conform. In cultivating the conscience we are set in social conflicts that condition us to moral independence and extreme individualism. This moral burden of the individual becomes almost unbearable in the weight of anxiety and guilt induced. To the Jew the law was such a burden, and for the Greek democracy perished in the conflicts of a heightened individualism that was merciless to individuals. The outcome is a self-will that separates us in tensions of opposition from other members of our society.

The Gospels show how Jesus taught men to love God and their neighbors as themselves. But the detailed questions of how to administer neighborly love in the many intricacies of human relationships are not yet answered. Paul in his letters to the churches works out detailed answers in the framework of the Christian community. The Beloved Community is a third object of love with love of God and neighbor. We are members one of another in the body of Christ, said Paul. This unity is not a bondage of the flesh in which rivalry and individualism produce natural hate along with natural love. It is a unity of the spirit in a new life miraculously created from heaven by divine grace. It is the spiritual community of love, the realm of heaven in the loving persons who love as members of one body whose head and spirit is Christ. By the Beloved Community the individual is saved from his original sin of isolation and enmity into a new spirit of love and peace which the world can neither give nor take away—the spirit of the risen and universal Christ. So Paul writes to the church in Ephesus:

But now in Christ Jesus you who once were far off have been brought near in the blood of Christ. For he is our peace, who has made us both one, and has broken down the dividing wall of hostility, by abolishing in his flesh the law of commandments and ordinances, that he might create in himself one new man in place of the two, so making peace, and might reconcile us both to God in one body through the cross, thereby bringing the hostility to an end. . . . So then you are no longer strangers and sojourners, but you are fellow citizens with the saints and members of the household of God, built upon the foundation of the apostles and prophets, Christ Jesus himself being the chief cornerstone, in whom the whole structure is joined together and grows into a holy temple in the Lord; in whom you also are built into it for a dwelling place of God in the Spirit. (Eph. 2:13-22 R.S.V.)

Again, writing to the church in Corinth, he says:

For just as the body is one and has many members, and all the members of the body, though many, are one body, so it is with Christ. For by one Spirit we were all baptized into one body—Jews or Greeks, slaves or free—and all were made to drink of one Spirit. For the body does not consist of one member but of many. . . . The eye cannot say to the hand, "I have no need of you," nor again the head to the feet, "I have no need of you." On the contrary, the parts of the body which seem to be weaker are indispensable. . . . But God has so adjusted the body, giving the greater honor to the inferior part, that there may be no discord in the body, but that the members may have the same care for one another. If one member suffers, all suffer together; if one member is honored, all rejoice together. (I Cor. 12:12-17 R.S.V.)

The genius of Christian communities is a spirit of organic unity rising from faith in a divine leader with whom all members share in redemptive love. This unifying spiritual love is creative of new life that forgives enemies, reconciles hostility in sympathy, returns good for evil, and aspires to extend a universal loyalty to every creature. The Christian Church is a beloved community that saves the lonely, guilt-ridden individual from self-consciousness and self-will by enfolding him in one body of new life by energies that seem to come from a higher order of reality. To the psychologist that reality remains a mystery, but the consequences of a spiritual energizing are evident in the new life of unity and love. That Christians are human enough to quarrel and separate in church divisions no one can deny. The visible church with all its failures and imperfections has this treasure of community love in earthen vessels. Nevertheless the treasure appears again and again, often enough to give evidence of a church invisible, a spirit of love that has universal dimensions—"that they all may be one" (John 17:21).

3. Can Modern Society Be Christian?

Twenty centuries have passed across the stage of world history since Jesus and his disciples founded their Beloved Community. To them the time was short; they lived in daily expectation of the end of their world and the coming of a new era. They were children of Israel who inherited from that culture a lively apocalyptic faith that God was about to intervene in the affairs of men by a sudden catastrophe that would overturn the kingdoms of earth and establish a millennium of divine government from heaven. Jesus seemed to fulfill the prophecy that a Messiah would come from God to lead his people and usher in a new Kingdom of Heaven. There were many who desired to make him king of Israel, but he rejected the role of political and military leader to be the Suffering Servant portrayed in Isaiah, one who would take upon himself the sins and sorrows of the world to free men by voluntary sacrifice from their bondage to evil. He accepted the cross as his sacrifice and God's willingness to save men at any cost.

At first the disciples were bewildered at the tragic and humiliating crucifixion of their leader, until convinced by his resurrection and ascension that he was now in a larger and more powerful way active in world history. Would he not soon return from the clouds and set aside earthly kingdoms and establish the reign of God on earth for a thousand years to come? As the years and centuries moved on, the followers of Jesus have seen many kingdoms overturned, but the visible intervention from heaven which they looked for so ardently has not come. Perhaps they misunderstood Jesus after all, to clothe in physical terms what was to him a spiritual movement. "The kingdom of God is within you" (Luke 17:21), he said. It is like a bit of yeast hidden within a lump of meal that quietly expands until the whole is leavened (Luke 13:21). His second coming was then viewed as a spiritual advent into the lives of those who accept him and live in his spirit. As Paul said, "I live; yet not I, but Christ liveth in me" (Gal.

CHRISTIAN LOVE

2:20). In the fellowship of the Beloved Community the spirit of Christ was felt to be present. "For where two or three are gathered together in my name, there am I in the midst of them." (Matt. 18:20.)

From such experiences Christian communities were established in the cities of the Mediterranean world and eventually spread to every continent, until today the Christian religion numbers 592,406,542 adherents.[2] The expansion of Christian movements is impressive indeed. But the tide may be turning as other interests gain momentum in our time. There are indications that the influence of Christianity may be declining due to several reasons. The strength of Christianity is weakened by divisions into rival sects and denominations. It is weakened even more by the indifference and preoccupation of its members. It is neglected by a surge of popular interest in counter-attractions that take people away from church on Sunday—such as sports, theaters, recreation, motoring—and absorb them exhaustively every day—in business, shopping, politics, industrial bargaining, and struggles for power. It is vigorously threatened by anti-Christian movements that ridicule, restrain, ban, or persecute Christian organizations and activities in many countries.

In the face of these conditions can modern society be Christian? To an impartial observer the answer is likely to be No. The modern social trends are increasingly secular. The astonishing achievements of the natural sciences with their harvest of practical inventions and technics have so caught the popular imagination that our generation turns less to God and more to man for the answers to its needs. Modern communications bring human events before us hourly, until we are so absorbed in keeping up with human affairs by radio, video, and the printed page there is little time to seek God and the less obvious realm of heaven. The mass production and distribution of economic goods awaken acquisitive desires insatiably to gain and possess more and more material things to the neglect of spiritual values. The competitive struggle for power and social status keeps us anxiously driving on in frantic efforts to arrive, to overtake, and to get ahead of others, or else. Altogether these compulsive drives and social pressures add

[2] *The World Almanac* (New York World-Telegram, 1948), p. 572.

210

up to a sensate culture that neglects spiritual interests and a naturalism that denies spiritual realities. In such a climate religion and morality, truth, beauty, and unselfish love are bound to suffer.[3]

So far as eye can see there is slight probability that modern society will be *inclusively* Christian in our time. An inclusive Christian society to govern all men belongs to another world than ours, as the apocalyptic view has recognized, requiring the end of this social order to begin a new one. Whether the church will ever again hold as dominating a position as in medieval European society is doubtful. One may question also whether it is psychologically healthy for persons to be dominated by any external authority, whether sacred or secular. At any rate the tides of secularism are too lusty and powerful in our society to predict their unconditional surrender to a religious authority unless that religion exerts temporal power and glory to outrival secular power and prestige. In this case religious motivations will become so entangled with sensate lusts that power would then actually be more secular than Christian. And men would again revolt and seek to overthrow a church that assumed the role of dominating temporal power.

There is little more probability that modern society will be *exclusively* Christian. For other religions will rightly claim a place in the sun and appeal to our sense of religious tolerance, fair play, freedom of conscience in a democracy that is safe for differences. A Christian zeal to exterminate or replace other religions would prove a boomerang of feudal and suicidal proportions, as holy wars have always proved to be. Furthermore, any exclusive spirit would contradict the inherent principle of Christianity to express universal love and loyalty. Men would rise up against a religion that sought to be exclusive, and the most conscientious Christians would be the first to protest against a church that seeks to dominate or exclude others. Even when Christian communities are separatist, to have freedom of conscience they are open to any who desire to join who will accept the rules of the order. An exclusive society is not a Christian society.

[3] See P. A. Sorokin, *The Crisis of Our Age* (New York: E. P. Dutton & Co., 1941); and *The Reconstruction of Humanity* (Boston: The Beacon Press, 1948).

What then is the aim of Christianity in any society? Is it not to be *contagiously* Christian? Rather than to dominate or exclude the Christian movement aims to attract others by the character of its life. As a missionary religion the principle of universal love and loyalty has sought to share Christian values with all who desire them. Its evangelistic effort has mistakenly appeared as a desire to make converts and win new members to the church, even by proselyting or taking them away from rival religious groups. But the essence of Christian evangelism, manifest by Jesus and his followers who best understand him, is to serve every person according to his need at whatever cost. This evangelism of the unselfish deed is far more eloquent than the persuasive word, for it is a demonstration of the Christian spirit of universal love. And the psychological effect of an act of unselfish love is to reproduce itself by the contagious power of example, the irresistible attraction of love to invite a loving response.

The test of Christian influence is not how many persons join the church, significant as that may be to the organization and support of a church program. The actual test is not statistical or organizational but psychological. It is the Christian spirit that is decisive, the inner motives and attitudes that come to social expression in redemptive love. To bear the name of a Christian is not so genuine a sign as to express the Christian spirit in attitudes and acts of unselfish love. Deeper than the verbal level of identity and communication is the dynamic motive power of identification and community. A person who expresses a Christian spirit of love is a contagious center of enlarging community fellowship.

We have defined Christian love as the experience of family love centered in God as heavenly Father. The test of Christian progress is the manifestation of such love. Is Christian love increasing or decreasing in our society? Do more people increasingly care and feel responsible for the welfare of others? Is the spirit of one human family of active social responsibility waxing or waning in society at large? Are we like Paul surrounded by a cloud of witnesses, an invisible community of love beyond the visible church? Let us examine the evidences of unselfish love and service in our society.

There is in our time no little concern to provide relief and re-habilitation to people in distress. This unwillingness to let strangers starve or suffer unattended is a motive equivalent to Christian love as portrayed by Jesus in the parable of the good Samaritan, who rescued the wounded man on the Jericho road (Luke 10:33). This motive is not confined to members of Christian churches; it is an obligation increasingly accepted by citizens and governments in our world today. The American Red Cross, founded by Clara Barton in 1881, and the International Red Cross, founded in 1884, have for over sixty years responded to crises of war, disaster, and famine with relief provided by the voluntary contributions of millions of unnamed, unselfish do-nors, many of whom give not only money but life blood for un-known strangers. Public and private welfare agencies in town, coun-ty, and state administer relief to those in need as a matter of course without a doubt as to the responsibility of all to care for each one who may be unable to support himself. During and since World War II overseas relief to the impoverished and dispossessed of other conti-nents has been led by religious bodies as the American Friends Service Committee, the United Jewish Appeal, the World Council of Church-es service representing major Protestant denominations, and the Catholic Charities. But it has not ceased with religious movements; the responsibility to rescue the perishing is accepted by countless others in friendship trains, CARE packages, the United Nations Relief and Rehabilitation Administration, followed by the European Recovery Program, the United Nation's International Children's Emergency Fund, the Silent Guest Plan, and tons of packages privately mailed to persons in other countries.

Social work, first pioneered by religious groups, has been extended in secular agencies whose skilled professional and volunteer workers serve their fellow men in unselfish devotion. Social settlements and neighborhood houses in city slums, playgrounds and recreational fa-cilities, scouting and camping agencies to build character, child guid-ance agencies, foster homes, Big Brother and Sister movements, Alcoholics Anonymous, juvenile courts and training schools for de-linquents or the feebleminded, are but a few of the social services offered. Case work supplements group work with individual diagnosis and treatment for struggling families and unadjusted persons of every age and condition. It would be impressive to add up the number of people who contribute to the support and leadership of these social services, expressing the motive of love as responsible citizens and good neighbors. Why should so many be interested in the welfare of strangers whom they do not know and who have no legal charge upon them? Our secular society is adopting to this extent the contagious spirit of a Beloved Community.

Health services in our society also enact the spirit of healing love. The hospitals may not bear a Christian name—though many do—but they are standing with open doors to care for the sick and afflicted. They are supported by community funds and professions which may not confess but actually demonstrate motives of religious love and service. Physicians and nurses, laboratory technicians, occupational therapists, social workers, clinical psychologists, and chaplains work on health teams with unsparing devotion to heal strangers who have no claim upon them but that of suffering fellow creatures. Health services are psychological and social as well as physical treatments to meet the spiritual needs so inextricably involved in health. The health of every man, woman, and child is a responsibility recognized by many communities. Public health services are moving from the local to the international level in the World Health Organization, an outgrowth of the League of Nations and the United Nations. Sixty-three nations have agreed in the first clause of the W.H.O. constitution that "health is a state of complete physical, mental, and social well-being and not merely the absence of disease or infirmity."

This means a new social responsibility, says Brock Chisholm, executive secretary of the W.H.O., upon each individual to live in peace and contribute to the welfare of others. Never before, he observes, has social responsibility been recognized on such a wide international basis. What is most pressing is the translation of what we know into practice. It is quite possible now to eradicate almost all the major diseases of the world. Nothing keeps these diseases alive but ignorance and self-interest.

The problem facing the world is not a problem between governments, but of individual people all over the world. It is the problem of individuals reaching out toward maturity, becoming adults. . . .

Until recently we could progress from infantile loyalties through those that attached to the immediate community of the family and later to the little group outside the family; it did not matter if millions of people did not get beyond a provincial loyalty to a relatively small group. Now it is of great concern that loyalty should not stop at anything short of world loyalty. No citizen is fully developed short of the status of world citizen.[4]

To implement this world-wide responsibility for the health of others an International Congress on Mental Health was held in London, August 11 to 21, 1948. Preparatory commissions in some forty-seven countries were at work during the year preceding to explore problem areas by informal discussions and report to the international congress. The congress considered the problems of world citizenship and group relationships, wartime experiences, economic security, cultural clashes and fascist infection, family problems and psychological disturbance, mental health in industry and industrial relations, planning for mental health, organizing and training health teams, public relations, and the like. From this London conference has come a permanent World Federation for Mental Health with representatives in each member country to work for better human relations.

The largest educational project today is the United Nations Educational, Scientific and Cultural Organization (UNESCO), whose purpose is stated in its constitution to which thirty-eight nations have adhered:

To contribute to peace and security by promoting collaboration among the nations through education, science and culture in order to further universal respect for justice, for the rule of law and for the human rights and fundamental freedoms which are affirmed for the peoples of the world, without distinction of race, sex, language or religion, by the Charter of the United Nations.[5]

[4] Brock Chisholm, "Organization for World Health," *Mental Hygiene*, XXXII (July, 1948), 368. Used by permission.
[5] M. S. Eisenhower, *UNESCO and You*, Department of State Publication 2904 (Washington, D.C.: U.S. Govt. Printing Office, Sept., 1947), p, l.

At the first session of the general conference of UNESCO, held in Paris, 1946, a program of over two hundred projects was proposed to be carried out, but only a small number were feasible under the first annual budget of $6,000,000. The program adopted at the second session of UNESCO at the Mexico City Conference in 1947 had a budget voted for each item. This program for 1948 is grouped under six heads as follows:

1. *Reconstruction* of schools, libraries, museums, laboratories, publications, press, radio, films, youth camps and duty-free educational materials in the war-devastated areas of Asia and Europe. The United States Commission has already raised over $100,000,000 for such reconstruction from 300 voluntary organizations.

2. *Communication* or international exchange of persons, information, and materials. UNESCO will facilitate exchange of students and scholars; remove obstacles to the free flow of ideas through press, radio, and films; promote public libraries and the distribution of publications.

3. *Education* is to be enlarged by pilot projects on modern methods of adult education, seek to form an international association of universities to encourage international relations and equivalence of academic degrees, hold educational seminars, promote understanding of the United Nations, improve textbooks and teaching materials, send educational missions on request of member states, draft charters for teachers and youth, and further the education of labor and of women.

4. *Cultural interchange* in the arts, letters, philosophy, and museums by international institutes, articles to journals, world catalogs, production of films to stimulate arts, translation of great books, exchange of museum exhibits, free access to archaeological sites, international round-table discussions, and regional centers of cultural co-operation.

5. *Human and Social Relations.* Searching inquiries into the tensions affecting international understanding will be carried out by UNESCO and leading social scientists in 1948. A philosophical analysis of current ideological conflicts will be pursued, also a study of international collaboration as a new social development, forums held by scientific organizations for popular discussion of recent developments, preparation of a scientific and cultural history of mankind, and a world register of workers, institutes, activities and research resources in selected fields.

6. *Natural sciences*, pure and applied, need international co-operation. UNESCO will maintain field science co-operation offices to perform liaison tasks between advanced and less advanced regions, convene a panel

of experts to advise on the development of science in Latin America, consult with governments on high altitude stations for scientific study, stimulate co-ordination of cartographic activities, provide grants to international scientific organizations; co-operate in the enterprises of the United Nations and its specialized agencies, as the forthcoming conference on the preservation of natural resources.[6]

The launching of these projects in developing a world community of understanding, appreciation, and co-operation at national and international levels is only a beginning. UNESCO also urges each national commission to form local councils in various cities and districts to promote discussion and arouse grass-roots participation by as many citizens as possible. Our national commission for UNESCO is urging every citizen to aid in educational reconstruction in war-devastated countries, to make personal exhibits and programs to portray UNESCO aims and projects, to take an active part in training the young generation for peace, to join in adult education, and to help promote good will and understanding among racial and religious groups. Voluntary organizations are invited to affiliate, and many have already done so to further the aims of UNESCO in creating a universal community of mankind.

These activities and services briefly surveyed are specimens of a dawning sense of responsibility for other people in one world community. This evidence is submitted in answer to the question, How Christian is our society today? Our society, we conclude, will not be Christian in an inclusive or exclusive sense. But it may become more Christian in a contagious sense. For the spirit of love is abroad in the world, and many people are responding to invitations to love one another. It is more urgent to work for the contagious spread of the spirit of love in a divided world than it is to win converts to any one of the many rival religious bodies. When a church is a useful means of grace and an open channel of love to all people, then the more active members the better. But the great need and the task of incomparable urgency is to spread the contagion of love in the motives and

<hr />

[6] *Digest of UNESCO Program for 1948*, Department of State Publication 3081 (Washington, D.C.: U.S. Govt. Printing Office, March, 1948).

actions of human beings. To the extent love goes outward it will strengthen the resources and membership of a world community.

4. WHAT CAN WE EXPECT OF THE CHURCH?

The need for a world community has never been more urgent than today. Does the Christian Church meet that need? The first Christian body in Jerusalem aroused great enthusiasm. Through the centuries the idea of the church as one body in Christ has awakened many hopes. Has this ideal come true, or does its glowing promise turn out to be an empty mirage? Is the church actually the Beloved Community the world is waiting for? To what extent is the church a manifestation of contagious Christian love?

A fair appraisal will recognize that the church has not yet become a completely loving community. The followers of Jesus have acknowledged his spirit of love and sought to follow him, but hesitate and lag behind. There are limitations and resistances, oppositions and differences, that delay our progress in love.

Christian unity is broken by divisions within the church. Controversies and dissensions have plagued the church in every generation from its beginning. It is natural that earnest minds will differ in their view of doctrine and organizational procedure. But why do differences become separations? If there is no room for difference of opinion in a community, the unity is brittle and fragile indeed. And if friends differ, why does that make them enemies? Must we disagree disagreeably? This divisive tendency is a serious historical weakness in Protestantism. The habit of solving differences by separation and registering protests with walkouts continues to break churches apart into splinter-parties that turn against each other in unchristian rivalry. Love is lost in the scuffle, yielding to pride and stubborn resistance. Will Christians learn how to differ and yet resolve to love?

Christian love is further retarded by coercive intolerance. When a church coerces its members to believe one way and no other, freedom is denied and democracy fails. The right of the individual conscience is crushed, and respect for personality is forgotten in the pressures of conformity. Such intolerance drives the dissenter to revolt and makes separation appear as the only recourse of a free conscience. In this way divisions are created by intolerance. Religious convictions are deep; they mean so much to the earnest believer. Consequently religious people have shown a fanatical zeal in persecuting the heretic who believes differently. We have seen in the family how coercion defeats love; so in the church coercive intolerance rouses enmities, anathemas, and excommunications. It denies the right to be right to anyone who differs, and refuses to recognize as a church any other religious group than one's own. Scorn and rejection are not the best traits of love.

Hunger for power and prestige also vies with Christian love. The wiles of the ego are subtle and deceptive. A person may renounce his egoistic striving and devote himself to his church. Then his church becomes the mask for his ego, and he vests the untamed and displaced ego drives in jealous ambition for its power and prestige. His pride and superiority are gratified unconsciously in belonging to a church that is superior to others, of which he can be proud. His boasting and striving is not for himself; neither is the lofty grandeur of its spires, the wealth of its treasury, or the power to overwhelm its enemies and build an empire on earth to which politicians and rulers will defer with subservient homage. When men identify their ego hungers with a church, it becomes an insatiable power interest that crushes opposition and rides over the individual for the inexorable destiny. Love is then sacrificed on the altar of power.

These drives produce hostility when rival sects are viewed as enemies. Intolerance channels hostile motives of coercion, persecution, and rejection against the dissenter. Hunger for power and prestige turns hostile energies into gaining the superiority of one church over others. Hostility is the mortal enemy of love; they are opposite moods that contradict each other. If we love enough, we can differ without division, intolerance, or struggle for power; but every hostility, whether sacred or secular, is a threat to love. Love and hostility cannot dwell in peace together; they may alternate, but one is always on top, and the gain of one is the loss of the other.

Love has another enemy equally dangerous. Indifference kills love as surely as hostility. The angry person is very much in earnest, giving full attention and energy to the object of his hostility. But the indifferent person is uninterested, inattentive, and inactive. Churches falter more from the indifference of their members than from any other cause. The man who joins the church reluctantly, takes his vows carelessly, attends rarely, declines to take responsibility, or participate actively is dead weight. When the majority are inactive, a church has little vitality or strength to do more than go through the formalities of keeping up appearances. This inertia is prevalent in many Protestant churches today whose influence is thereby declining. To the question of survival is added the question of futility. Churches may keep open, but little more. The loss of contagious love is the most devastating effect of indifference, for the indifferent church is not meeting the needs of men with the deeds of love. There is no overflow of loving service in feeding the hungry, clothing the naked, visiting the sick, uplifting the poor, releasing the captive and oppressed, comforting the lonely and brokenhearted. The contagious dynamic of Christian love is sapped by indifference until it becomes nothing more than a quiescent memory of a forgotten word.

But this is not the whole story. There are Christians who have not succumbed entirely either to hostility or to indifference, who find in their church fellowship potential resources for enlarging love. Their church is not a communion of saints who have arrived at final perfection, but a body of fellow workers and worshipers who are ready to grow in Christian love together. This calls for earnest dedication and faithful labors in the contagious spirit of redemptive love. There will be mistakes and failures, differences and misunderstandings, but there will also be readiness to admit errors, willingness to forgive and try again in renewed love. There will be those who feel an urgent responsibility to reach out beyond the favored few to other people who are lonely or left out or caught in the bitter pangs of enmity. There will be those who have serious discontent with sectarian rivalry that dwells in smug aloofness and assumed superiority, who are tireless in seeking for common ground, generous in compromise to find ways of agreement by understanding that will bring church union in reconciling love.

There is no denying the fact of Christian love. Even in the midst of hostility and indifference love is active in religious and secular movements of our time. It is not within our power to predict the ultimate outcome of these movements. One may not wisely under-estimate the power of hostility or the attrition of indifference. But the contagious power of love is no less dynamic than its enemies. It is the genius of redemptive love to forgive and transform enemies (hostility) and strangers (indifference) into friends. And there is reason to believe in the power of this responsible love.

Christian love will make common cause with all who honestly and earnestly desire to love in the spirit of Jesus. This will bring Christians into harmony with others of whatever denomination or creed so long as such love is the basic motive. Love will bring us into unity with Jews and Moslems, with Hindus and followers of every faith who are devoted to unselfish love. What about the Communists; are they not open enemies toward the Christian faith? Even so, Jesus asks his followers to love their enemies, to bless persecutors and pray for their welfare. In so far as Communists work for social justice, sharing, and voluntary co-operation in love, they are to that extent with and not against us. And if there are evildoers among us by whatever name, are they not also children of our Father in heaven, for whom Christ died and to whom Christians are to show forgiving love? Such love will seek common ground where all may meet as brothers and labor together for an honest community of understanding. There is a search for unity that is deeper than a passing ripple; it is a moving tide that is gaining momentum to overflow the barriers and suspicions of a divided world.

On August 22, 1948, a World Council of Churches was established. Meeting in Amsterdam, delegates from 135 denominations with head-quarters in 44 countries joined together in a united church council that may well prove to be the most significant of all councils in the long history of the Christian Church. It was the culmination of years of planning and working toward unity, drawing together the major

Protestant and some of the Eastern Orthodox churches, who say, "We intend to stay together." This opens the way for continuous co-operation among these religious bodies with their full approval in a new atmosphere of brotherhood that declares disunity a sin. Though other churches of the Christian family were not represented, and the opportunities of the new World Council are far greater than budget or staff to implement them, yet it is the dawn of a new day in church unity.

The World Council of Churches has come into existence because we have already recognized a responsibility to one another's churches in our Lord Jesus Christ. There is but one Lord and one Body. Therefore we cannot rest content with our present divisions. Before God, we are responsible for one another. We see already what some of our responsibilities are, and God will show us more. But we embark upon our work in the World Council of Churches in penitence for what we are and in hope for what we shall be. At this inaugural Assembly, we ask for the continued prayer of all participating churches that God may guide it in his wisdom, saving us both from false claims and from faithless timidity.[7]

Is there a growing community life? The desire for unity is more a hope than a realization. Declarations and documents are historic, but the word is not yet the full-bodied organism of a living world community of love. But there are persistent gropings toward larger understanding and fellowship among the churches.

Such churches can be homes of Christian love. Yet Christian love is not content forever to remain at home. For it has a mission outgoing as well as incoming. This mission is to bring other people into its home and to extend the home out to other people wherever they may be. Christian love is ever building a larger home in the expanding appreciation of a universal loving community. Not to turn them away from their own homes, for every faith and every service is of unique value. But rather it is the task of love to surround every home with a larger community of redemptive love. Jesus called this the Kingdom of God. For this Christians pray; for this they wait in hope and faith; for this

[7] From the *Christian Century*, Oct. 6, 1948. Copyright by the *Christian Century* and reprinted by permission.

they need to work more ardently in the enlarging outreach of a love that flows wherever children of God find and follow the unerring purpose.

5. Achieving Maturity

As the secretary of the World Health Organization has said, the problem facing the world today is one of "reaching out toward maturity." A new kind of citizen is necessary if the human race is to survive, one who will outgrow infantile anxieties and loyalties to be at home with all peoples as members of a larger family. A mature person will replace hostility and suspicion with growing appreciation and responsible love for other persons. The urgent issue confronting us today is whether we can develop enough of that kind of maturity, soon enough in enough places. We have all been children, and we have a right to be children for a while, but the time comes when we must outgrow childishness or we become a serious problem to ourselves and to others. We cannot have the kind of society we need until each of us puts away childish attitudes and takes upon himself a mature responsibility for social values. As Paul confessed of his own need to grow, "When I was a child, I spake as a child, I understood as a child, I thought as a child: but when I became a man, I put away childish things" (I Cor. 13:11).

Not always do we succeed as adults in putting away childish things. No longer children, yet we may have childish impulses. Wishing to be dependent is childish; it is seeking authorities to think and decide for us because we feel more secure when we can lean on someone stronger. It is childish to enjoy the receiving of gifts more than giving or sharing them with others, hoping for a Santa Claus or a paternal government to supply every need from the cradle to the grave. Is it not just as childish to want a religion of absolute dependence, a God who does it all for us, a Saviour who paid it all so that salvation can be free, a world so evil that we can do nothing about it but wait for divine intervention at the end of the world? It is immature to be fixated in love, with no desire to grow or enlarge our love to the larger family of the whole earth. Growing love is mature, but its development is often arrested until we are content with partial interests or regress to infantile attitudes toward other persons.

Wishing to assert independence is another immaturity of arrested growth. It is adolescent to revolt against every authority, to assert my independence in every situation at whatever cost to the larger good, to seek to prove my superiority on every occasion by whatever devices will cast reflections on others to demonstrate how much better I am than you. In striving for superiority one may resist opportunities to learn in humility, taking the scornful pose of one who knows it all and cannot stoop to ask a question that may reveal ignorance or admit he could have been in error. It is immature to struggle to get ahead of others, unable to relax or enjoy present values in the nervous compulsion to push on beyond others, suspicious of friends and resentful of competitors who may be more successful, determined to rise to a dominant position of ascendant and self-sufficient glory.

The mature person is interdependent. By outgrowing the indulgent dependence of childhood and the assertive independence of adolescence he comes into a larger appreciation of others as well as of himself. He honestly recognizes his need of others at the same time he realizes their need of him. He is ready to learn of everyone he meets, as was Confucius in saying, "When three of us walk together, two shall be my teachers." He is also ready to help others in a responsible comradeship that does not hesitate to bear each other's burdens or to go a second mile in useful service for the larger good. Instead of working against others as rivals he works with them as fellow laborers in community enterprises that take account of the abilities of each and the needs of all. Mature persons have outgrown the crippling anxieties that impel them to move away from or against other persons; they have grown into a free association of open selves in an open society where each is welcome and worthy.

The true self, as Künkel shows, is not the aggressive-defensive ego which stands off in fear and anger from other separate and rival egos.[8] The true self is a we-experience in which one feels his

[8] *In Search of Maturity* (New York: Charles Scribner's Sons, 1943).

interdependent unity with others in a common life of sharing. The infant enjoys this close feeling of unity with the mother in the original we-experience of nourishing love. But then come separations and denials that disappoint and frustrate the infant in a sharp breach of the we, leaving him lonely and resentful. He is thereby forced to grow away from others and develop an independence of his own. But that is a halfway house along the trail of growing up, where he is anxious and hostile in his insecure efforts to establish independence. The next step, without which he remains immature, is to achieve the mature we, and restore a new social unity of sharing life with others in grateful and responsible fellowship.

The development of maturing is a growing series of linkages with other persons in social relationships. This process of expanding linkages is delineated by H. A. Overstreet as the building of many bridges outward as we overcome lonely reticence and fearful inadequacies in enlarging connections with others.[9] We are born inarticulate and must learn word linkages to our world; we are born self-centered and must grow into relationships with other persons; we are born irresponsible and must learn to take our share of the load; we are born isolated particulars and must grow into larger wholeness. This is the school of life to which we go as long as we live, never through learning, always needing to keep on growing with widening social relations.

How does Christianity affect this maturing process? The whole dynamic of the Christian movement at its best is to love more and more persons with growing interest, appreciation, and responsibility. From the Judaeo-Christian imperative of loving God with all one's mind and strength each growing person is urged to honor his father and mother, to cherish his brothers and sisters, to love his neighbors as himself, to open his hand to strangers, to love and forgive his enemies. It is for their sakes that Jesus consecrates himself to be faithful in his Father's business of healing and redeeming love, to draw everyone together in one family—"That they all may be one; as thou, Father, art in me, and I in thee" (John 17:21). In these developing interests there are widening and deepening linkages with other persons in the constructive relationships of maturity.

There are critics who insist that the Christian religion keeps people immature by encouraging them to feel dependent upon a God who is asked to do for them what they would otherwise do for themselves and to trust blindly in authorities who tell them what to believe and what not to do in restrictive moral codes of "thou shalt not." Did not Jesus require unquestioning faith and unswerving obedience with no hesitation or doubts in sacrificial devotion? Did he not enjoin his followers to be immature when he said, "Except ye be converted, and become as little children, ye shall not enter into the kingdom of heaven" (Matt. 18:3)? Why should he demand of adults that they become as little children?

It is not easy to understand exactly what Jesus meant in this saying. There are some who think he required his followers to be innocent as a child, but when we know children better, we see that they are not so innocent after all. There are others who think a follower of Jesus is to be as weak and dependent as a child, that man's weakness is God's opportunity to do what man in his pride cannot do for himself. Others expound the trusting attitudes of children, who are able to believe the impossible; accenting the folly of reason, they urge us to be irrational that faith may flourish the more to our salvation.

But none of these interpretations, ingenious as they are, seem to comprehend the meaning of Jesus. The key to his actual intention is the following verse, which declares that whoever shall "humble himself as this little child, the same is greatest in the kingdom of heaven" (Matt. 18:4). What Jesus requires is the humility to learn anew, to give up the pride of what is already attained, to start over again as a beginner. This is an arduous requirement, for we hold desperately to every gain we have made. Who wants to be a baby again, to know nothing and learn again the hard way? But Jesus asks his followers to give up their pride as well as their possessions. "Except a man be born again, he cannot see the kingdom of God" (John 3:3) was too much for the ruler who came by night. Yet Jesus requires no less than such humility, to be willing to give up every gain and start at a new beginning, to lay aside pretensions, to be teachable and willing to learn, flexible and willing to grow. There is nothing to lose but our chains of half-truths, halfway compromises, deceptions, and rigid defenses. To sell all for this new treasure is to take great risks, yet the adventure is well worth the cost if one has the courageous humility and devotion to start learning again in honest growth toward a new maturity.

What Jesus offers is a personal and social revolution. If a little child is greatest in the kingdom of heaven, then every established order of pride and position totters. The kingdoms of earth magnify the big fellows, the mighty, strong men of power and ruthless cleverness who have gained prestige and position by ruthless aggression. But the Kingdom of Heaven turns society upside down until the smallest is the greatest, the last is first, the least have the most value, the strong and wise are the devoted servants of the weak and ignorant. This is the blueprint which Jesus offers of a Christian society, in which all belong to each in one family of God. Instead of, as in a hierarchy, struggling to gain the highest position, we are advised to sit at the foot of the table in deference to others whom we are to serve in love. Instead of lifting ourself up above others we are to decrease that others may increase. Rather than puffing up in the fullness of pride we are to empty ourselves of such pretensions and descend to save the lowest and the least.

Maturity is the aim of all growth. Jesus sets a high standard for growth when he says, "Be ye therefore perfect (mature), even as your Father which is in heaven" (Matt. 5:48). How can he expect mortal men to be as mature as God is? Is not the gulf between the creature and the Creator too vast to mock us with an impossible perfectionism? But there may be ethical traits in which Jesus saw a genuine possibility of men and women becoming godlike. This John indicates to be a quality of love that is divine. God is love, and he loves us; so we are to love each other. Jesus demonstrates such an overflowing and outreaching love: As the Father has loved me, so have I loved you; in this spirit love one another (John 15).

Paul unfolds the self-giving divine love in his doctrine of kenosis. God as Father was willing to be Son; as Son he was willing to be born in a humble stable as a helpless infant. This Son of God came to save the least and the lost, to heal the sick and uplift the fallen, to wash his disciples' feet as their master-servant; to be mocked and spat upon, despised and rejected, crucified and buried, that others, even his enemies, might be forgiven and reconciled to God. Consequently he who so humbled and emptied himself in love for others was worthy to be exalted to the maturity of God, whose love is perfect.

Let this mind be in you, which was also in Christ Jesus: who, being in the form of God . . . made himself of no reputation, and took upon him the form of a servant . . . and being found in fashion as a man, he humbled himself, and became obedient unto death, even the death of the cross. . . . Having the same love . . . let nothing be done through strife or vainglory; but in lowliness of mind let each esteem others better than themselves. (Phil. 2:5-8, 2-3.)

How does Paul learn this? Evidently, he would declare, from his own experience of God as revealed in Jesus. Paul was childish when he sought to be wise and legalistic; he was immature when he became a zealous persecutor striving to prove himself better and more righteous than others. He put away childish ways when he was willing to begin again as a child, blinded by the overwhelming sense of previous failure, yet humbling himself, ready to be led and willing to be taught by the master Teacher.

How do we learn this maturing love? As we give up our pride of striving to be better and higher than others; as we learn to take new beginnings as humble learners, spontaneous to seek and eager to grow; such outward growing in love is the only way to mature. We are all children playing along a shore of infinite mystery, as one scientist in his humility has said. If we would launch forth upon that sea of mystery, or even begin to understand the wonder of a grain of sand between our fingers, we too shall need humility to keep on learning, and divine grace to keep on maturing forever. Life grows best in a loving community. In that spirit love will be with us even unto the end of the world.

Index

229

Illness, 199
Illusions, 74
Immaturity, 37, 147, 224, 226, 228
Immortality, 175
Impartial, 42
Impotence, 17, 75
Impulses, 18, 49, 51, 58, 59, 60, 61, 90, 103, 104, 165, 170, 181, 188, 191, 223
Inclusive, 211
Incompatibility, 151
Independence, 17, 62, 74, 111, 133, 224
India, 29, 169
Indifference, 13, 33, 83, 94, 176, 197, 210, 219
Individual, 199
Individualism, 207
Individuality, 122
Indulgent, 17
Industrial strife, 166
Infant, 67, 90, 131, 188, 225
Inferior, 57
Inferiority, 40, 138, 158, 178, 189
Inhibitions, 106, 189
Initiative, 23, 62, 133, 186, 197
Innate, 50, 52, 53
Inopportunism, 21
Insecurity, 38, 63, 185
Insight, 16, 60, 64
Inspiration, 85, 130
Instigators, 79
Instinct, 49-52, 53, 93
Institute for Pastoral Care, 161
Integration, 58
Integrity, 145
Intellect, 55
Intention, 52, 55, 63, 64, 92, 105, 117, 226
Interaction, 16, 93, 105, 126, 144, 146, 163, 172
Interchange, 19, 53
Interdependent, 82, 112, 224
Interest, 13, 16, 19, 26, 51, 56, 61, 63, 68, 74, 78, 88, 132, 134, 146, 177
Intergroup, 95
Interpersonal, 44, 48, 52, 63, 65, 66, 67, 92, 93, 95, 105, 147, 171, 173, 180
Interpersonal psychology, 56, 193
Interpersonal relationships, 15, 38, 63, 80, 108, 114, 121, 122, 125, 132, 135, 199
Interview, 87
Intolerance, 218
Introvert, 63, 132
Invent, 18
Isaiah, 209
Isolates, 76, 79, 225
Isolation, 74, 80, 101, 199

Jain, 48
James, 104, 126
James, William, 49, 52, 53, 104, 105, 195
Japan, 169, 178
Jealousy, 168, 219

Jeremiah, 62
Jerusalem, 128, 202
Jesus, 21, 23, 24, 25, 27, 28, 29, 30, 31, 32, 44, 45, 47, 48, 60, 61, 63, 64, 73, 85, 92, 97, 98, 103, 109, 110, 128, 165, 168, 201, 202, 203, 206, 207, 209, 212, 213, 218, 221, 226, 227, 228
Jew, 60, 128, 207, 221
Jewish Board of Guardians, 78, 94
John, 24, 28, 29, 30, 31, 47, 62, 64, 106, 121, 127, 165, 169, 205, 209, 226, 227
Johnson, P. E., 53, 104, 157
Joseph, 168
Joys, 12, 26, 45, 84, 129, 143, 149
Judaeo-Christian, 83, 144, 225
Judaism, 48, 60
Jung, C. G., 57, 60, 63
Justice, 12, 16, 86, 191, 221

Kagawa, Toyohiko, 11
Kant, Immanuel, 175
Kenosis, 228
Kierkegaard, Sören, 41
Kill, 72, 170
Kindness, 95
Kingdom, 38, 65, 165, 183, 184, 209, 227
Kingdom of God, 48, 98, 203, 204, 206, 209, 222, 226
Kinsey, A. C., 140
Kiss, 132, 138, 149, 183, 185
Knowledge, 18, 25, 44, 59, 67, 112
Knudson, A. C., 37, 166
Künkel, Fritz, 60, 224

Laborers, 24
Language, 13, 23, 51, 185
Lares, 127
Laws, 23, 42, 48, 62, 80, 87, 105, 111, 159, 191, 194
Leadership, 65, 86, 111, 125, 158, 197
League of Nations, 214
Learn, 18, 21, 23, 134
Learning, 50, 53, 63, 67, 68, 78, 88, 92, 150, 228
Lessons, 88, 90, 100, 129
Levite, 25
Libido, 51, 57, 58, 131
Liebman, J. L., 37
Life, 15, 22, 23, 31, 44, 49, 59, 62, 170, 192, 211
Life instinct, 167, 187
Light, 21, 22, 44
Ligon, E. M., 26, 85, 107
Lindemann, Erich, 125
Linkages, 225
Lippitt, Rosemary, 122
Lord, 24, 26, 30, 32, 44, 100, 208, 222
Lord's Prayer, 38
Love, 11, 13, 16, 21, 22, 24, 31, 33, 41, 49, 52, 63, 64, 71, 72, 80, 85, 121, 124, 127, 152, 167, 188, 198, 228
Love, heavenly, 23, 144, 165

Nonviolent, 65, 165, 205
Normal personality, 53
Nourish, 18, 92, 99
Nygren, Anders, 27, 29, 31, 36-37, 39, 42

Obedience, 99
Obligation, 14, 55
Occupational therapy, 16, 196, 214
Oedipus, 30, 133, 174
Old Testament, 24, 168
Opinions, 16
Opponents, 19
Opposites, 20
Opposition, 14, 83, 167, 175
Oral, 131
Organic, 54, 114, 181
Organism, 52
Organization, 50, 197
Organizations, 216
Organize, 18, 79
Overpowered, 17
Overprotective, 40
Overstreet, H. A., 225
Ownership, 174

Pacifists, 33, 165
Pair unity, 145
Pantheists, 29
Parables, 24, 45
Paranoia, 69, 189
Parental love, 26, 32, 49, 120
Parents, 18, 26, 64, 67, 68, 77, 79, 87, 98, 110, 135, 137, 144, 151, 158, 185, 191
Paris, 216
Parsee, 48
Parsonage, 91, 100
Participation, 16, 19, 38, 83, 84, 88, 92, 94
Passion, 61, 166, 171, 190
Passive, 79
Pastoral counseling, 161
Pastoral psychology, 161
Pastoral services, 100
Pastors, 135, 158, 161
Patient, 42
Patriotism, 14
Paul, 24, 25, 28, 41, 44, 60, 103, 128, 168, 202, 204, 207, 209, 212, 223, 228
Peace, 12, 29, 127, 165, 189
Pecking order, 109
Penates, 127
Pentecost, 21, 202
Perfectionism, 227
Permissive, 80
Persecution, 21, 28, 166, 169, 189, 203, 210
Persia, 169
Persistent, 19, 23, 56, 62, 85
Persona, 57, 93
Personality, 16, 27, 43, 54, 59, 61, 63, 87, 107, 118, 121, 153, 160

Persons, 19, 20, 22, 39, 43, 44, 47, 48, 56, 64, 66, 70, 71, 84, 98, 101, 112, 131, 143, 148, 173, 204, 223
Persuasion, 185
Peter, 31, 128, 165, 169
Philanthropy, 14
Philippians, 228
Philosophers, 192
Phobias, 104
Physician, 112, 158, 159, 200, 214
Pious, 20
Pity, 18, 94
Play, 18, 53, 79, 80, 147, 196
Playmates, 92
Pleasure, 51, 58, 107, 180
Plymouth, 201
Poliomyelitis, 94
Political, 70, 73, 84, 175, 190
Poor, 21, 35, 65, 95, 203, 204, 220
Portugal, 169
Position, 21
Possession, 174, 226
Potential, 25, 39, 61, 129, 142, 144, 171
Power, 17, 19, 22, 38, 44, 65, 73, 109, 111, 133, 167, 170, 187, 195, 210, 211, 219
   drive, 179
   destroy, 182-202
Practice, 20, 22, 83, 99, 120, 126
Praise, 92
Prayer, 30, 38, 45, 46, 47, 63, 89, 100, 105, 117, 148, 157, 203, 222
Preachers, 197
Preaching, 100
Preferences, 109
Prejudice, 90, 154, 161, 176
Premarital counseling, 158, 160, 162
Presence, 47
Prestige, 120, 134, 174, 176, 179, 211 219
Pride, 17, 46, 75, 126, 159, 170, 219, 226
Priest, 25, 145
Prison, 101
Private hell, 130
Private worlds, 13
Privileges, 31, 175
Procreation, 131, 163
Prodigal son, 24, 31
Production, 195
Profession, 21
Progress, 175, 212, 218
Projection, 126
Projective techniques, 16
Projects, 88-89
Propensity, 50
Property, 21, 98
Prophets, 30
Protective, 181
Protest, 201
Protestants, 21, 218, 220, 222
Providence, 42, 144
Psalm, 104
Psychiatric, 78

World—*cont'd.*
  Council of Churches, 213, 221
  family, 129, 130
  Health Organization, 214, 223
Worship, 20, 21, 24, 27, 35, 83, 89, 99, 100, 144

Worth, 38, 41, 97, 109, 120, 154, 181
Wright, Helena, 161

Yogi, 48
Young, P. T., 54
Youth Fellowship, 129, 137, 158